Project Maths

Text&Tests5

Leaving Certificate Higher Level Maths

Strand 1 – Probability & Statistics

Frances O'Regan · O. D. Morris

 The Celtic Press

Acknowledgements
We would like to express our deep gratitude to Robert Garland and Paul Behan for their invaluable help and contributions.

First published in 2011 by
The Celtic Press
Ground Floor – Block B
Liffey Valley Office Campus
Dublin 22

Reprinted May 2013; May 2014; July 2014
This Reprint (with minor corrections) March 2015

ISBN: 978-0-7144-2012-7

Layout and artwork: Tech-Set Limited, Gateshead

Contents

PROJECT MATHS – STRAND 1

chapter 1 **Probability 1** 1

1.1 Permutations 1
1.2 Combinations 8
1.3 Elementary probability 13
1.4 Experimental probability – Relative frequency 19
1.5 Mutually exclusive events – The addition rule 23
1.6 The multiplication law for independent events 30
1.7 Conditional probability 34
Test yourself 1 42

chapter 2 **Statistics 1** 48

2.1 Types of data 49
2.2 Collecting data 53
2.3 Populations and sampling 58
2.4 Measures of location 63
2.5 Measures of variability 70
2.6 Stem and leaf diagrams (stemplots) 79
2.7 Histograms 87
2.8 The shape of a distribution 90
Test yourself 2 96

chapter 3 **Probability 2** 104

3.1 Tree diagrams 104
3.2 Probability distributions – Expected value 109
3.3 Binomial distribution – Bernoulli trials 115
3.4 How to show events are independent 120
3.5 Probability involving permutations and combinations 124
3.6 The normal distribution 127
3.7 Probability simulations 135
Test yourself 3 140

Preface

This book was compiled and written for ***Project Maths – Strand 1*** of the Leaving Certificate, Higher Level Course for examination in 2015 and onwards. The book reflects the overall approach to the teaching of maths as stated in the learning outcomes for *Project Maths*. It encourages the development of not only the students' mathematical knowledge and skills, but also the understanding necessary to apply these skills.

There is an excellent range of imaginatively-written and probing questions on each topic which will help students to understand what they are doing and to develop their problem-solving skills. A sufficient number of questions in varying degrees of difficulty have been provided to satisfy the needs of the vast majority of students at this level.

The motivating and stimulating full-colour design, together with the large number of well-constructed diagrams, should help the student's understanding of the topic being studied. At the beginning of each chapter, there is a list of ***Key Words*** that students are expected to know and understand when the chapter is completed. Each chapter concludes with a blue-coloured ***Test Yourself*** section which provides comprehensive consolidation and revision. This section is divided into A-questions, B-questions and C-questions. These questions are graded in order of difficulty and thus enable the student to revise the basics of any topic before moving on to the more challenging exercises.

The eBook for Text and Tests 5 is available from The Celtic Press.

Frances O'Regan
O. D. Morris
March 2014

Probability 1

chapter 1

Key words

> **the fundamental principle of counting**   **permutations**   **factorial**
> **combinations**   **relative frequency**   **expected frequency**   **addition rule**
> **mutually exclusive**   **exhaustive events**   **Venn diagrams**
> **independent events**   **multiplication rule**   **conditional probability**

Section 1.1 Permutations

1. The fundamental principle of counting

The diagram below shows three towns A, B and C.
There are 2 roads from A to B and 3 roads from B to C.

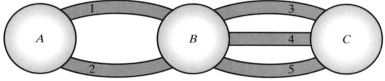

The number of ways a person can travel from A to C is 6. These are listed as follows:

> $(1, 3), (1, 4), (1, 5),(2, 3), (2, 4), (2, 5)$.

This illustrates that there are 2 ways of going from A to B and for **each** way of going from A to B, there are 3 ways of going from B to C.
Thus there are $3 \times 2 = 6$ ways of going from A to C.

Similarly, if a car manufacturer produces 5 different models of a car and each model comes in 4 different colours, then a customer has 5×4 i.e. 20 different ways in which he can select a car.

These examples illustrate what is generally referred to as the **Fundamental Principle of Counting** which can be stated as follows:

Fundamental Principle of Counting

> If one task can be accomplished in m ways **and** following this a second task can be accomplished in n ways, then the first task followed by the second task can be accomplished in $m \times n$ ways.

Example 1

From the given number of names and surnames, determine how many different name–surname pairs are possible.

There are 6 names and for each of these, there are 5 surnames.

Number of possible different pairs = 6 × 5
= 30

Name	Surname
Mary	Mooney
Jennifer	Byrne
Cormac	O'Brien
Kate	Lawiski
Barry	
Shane	McCarthy

Note: The *Fundamental Principle of Counting* can be extended to any number of tasks. For example, if there are 3 roads from A to B, 2 roads from B to C and 4 roads from C to D, then there are

$3 \times 2 \times 4$ i.e. 24 ways of going from A to D.

2. Permutations

A permutation is an arrangement of a number of objects in a certain order.

If the letters A, B and C are written in a row, one after another, there are 6 possible arrangements as follows:

$ABC \quad ACB \quad BAC \quad BCA \quad CAB \quad CBA$

Each arrangement is called a **permutation**; so there are 6 different permutations possible.

When calculating the number of permutations that can be made from a number of items, it is convenient to use "boxes", and working from the left, write down the number of ways in which each box can be filled.

Again, returning to the permutations of the letters A, B and C.
The first letter can be selected in 3 different ways.
Once the first place has been filled, there are only two letters left to choose from.
Thus the second place can be filled in 2 ways.
Similarly the third place can be filled in 1 way only.
Thus the letters A, B and C can be arranged in

$\boxed{3}\,\boxed{2}\,\boxed{1} = 3 \times 2 \times 1 = 6$ ways

3. Factorial notation

To represent $3 \times 2 \times 1$, we write 3!, pronounced "three factorial".
Similarly, $8 \times 7 \times 6 \times 5 \times 4 \times 3 \times 2 \times 1 = 8!$

In general, the product of all natural numbers from any number, n, down to 1 is called **n factorial**, and written as **$n!$**.

Definition

$n!$ is the number of permutations of n different objects when all the objects are included in each arrangement.

Thus (i) 5 different objects can be arranged in 5! i.e. 120 ways
(ii) 8 different objects can be arranged in 8! i.e. 40320 ways.

Example 2

There are 6 different books, including a science book, on a shelf.
(i) In how many different ways can the 6 books be arranged on the shelf?
(ii) In how many ways can the 6 books be arranged if the science book is always on the extreme left?

(i) The number of permutations of 6 different books is 6!
$$6! = 6 \times 5 \times 4 \times 3 \times 2 \times 1 = 720$$

(ii) If we use "boxes", it is clear that the box on the extreme left can be filled in 1 way only (i.e. with the science book).

1	5	4	3	2	1

The next box can be filled in 5 ways, the next in 4 ways and so on.
∴ the number of permutations is $1 \times 5 \times 4 \times 3 \times 2 \times 1$
$$= 120 \text{ ways}$$

Example 3

In how many ways can the letters of the word SCOTLAND be arranged in a line?
(i) In how many of these arrangements do the two vowels come together?
(ii) How many of the arrangements begin with S and end with the two vowels?

The letters of the word SCOTLAND can be arranged in 8! ways.
$$8! = 8 \times 7 \times 6 \times 5 \times 4 \times 3 \times 2 \times 1 = 40320 \text{ ways}$$

(i) If the two vowels come together, we treat them as one 'unit'.

There are now seven 'units' (or boxes) and these can be arranged in 7! ways, i.e., 5040 ways. For each arrangement of these seven boxes, the box containing AO can be arranged in 2! ways.
∴ the number of arrangements is $7! \times 2!$
$$= 5040 \times 2 = 10080 \text{ ways}$$

(ii) Arrangements beginning with S and ending with AO or OA:

S					AO

The S is fixed and we treat AO as one 'unit' and that is also fixed.
The remaining 5 letters can be arranged in 5! ways.
For each of these arrangements, AO can be arranged in 2! ways.
∴ the number of arrangements is $5! \times 2!$
$$= 120 \times 2 = 240$$

Example 4

How many four-digit numbers can be formed using the digits 0, 2, 5, 7, 8 if a digit cannot be used more than once in any number?
 (i) How many of these numbers are greater than 5000?
 (ii) How many of these numbers are odd?

Using boxes for the digits, the first box can be filled in 4 ways as 0 cannot be used as a first digit.

$$\boxed{4}\,\boxed{4}\,\boxed{3}\,\boxed{2}$$

The second box can also be filled in 4 ways as one digit is used but the zero can now be used.
The third box can be filled in 3 ways and the fourth in 2 ways.
∴ the number of numbers is $4 \times 4 \times 3 \times 2 = 96$

 (i) If a number is greater than 5000, the first digit must be either 5, 7 or 8.
 Therefore the first box can be filled in 3 ways.

$$\boxed{3}\,\boxed{4}\,\boxed{3}\,\boxed{2}$$

 The remaining boxes can be filled in 4, 3 and 2 ways.
 ∴ the number of numbers is $3 \times 4 \times 3 \times 2 = 72$

 (ii) If one of these numbers is odd, it must end with 5 or 7.
 Therefore the last box can be filled in 2 ways only.

$$\boxed{3}\,\boxed{3}\,\boxed{2}\,\boxed{2}$$

 We then go to the first box and, as either 5 or 7 is used and zero cannot be used, this box can be filled in 3 ways.
 The zero can now be used and 2 digits are already used, so the second and third boxes can be filled in 3 and 2 ways.
 ∴ the number of 4-digit odd numbers is $3 \times 3 \times 2 \times 2 = 36$

4. Permutations of n different objects taking r of them at a time

To find the number of ways the five letters A, B, C, D, E can be arranged in a line when taking 3 at a time, we could use boxes as follows:

$$\boxed{5}\,\boxed{4}\,\boxed{3} = 5 \times 4 \times 3 = 60 \text{ ways.}$$

The first box can be filled in 5 ways, the second in 4 ways and the third in 3 ways.

Notice that $5 \times 4 \times 3 = \dfrac{5 \times 4 \times 3 \times 2 \times 1}{2 \times 1} = \dfrac{5!}{2!} = \dfrac{5!}{(5-3)!}$

We use the notation $^5P_3$ to denote the number of permutations of 5 objects, taking them 3 at a time.

$^5P_3 = 5 \times 4 \times 3$ ... starting at 5 and going down 3 numbers

Similarly, $^8P_4 = 8 \times 7 \times 6 \times 5 \left(\text{or } \dfrac{8!}{(8-4)!}\right)$

> In general, the number of arrangements of n objects, taking r at a time, is given on the right.
>
> $$^nP_r = \dfrac{n!}{(n-r)!}$$

Example 5

(i) Evaluate $^{10}P_3$ (ii) Find n if $7[^nP_3] = 6[^{n+1}P_3]$

(i) $^{10}P_3 = 10 \times 9 \times 8 = 720$

(ii) $7[^nP_3] = 6[^{n+1}P_3] \Rightarrow 7n(n-1)(n-2) = 6(n+1)(n)(n-1)$
$\Rightarrow 7(n-2) = 6(n+1)$
$\Rightarrow 7n - 14 = 6n + 6$
$\Rightarrow n = 20$

Example 6

How many different four-letter arrangements can be made from the letters of the word THURSDAY if a letter cannot be repeated in an arrangement?
How many of the arrangements begin with the letter D and end with a vowel?

There are 8 letters in THURSDAY.
The number of four-letter arrangements $= {}^8P_4 = 8 \times 7 \times 6 \times 5$
$= 1680$

To find the number of arrangements that begin with D and end with a vowel, we will use 'boxes'.

| D | 6 | 5 | 2 |

The first box can be filled in one way only, i.e. with D.
The last box can be filled in 2 ways, i.e., U or A.

Having used two letters, the remaining two boxes can be filled in 6 and 5 ways.
∴ the number of arrangements $= 1 \times 6 \times 5 \times 2$
$= 60$ ways

Exercise 1.1

1. A three-course lunch menu consists of four starters, three main courses and five desserts. In how many ways can a three-course lunch be chosen?

2. There are six nominations for the post of Chairman and seven nominations for the post of Secretary of a committee.
   In how many ways can a Chairman and Secretary be elected?

3. A code consists of a letter of the alphabet followed by two digits from 1 to 9, e.g. A34. How many different codes are possible if a digit cannot be repeated in the same code?

4. Jack has 10 shirts, 6 pairs of shoes and 4 pairs of trousers.
   In how many different ways can he dress himself?

5. In how many ways can six books be arranged on a shelf?

6. In how many ways can seven children sit on a bench?
   In how many of these arrangements are the two oldest always together?

7. In how many ways can the letters A, B, C, D and E be arranged in a row?
   In how many of these arrangements
   (i)   is D always first?
   (ii) is A first and E last?

8. How many different arrangements can be made from the letters of the word PROBLEM?
   (i)   How many of these arrangements begin with a vowel?
   (ii) In how many of these arrangements do the two vowels come together?

9. How many different arrangements can be made from the letters of the word PRINCE if
   (i)   the first letter must be a consonant
   (ii)   the last letter must be a vowel
   (iii) the letters P and R must be together?

10. In how many ways can the letters of the word LEAVING be arranged if
    (i)   L is always at the beginning
    (ii) the letters E and A are always together?

11. In how many ways can the letters of the word IRELAND be arranged if each letter is used exactly once in each arrangement?
    In how many of these arrangements do the three vowels come together?

12. Three girls and four boys are to sit in a row of seven chairs.
    How many different arrangements are possible
    (i)   if the girls sit beside one another
    (ii) if no two boys may sit beside each other?

13. In how many ways can 7 books be arranged on a shelf, taking 4 at a time?

14. In how many ways can the letters of the word BRIDGE be arranged in a row taking 4 at a time?

15. There are eight horses in a race.
    In how many ways can the first three places be filled if there are no dead-heats?

16. A code consists of two vowels followed by two of the digits 1 to 9, e.g. AE29.
    How many different codes are possible if no repetition is allowed in a code?

17. How many three-digit numbers can be formed using the digits
    (i) 1 to 9   (ii) 0 to 9
    if a digit cannot be repeated in the same number?

18. How many 4-digit numbers can be made from the digits 4, 5, 6, 7 if no digit is repeated in the same number?
    (i)   How many of these numbers are greater than 7000?
    (ii) How many of these numbers end in 7?
    (iii) How many of these numbers are less than 6000?

19. How many four-digit numbers can be formed from the digits 0, 1, 2, 3, …, 9, if no digit is repeated in a number?
    How many of these numbers
    (i) are greater than 8000   (ii) are divisible by 10?

20. How many different four-digit numbers greater than 5000 can be formed from the digits 2, 4, 5, 8, 9 if each digit can be used only once in any given number?
    How many of these numbers are odd?

21. How many different three-digit numbers can be formed with the digits 0, 1, 4, 6, 7, 8 if each digit can be used once only in a number?
    (i) How many of these numbers are greater than 600?
    (ii) How many of the numbers begin with 1?

22. A security lock requires a four-digit code to be keyed in before it can be released.
    The digits can be 0, 1, 2, 3, 4 or 5 but the four-digit code cannot start with the digit 0.
    How many different codes are there if
    (i) all the digits are different
    (ii) the first digit is 5 and no digit is repeated?

23. A code consists of any permutation of the letters A, B and C followed by any permutation of the numbers 1, 2, 3.
    How many different codes can be made if no letter or number can be repeated in a code?

24. A woman has 10 ornaments, including a clock, of which only 7 will fit on the mantelpiece. If the clock must go in the centre, how many different arrangements can be made with the ornaments?

25. Seven children, including one set of twins, are arranged in a line.
    How many different arrangements can be made?
    In how many of these arrangements are the twins
    (i) always together   (ii) always apart?

26. A competition has a first prize, a second prize and a third prize. 10 competitors enter
    this competition and the 3 prizes are awarded in order of merit.
    (i)   Find the number of different ways in which these prizes could be won.

    Smith and Jones are 2 of the 10 competitors. Find the number of different ways in which
    the prizes could be won if
    (ii)   neither Smith nor Jones wins a prize
    (iii)   each of Smith and Jones wins a prize.

Section 1.2 Combinations

A **combination** is a selection of objects chosen from a given set.
When we select, for example, three letters from A, B, C, D and E, then the combination ABC
is the same as the combination BCA.
Thus in combinations, unlike permutations, the order is not important.

We use the notation $\binom{7}{3}$ to denote the number of ways in which three objects can be chosen
from seven different objects.

The value of $\binom{7}{3} = \dfrac{7 \times 6 \times 5}{3 \times 2 \times 1}$ ... start at 7 and go down 3 factors
... start at 3 and go down to 1

$$= \frac{210}{6} = 35$$

Similarly   (i) $\binom{8}{4} = \dfrac{8 \times 7 \times 6 \times 5}{4 \times 3 \times 2 \times 1} = 70$

(ii) $\binom{10}{3} = \dfrac{10 \times 9 \times 8}{3 \times 2 \times 1} = 120$

In general, $\binom{n}{r} = \dfrac{n(n-1)(n-2) \dots (n-r+1)}{r!} = \dfrac{n!}{r!(n-r)!}$

Combinations

> The number of combinations of r objects, chosen from a set
> of n different objects, is denoted by $\binom{n}{r}$ where
> $$\binom{n}{r} = \frac{n(n-1)(n-2) \dots (n-r+1)}{r!} = \frac{n!}{r!(n-r)!}$$

Again $\binom{10}{6} = \dfrac{10 \times 9 \times 8 \times 7 \times 6 \times 5}{6 \times 5 \times 4 \times 3 \times 2 \times 1}$ → start at 10 and go down 6 factors
→ start at 6 and go down to 1.

$$= 210$$

Also $\binom{10}{4} = \dfrac{10 \times 9 \times 8 \times 7}{4 \times 3 \times 2 \times 1} = 210$

This shows that $\binom{10}{6} = \binom{10}{4}$ i.e. $\binom{10}{6} = \binom{10}{10-6}$

In general, it can be shown that $\binom{n}{r} = \binom{n}{n-r}$ as follows:

$$\binom{n}{r} = \dfrac{n!}{r!(n-r)!} \text{ and } \binom{n}{n-r} = \dfrac{n!}{(n-r)![n-(n-r)]!}$$

$$= \dfrac{n!}{(n-r)!r!} = \dfrac{n!}{r!(n-r)!}$$

$$\Rightarrow \qquad \boxed{\binom{n}{r} = \binom{n}{n-r}}$$

Also since $\binom{n}{r} = \binom{n}{n-r} \Rightarrow \binom{n}{n} = \binom{n}{n-n} = \binom{n}{0} = 1$
$\boxed{0! = 1}$

$$\Rightarrow \qquad \boxed{\binom{n}{n} = \binom{n}{0} = 1}$$

The fact that $\binom{n}{r} = \binom{n}{n-r}$ is very useful for shortening the calculation involved in evaluating $\binom{16}{12}$, for example.

$$\binom{16}{12} = \binom{16}{16-12} = \binom{16}{4} = \dfrac{16 \times 15 \times 14 \times 13}{4 \times 3 \times 2 \times 1} = 1820$$

Note: $\binom{n}{r}$ may also be written as ${}^{n}C_{r}$.

The notation nCr is generally used on calculators.

To find $\binom{16}{12}$ on your calculator, key in

$\boxed{16}\,\boxed{\text{Shift}}\,\boxed{nCr}\,\boxed{12}\,\boxed{=}$ The result is 1820.

Example 1

(i) In how many ways can a team of 5 players be chosen from 9 players?
(ii) In how many ways can this be done if a certain player must be selected in each team?

(i) 5 players can be selected from 9 players in $\binom{9}{5}$ ways.

$$\binom{9}{5} = \binom{9}{4} = \dfrac{9 \times 8 \times 7 \times 6}{4 \times 3 \times 2 \times 1} = 126$$

(ii) If a certain player must be included, this results in 4 players being selected from the remaining 8.

4 players can be selected from 8 in $\binom{8}{4}$ ways.

$$\binom{8}{4} = \frac{8 \times 7 \times 6 \times 5}{4 \times 3 \times 2 \times 1} = 70$$

Example 2

In how many ways can a group of five be selected from ten people?
How many groups can be selected if two particular people from the ten cannot be in the same group?

Five people can be selected from ten in $\binom{10}{5}$ ways.

$$= \frac{10 \times 9 \times 8 \times 7 \times 6}{5 \times 4 \times 3 \times 2 \times 1} = 252 \text{ ways}$$

If two particular people cannot be in the same group, we find
 (i) the total number of ways 5 people can be selected from 10, i.e., 252, from above
(ii) the number of ways the group can be selected if the two people are **always** included.

If the 2 people are in each group, the number of ways is

$$\binom{8}{3} = \frac{8 \times 7 \times 6}{3 \times 2 \times 1} = 56 \dots \text{ select 3 from 8}$$

Therefore the number of ways the group can be selected if the two people cannot be in the same group is (i) less (ii).
∴ the number is $252 - 56 = 196$ ways

Combinations from two different sets

If we have two different sets, one containing m different things and the other containing n different things, the number of combinations which can be made containing r of the first and s of the second is,

$$\binom{m}{r} \times \binom{n}{s}$$

The selections of $\binom{m}{r}$ and $\binom{n}{s}$ are **multiplied** because for each selection from $\binom{m}{r}$ we can

associate every selection from $\binom{n}{s}$.

Example 3

Find the number of ways in which a panel of four men and three women can be chosen from seven men and five women.

4 men can be selected from 7 men in $\binom{7}{4}$ ways.

3 women can be selected from 5 women in $\binom{5}{3}$ ways.

With each of the $\binom{7}{4}$ selections, we may associate one of the $\binom{5}{3}$ selections.

$\Rightarrow$ the panel can be selected in $\binom{7}{4} \times \binom{5}{3}$ ways

$$= 35 \times 10$$
$$= 350 \text{ ways}$$

Example 4

In how many ways can a committee of six be formed from 5 teachers and 8 students if there are to be more teachers than students on each committee?

If there are more teachers than students on each committee, the committee will consist of either of the following combinations:
 (i) 4 teachers and 2 students
 (ii) 5 teachers and 1 student

 (i) 4 teachers and 2 students can be selected in $\binom{5}{4} \times \binom{8}{2}$ ways

$$= 5 \times 28 = 140 \text{ ways}$$

 (ii) 5 teachers and 1 student can be selected in $\binom{5}{5} \times \binom{8}{1}$ ways

$$= 1 \times 8 = 8 \text{ ways}$$

The total number of possible committees is $140 + 8$
$$= 148 \text{ committees}$$

Note: In example 4 above, the committee could consist of combinations (i) **or** (ii). Notice that these results were **added**.

In general, when dealing with problems involving permutations, combinations or probability, the word **or** indicates that results are **added**.

Exercise 1.2

1. Evaluate each of the following:

   (i) $\binom{6}{2}$ (ii) $\binom{7}{3}$ (iii) $\binom{10}{2}$ (iv) $\binom{12}{10}$ (v) $\binom{18}{16}$

2. Show that (i) $\binom{12}{9} + \binom{12}{8} = \binom{13}{9}$ (ii) $8\binom{10}{2} = 3\binom{10}{3}$

3. In how many ways can a committee of 5 be selected from 8 people?

4. In how many ways can a team consisting of 11 players be selected from a panel of 14 players?
   If the 14 players include only one goalkeeper, how many different teams can be selected if the goalkeeper is included in each team?

5. How many different selections of 5 letters can be made from the letters of the word CHEMISTRY?
   (i) How many 5-letter selections can be made if the letter C is included in each selection?
   (ii) How many 5-letter selections can be made if the letter C is always included and Y is always excluded?

6. An examination paper consists of 9 questions.
   In how many ways can 5 questions be selected?
   If Question 1 is compulsory, in how many ways can 5 questions then be selected?

7. From a pack of 52 cards, how many different hands of 3 cards can be selected?
   How many different hands of 3 spades can be chosen from the 52 cards?

8. In how many different ways may 5 colours be selected from 10 different colours including red, blue and green,
   (i) if blue and green are always included
   (ii) if red is always excluded
   (iii) if red and blue are always included but green excluded?

9. In how many ways can a committee of six persons be chosen from five men and four women if each committee is to consist of 3 men and 3 women?

10. A school council consists of 10 teachers and 12 students.
    In how many ways can a group of 6 be selected if the group consists of
    (i) 3 teachers and 3 students
    (ii) 2 teachers and 4 students?

11. How many subsets, each containing three letters, can be made from the set $\{a, b, c, d, e, f\}$?
    How many such subsets can be formed if
    (i) each subset contains one vowel and two consonants
    (ii) each subset contains at least one vowel?

12. In how many ways can a jury of 6 persons be chosen from 4 men and 4 women?
    In how many of these ways will all the women have been chosen?

13. A board of six persons is to be chosen from five men and three women.
    In how many ways can this be done
    (i) when there are 4 men on each board
    (ii) when there is a majority of men on each board?

14. There are 3 goalkeepers, 6 backs and 4 forwards available for selection on a 6-man team. How many different teams can be selected if each team has a goalkeeper, three backs and two forwards?

15. There are eight people, including Mr. and Mrs. Jones, on a committee.
    How many subcommittees of four can be selected
       (i)   if all members are eligible for the subcommittee
      (ii)   if Mr. and Mrs. Jones are included on each subcommittee
     (iii) if neither Mr. nor Mrs. Jones can be included on the subcommittee?

16. Five points are marked on a plane. No three of them are collinear.
    How many different triangles can be formed using these points as vertices?
    Two of the five points are labelled X and Y respectively.
    How many of the above triangles have [XY] as a side?

17. Six points A, B, C, D, E, F are marked on a sheet and no three of them are collinear.
       (i)   How many different quadrilaterals can be formed using these points?
      (ii)   How many of these quadrilaterals have A and B as one side?

18. Nine friends, including Ann and Barry, wish to go to a show but only five tickets are available.
    In how many ways can the group of five be selected if
       (i)   both Ann and Barry are included
      (ii)   either Ann or Barry is included, but not both?
    Another member of the group is named Claire.
     (iii) In how many ways can the group of five be selected, given that at least one of Ann, Barry and Claire must be included?

19. An examination paper consists of 12 questions, 5 in Section A and the remainder in Section B. A candidate must attempt 5 questions, at least 2 of which must be from each section. In how many different ways may the candidate select the 5 questions?

20. A registration system consists of the four letters A, B, C, D and the four digits 2, 4, 6, 8. Find the maximum number of registrations the system can have if each registration consists of 2 letters followed by 3 digits, none of which may be repeated in a registration.

21. Find the value of $n \in N$ in each of the following:
      (i) $\binom{n}{2} = 10$ (ii) $\binom{n}{2} = 45$ (iii) $\binom{n+1}{2} = 28$

Section 1.3 Elementary probability

Probability uses numbers to tell us how likely something is to happen.
The **probability** or **chance** of something happening can be described by using words such as:

    Impossible   **Unlikely**   **Even Chance**   **Likely**   **Certain**

An event which is **certain to happen** has a **probability of 1**.

An event which **cannot happen** has a **probability of 0**.

All other probabilities will be a number greater than 0 and less than 1.

The more likely an event is to happen, the closer the probability is to 1.

The line shown below is called a **probability scale**.

Before you start a certain game, you must throw a dice and get a 6.
The act of throwing a dice is called a **trial**.
The numbers 1, 2, 3, 4, 5 and 6 are all the possible **outcomes** of the trial.
The required result is called an **event**.

If you require an even number when throwing a dice, then the
event or **successful outcomes** are the numbers 2, 4 and 6.

> The result we want
> is called an **event**.

The chance of getting a red with this spinner is the same as the chance
of getting a blue. Getting a red and getting a blue are **equally likely**.

In general, if E represents an event, the probability
of E occurring, denoted by $P(E)$, is given below:

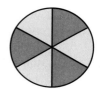

$$P(E) = \frac{\text{number of successful outcomes in } E}{\text{number of possible outcomes}}$$

Note: 1. The probability of any event E cannot be less than 0 or greater than 1, i.e.,
   $0 \leqslant P(E) \leqslant 1$.
   2. The probability of a certainty is 1.
   3. The probability of an impossibility is 0.
   4. If E is an event, then the probability that E does not occur is 1 minus the
   probability that E occurs.
   This is written as **P(E not occurring) = 1 − P(E)**.

> If A is an event, it will either happen or not happen.
>
> $P(A$ happening$) = 1 - P(A$ not happening$)$.

Example 1

If a card is drawn from a pack of 52, find the probability that it is
(i) an ace   (ii) a diamond   (iii) a red card.

(i)   There are 4 aces in the pack $\Rightarrow P(\text{ace}) = \frac{4}{52} = \frac{1}{13}$

(ii) There are 13 diamonds in the pack $\Rightarrow P(\text{diamond}) = \frac{13}{52} = \frac{1}{4}$

(iii) There are 26 red cards in the pack $\Rightarrow P(\text{red card}) = \frac{26}{52} = \frac{1}{2}$

Example 2

A letter is selected at random from the letters of the word STATISTICS.
Find the probability that the letter is
(i) C   (ii) S   (iii) S or T   (iv) a vowel.

There are 10 letters in the word STATISTICS.

(i)   There is just one C.   (ii) There are 3 Ss.
$\Rightarrow P(\text{C}) = \frac{1}{10}$ $\Rightarrow P(\text{S}) = \frac{3}{10}$

(iii) There are 3 Ss and 3 Ts, i.e. 6 altogether
$\Rightarrow P(\text{S or T}) = \frac{6}{10} = \frac{3}{5}$

(iv) There is one A and two Is in the word, i.e., 3 vowels.
$\Rightarrow P(\text{vowel}) = \frac{3}{10}$

Two events – use of sample spaces

When two coins are tossed, the set of possible outcomes is

$\{HH, HT, TH, TT\}$, where H = head and T = tail.

This set of possible outcomes is called a **sample space**.

By using this sample space, we can write down the probability of getting 2 heads, for example.

$P(HH) = \frac{1}{4}$ and $P(\text{one head and one tail}) = \frac{2}{4} = \frac{1}{2}$

In an experiment such as throwing two dice, for example, the construction of a sample space showing all the possible outcomes can assist in finding the probability of a given event.

Example 3

If two dice are thrown and the scores are added, set out a sample space giving all the possible outcomes. Find the probability that
  (i) the total is exactly 7
  (ii) the total is 4 or less
  (iii) the total is 11 or more
  (iv) the total is a multiple of 5.

The sample space is set out on the right.
There are 36 outcomes.

  (i) There are 6 totals of 7.
    $\Rightarrow P(7) = \frac{6}{36} = \frac{1}{6}$

  (ii) There are 6 totals of 4 or less.
    $\Rightarrow P(4 \text{ or less}) = \frac{6}{36} = \frac{1}{6}$

  (iii) There are 3 totals of 11 or more.
    $\Rightarrow P(11 \text{ or more}) = \frac{3}{36} = \frac{1}{12}$

  (iv) The multiples of 5 are 5 and 10.
    There are 7 totals of 5 or 10.
    $\Rightarrow P(\text{multiple of 5}) = \frac{7}{36}$

	1	2	3	4	5	6
1	2	3	4	5	6	7
2	3	4	5	6	7	8
3	4	5	6	7	8	9
4	5	6	7	8	9	10
5	6	7	8	9	10	11
6	7	8	9	10	11	12

Exercise 1.3

1. There are seven labels on the probability scale below:

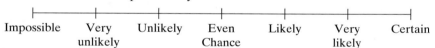

Impossible   Very unlikely   Unlikely   Even Chance   Likely   Very likely   Certain

Which of these labels best describes the likelihood of each of these events occurring?
  (i) You will score 10 in a single throw of a normal dice.
  (ii) It will rain in Ireland sometime in the next week.
  (iii) You will win a prize in the club lottery with a single ticket.
  (iv) You will live to be 100 years old.
  (v) If I toss a coin, it will show tails.
  (vi) A day of the week ending with the letter Y.
  (vii) You will draw an even number from these cards.

2. Yoghurt is sold in packs of 12.
   Robbie is going to take one without looking.

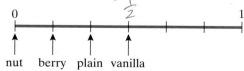

   0                    $\frac{1}{2}$ 1

   nut   berry   plain   vanilla

   Use the probability scale to work out how many of these flavours are in a pack:
   (i) vanilla   (ii) plain   (iii) nut   (iv) berry.

6

3.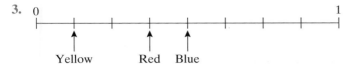

0 ├─┼─┼─↑─┼─↑─↑─┼─┼─┼─┼─┤ 1
    Yellow   Red Blue

In a game, Todd spins an arrow. The arrow stops on one of sixteen equal sectors of a circle. Each sector of the circle is coloured. The probability scale shows how likely it is for the arrow to stop on any one colour. How many sectors are
(i) coloured red   (ii) coloured blue   (iii) coloured yellow?

4. A fair dice is rolled.
What is the probability of getting
(i)   a 5   (ii) a 1 or a 2   (iii) 4 or more
(iv) an odd number   (v)   less than 3   (vi) a prime number?

5. If one card is selected at random from a pack of 52 cards, what is the probability of getting
(i)   a king   (ii) a diamond   (iii) a picture card
(iv) a black queen   (v)   an even number on the card?

6. Tickets numbered 1 to 17 are placed in a box.
If one ticket is drawn at random, what is the probability that it has
(i)   an odd number   (ii) a 2-digit number
(iii) a multiple of 3   (iv) a perfect square?

7. A letter is selected at random from the word ADDITION.
Find the probability that the letter is
(i) T   (ii) I   (iii) T or D   (iv) a vowel.

8. A counter is drawn from a box containing 15 red, 10 black and 5 green counters.
Find the probability that the counter is
(i) red   (ii) green   (iii) red or green   (iv) not red.

9. Two unbiased dice are thrown. Using the sample space given in Example 3 of this section, find the probability that
(i)   the total is 10   (ii) both numbers are odd
(iii) the total is 4 or less (iv) the total is odd and greater than 6.

10. Two dice are thrown simultaneously. The scores are to be multiplied.
If $P(n)$ is the probability that the number n is obtained, find
(i) $P(9)$ (ii) $P(4)$ (iii) $P(12)$.

11. There are 6 counters in a box.
The probability of taking a green counter out of the box is $\frac{1}{2}$.
A green counter is taken out of the box and put to one side.
Gerry now takes a counter from the box at random.
What is the probability it is green?

12. There are some yellow and purple blocks in a toddlers toy bin.
The probability of getting a yellow block, if you take a block at random out of the bin, is $\frac{2}{5}$
.
   (i) What is the probability the block will be purple?
  (ii) Karl takes one block out of the bin.
        It is yellow.
        What is the smallest number of purple blocks there could be in the bin?
 (iii) Karl then takes another block out of the bin and it is also yellow.
        What is the smallest number of purple blocks there could be in the bin?

13. You play a game with two spinners, as shown.
They are spun at the same time and the scores are added.
Make out a sample space for the possible results and
write down the probability of getting a total of
(i) 6   (ii) 10   (iii) an even number.
Which score do you get most often?
Hence write down the probability of getting this score.

14. In a particular game, a player throws two fair dice together.
If their total is 7 or 11 he wins.
If their total is 2, 3 or 12 he loses.
For any other total, he neither wins nor loses.
 (i) Find the probability of winning.
(ii) Find the probability of losing.

15. Three coins are tossed, each toss resulting in a head (H) or a tail (T).
Make out a sample space for the possible results and write down the probability that
the coins show
(i) *HHH*   (ii) *HTH* in that order   (iii) 2 heads and 1 tail in any order.

16. This two-way table shows the
numbers of males and females
in a group of 50 who wear or
do not wear glasses.

	Male	Female	Total
Wearing glasses	16	18	34
Not wearing glasses	9	7	16
Total	25	25	50

Work out the probability that
a person chosen at random is:
(i) female   (ii) not wearing glasses   (iii) a male who wears glasses.
If a male is chosen at random, find the probability that he wears glasses.

17. The pie chart gives information about how some
students travelled to school one day.
One of these students is chosen at random.
Use the information in the pie chart to work
out the probability that the student:
 (i) travelled to school by bus
(ii) walked to school.

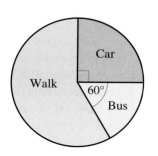

Section 1.4 Experimental probability
– Relative frequency

In the previous section, we calculated probabilities on the basis that all outcomes are equally likely to happen. However in real-life situations, events are not always equally likely. For example, the probability of a football team winning a game, or the probability that the next car that passes the school gate will be coloured red, can only be estimated by analysing previous results or carrying out an experiment or survey.

Experiment

John suspects that a coin is biased. In an experiment, he tossed the coin 200 times and recorded the number of heads after 10, 50, 100, 150 and 200 tosses.

The results are shown in the table on the right:

As the number of tosses increase, the number of heads divided by the number of tosses gets closer to 0.5, i.e., $\frac{1}{2}$.

This value is called **relative frequency** and it gives an **estimate of the probability** that the event will happen.

Number of tosses	Number of heads	Heads ÷ tosses
10	7	0.7
50	28	0.56
100	53	0.53
150	78	0.52
200	103	0.515

Thus an estimate of the probability that an event will occur, by carrying out a survey or experiment, is given by

$$\text{Relative frequency} = \frac{\text{Number of successful trials}}{\text{Total number of trials}}$$

In general, as the number of trials or experiments increases, the value of the relative frequency gets closer to the true or theoretical probability.

Example 1

Dara collected data on the colours of cars passing the school gate.
His results are shown on the table below.

Colour	White	Red	Black	Blue	Green	Other
Frequency	24	32	14	16	10	4

(i) How many cars did Dara survey?
(ii) What was the relative frequency of blue cars?
(iii) What was the relative frequency of red cars?
Give your answer as a decimal.
(iv) Write down an estimate of the probability that the next car passing the school gate will be green.
(v) How can the estimate for the probability of green cars be made more reliable?

(i) The number of cars in the survey is the sum of the frequencies.
This is 100 cars.

(ii) Relative frequency of blue cars $= \frac{16}{100} = \frac{4}{25}$

(iii) Relative frequency of red cars $= \frac{32}{100} = 0.32$

(iv) Probability of next car green = relative frequency of green cars
$$= \frac{10}{100} = \frac{1}{10}$$

(v) The estimate for the probability of green cars can be made more reliable by increasing the number of cars observed. Five hundred cars would give a very accurate estimate of the true probability.

Expected frequency

A bag contains 3 red discs and 2 blue discs.
A disc is chosen at random from the bag and replaced.
The probability of getting a blue disc is $\frac{2}{5}$.
This means that, on average, you expect 2 blue discs
in every 5 chosen or 20 blue discs in every 50 chosen.

To find the expected number of blue discs when you choose a disc 100 times,

(i) Work out the probability that the event happens once.
(ii) Multiply this probability by the number of times the experiment is carried out.
Thus the expected number of blue discs is

$\frac{2}{5} \times \frac{100}{1} = 40.$

> Expected frequency is
> probability × number of trials.

Example 2

This spinner is biased.
The probability that the spinner will land on each of
the numbers 1 to 4 is given in the table below.

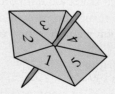

Number	1	2	3	4	5
Probability	0.35	0.1	0.25	0.15	k

The spinner is spun once.
(i) Work out the probability, k, that the spinner will land on 5.
(ii) Write down the number on which the spinner is most likely to land.
(iii) If the spinner is spun 200 times, how many times would you expect it to land on 3?

(i) The sum of the probabilities is 1.
$$\therefore\ 0.35 + 0.1 + 0.25 + 0.15 + k = 1$$
$$\Rightarrow 0.85 + k = 1$$
$$\Rightarrow k = 1 - 0.85 \Rightarrow k = 0.15$$

(ii) The spinner is most likely to land on 1 as it has the highest probability.

(iii) $P(3) = 0.25$
Expected frequency of $3 = P(3) \times$ number of trials
$$= 0.25 \times 200$$
$$= 50$$
You would expect to land on a three 50 times.

Exercise 1.4

1. A fair dice is thrown 900 times.
   (i) How many twos would you expect to get?
   (ii) How many sixes would you expect to get?
   (iii) How many twos or sixes would you expect to get?

2. One ball is selected at random from the bag
   shown and then replaced. This procedure
   is performed 400 times.
   (i) What is the probability of getting a red ball?
   (ii) How many times would you expect to select
      (a) a red ball   (b) a white ball?

3. Ben tosses a coin 100 times.
   His results are shown on the right.
   (i) Find the relative frequency of getting a head.
   (ii) Is the coin fair? Explain your answer.

Outcome	Frequency
Head	34
Tail	66

4. Helen wanted to find out if a dice was biased. She threw the dice 300 times.
   Her results are given in the table below.

Number on dice	1	2	3	4	5	6
Frequency	30	40	55	65	50	60

   (i) For this dice, calculate the experimental probability of obtaining
      (a) a 6   (b) a 2.
   (ii) For a fair dice, calculate the probability of scoring
      (a) a 6   (b) a 2.
   (iii) Do your answers suggest that this dice is fair?
      Give your reasons.

5. The sectors of a 3-sided spinner are each coloured red or orange or green.
The table gives the results when the spinner is spun 300 times.

Colour	Red	Orange	Green
Frequency	154	56	90

   (i) Use the information in the table to find an estimate for getting red.
   (ii) Is this a fair spinner? Give a reason for your answer.

6. A spinner has 10 equal sectors, 5 red and 5 green.
Dave carries out an experiment.
He spins the spinner 300 times.
The spinner lands on red 120 times.
Is the spinner fair? Explain your answer.

7. The probability that a biased dice will land on each of the numbers 1 to 6 is given in the table below:

Number	1	2	3	4	5	6
Probability	x	0.2	0.1	0.3	0.1	0.2

   (i) Calculate the value of x.
   (ii) If the dice is thrown once, find the probability that the dice will show a number higher than 3.
   (iii) If the dice is thrown 1000 times, estimate the number of times it will show a 6.

8. Gemma keeps a record of her chess games with Helen.
Out of the first 10 games, Gemma wins 6.
Out of the first 30 games, Gemma wins 21.
Based on these results, estimate the probability that Gemma will win her next game of chess with Helen.

9. Paula records the number of 6s she gets when she rolls a dice 10, 100 and 1000 times.
The table below shows her results.

Number of rolls	10	100	1000
Number of 6s	1	15	165

Use this information to work out the best estimate for getting a 6 on Paula's dice.
Give a reason for your answer.

10. Four friends are using a spinner for a game and they wonder if it is perfectly fair.
They each spin the spinner many times and record the results.

Name	Number of spins	Results		
		0	1	2
Alan	30	12	12	6
Keith	100	31	49	20
Bill	300	99	133	68
Ann	150	45	73	32

(i) Whose results are most likely to give the best estimate of the probability of getting each number?

(ii) Make a table by adding together all the results.
Use the table to decide whether you think the spinner is biased or unbiased.

(iii) Use the results to work out the probability of the spinner getting a '2'.

(iv) If the spinner is spun 1000 times, use the table in (ii) to write down the number of zeros you could expect.

11. (i) Sarah takes a cube and writes these numbers on its six faces: 1, 1, 2, 2, 2, 3.
She then rolls the cube.
What is the probability that the number 1 is uppermost?

(ii) David writes numbers on the faces of a different cube.
He rolls the cube many times and makes this record of how it lands.

Number uppermost	1	2	3	4
Frequency	42	79	85	34

What numbers do you think he wrote on the six faces of the cube?

Section 1.5 Mutually exclusive events – The addition rule

Consider the following two events when drawing a card from a pack of 52 playing cards:

A = drawing an ace   B = drawing a king.

These two events are said to be **mutually exclusive** as they cannot occur together.

If the events A and B cannot happen together, then

P(A or B) = P(A) + P(B)

This is called the **addition law** for mutually exclusive events.

> Outcomes are mutually exclusive if they cannot happen at the same time.

So P(draw an ace **or** king) = P(ace) + P(king)

$$= \frac{4}{52} + \frac{4}{52}$$
$$= \frac{8}{52} = \frac{2}{13}$$

When events are not mutually exclusive

We will now consider events which may occur at the same time.
If A is the event: selecting an ace from a pack of cards and
   B is the event: selecting a heart from a pack of cards
   then $P(A) = \frac{4}{52}$ and $P(B) = \frac{13}{52}$

In this situation, both events may occur at the same time since the *ace of hearts* is common to both.

In general, when two events A and B can occur at the same time,

$$P(A \text{ or } B) = P(A) + P(B) - P(A \text{ and } B)$$

Thus in the example given above,

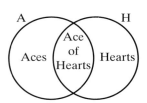

$$P(\text{ace or heart}) = P(\text{ace}) + P(\text{heart}) - P(\text{ace and heart})$$
$$= \tfrac{4}{52} + \tfrac{13}{52} - \tfrac{1}{52}$$
$$= \tfrac{16}{52}$$

This result can be verified as there are 4 aces and 13 hearts in a pack of cards. Since one of the aces is the ace of hearts, there are 16 aces or hearts in the pack.

i.e. $P(\text{ace or a heart}) = \tfrac{16}{52}$, as already found.

Example 1

A card is drawn at random from a pack of 52.
What is the probability that the card is
   (i) a club   (ii) a king   (iii) a club or a king
   (iv) a red card   (v) a queen   (vi) a red card or a queen

(i) $P(\text{club}) = \tfrac{13}{52} = \tfrac{1}{4}$

(ii) $P(\text{king}) = \tfrac{4}{52} = \tfrac{1}{13}$

(iii) $P(\text{a club or a king}) = P(\text{club}) + P(\text{king}) - P(\text{club and king})$
$$= \tfrac{13}{52} + \tfrac{4}{52} - \tfrac{1}{52}$$
$$= \tfrac{16}{52} = \tfrac{4}{13}$$

(iv) $P(\text{red card}) = \tfrac{26}{52} = \tfrac{1}{2}$

(v) $P(\text{queen}) = \tfrac{4}{52} = \tfrac{1}{13}$

(vi) $P(\text{a red card or a queen}) = P(\text{red card}) + P(\text{queen}) - P(\text{red card and queen})$
$$= \tfrac{26}{52} + \tfrac{4}{52} - \tfrac{2}{52}$$
$$= \tfrac{28}{52} = \tfrac{7}{13}$$

Venn diagrams for mutually exclusive events

(i) Mutually exclusive

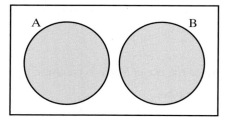

$P(\text{A or B}) = P(\text{A}) + P(\text{B})$
$P(\text{A} \cup \text{B}) = P(\text{A}) + P(\text{B})$

(ii) Non-mutually exclusive

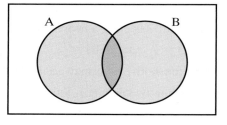

$P(\text{A or B}) = P(\text{A}) + P(\text{B}) - P(\text{A} \cap \text{B})$
$P(\text{A} \cup \text{B}) = P(\text{A}) + P(\text{B}) - P(\text{A} \cap \text{B})$

Example 2

A and B are two events such that $P(A) = \frac{19}{30}$, $P(B) = \frac{2}{5}$ and $P(A \cup B) = \frac{4}{5}$.
Find $P(A \cap B)$.

Using $P(A \cup B) = P(A) + P(B) - P(A \cap B)$

$$\frac{4}{5} = \frac{19}{30} + \frac{2}{5} - P(A \cap B)$$

$$P(A \cap B) = \frac{19}{30} + \frac{2}{5} - \frac{4}{5}$$

$$= \frac{19}{30} + \frac{12}{30} - \frac{24}{30}$$

$$= \frac{7}{30}$$

Exhaustive events

Consider these events when throwing a dice:

    A: Getting an odd number
    B: Getting an even number

These two events contain all the possible outcomes
when a dice is thrown.
These events are said to be **exhaustive**.
If A and B are exhaustive events, then

    $P(A) + P(B) = 1$.

> A set of events is exhaustive
> if the set contains all
> possible outcomes.

Venn diagrams

A Venn diagram is a useful way to represent data or probabilities.
Each region of a Venn diagram represents a different set of data.

The Venn diagram on the right shows two sets, A and B,
in the sample space S.

The number of elements in each region is also shown.

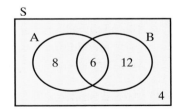

8 is the number of elements in A but not in B. This is written as A/B.
12 is the number of elements in B but not in A. This is written as B/A.
6 is the number of elements in A and B. This is written as A ∩ B.
4 is the number of elements in neither A nor B.
This is written as (A ∪ B)′.

If information is presented in the form of a Venn diagram, it is easy to write down the
probability of different events occurring.

In the diagram on the previous page, the probability of either A or B is given by $P(A \cup B)$.

$$P(A \cup B) = \frac{8 + 6 + 12}{8 + 6 + 12 + 4} = \frac{26}{30} = \frac{13}{15}$$

Example 3

The given Venn diagram represents the subjects taken by a group of 50 pupils.
  (i) Find the value of x.

Now find the probability that a person chosen at random takes
(ii) both subjects
(iii) neither subject
(iv) Science but not Maths
(v) Maths or Science or both.

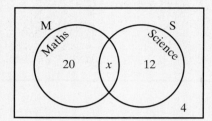

(i) $x = 50 - (20 + 12 + 4)$ i.e. $x = 14$

(ii) $P(\text{both}) = \dfrac{x}{50} = \dfrac{14}{50} = \dfrac{7}{25}$

(iii) $P(\text{neither}) = P(M \cup S)' = \dfrac{4}{50} = \dfrac{2}{25}$

(iv) $P(\text{Science but not Maths}) = \dfrac{12}{50} = \dfrac{6}{25}$

(v) $P(\text{Science or Maths or both}) = \dfrac{20 + 14 + 12}{50} = \dfrac{46}{50} = \dfrac{23}{25}$

Exercise 1.5

1. A box contains discs numbered 1 to 16.
   If a disc is selected at random, what is the probability that it is
     (i) an odd number   (ii) a multiple of 4
   (iii) an odd number or a multiple of 4?

2. A card is selected at random from a pack of 52 playing cards.
   What is the probability that it is
     (i) a spade   (ii) a red picture card
   (iii) a spade or a red picture card?

3. A number is selected at random from the integers 1 to 30 inclusive.
   Find the probability that the number is
     (i) a multiple of 3   (ii) a multiple of 5
   Explain why events (i) and (ii) are not mutually exclusive.
   Now find the probability that a multiple of 3 or 5 is selected.

4. A number is selected at random from the integers 1 to 12 inclusive.
   Find the probability that the number is
      (i)   even   (ii) a multiple of 3   (iii) even or a multiple of 3.

5. A card is drawn at random from a pack of 52.
   What is the probability that the card is
      (i)   a club   (ii) a king   (iii) a club or a king
      (iv) a red card   (v) a queen   (vi) a red card or a queen?

6. If two fair dice are thrown, what is the probability of getting
      (i)   the same number on both dice
      (ii) a total of 8
      (iii) the same number on both dice or a total of 8?

7. In a small school, a class consists of children of a variety of ages as given in the table.

5-year-old girls	5-year-old boys	6-year-old girls	6-year-old boys	7-year-old girls	7-year-old boys
3	4	6	8	5	2

   A pupil is selected at random.
   What is the probability that the pupil is
      (i)   a girl   (ii) not 5 years old
      (iii) a boy and 6 years old   (iv) a girl or 6 years old
      (v)   6 or 7 years old   (vi) 6 and 7 years old?

8. The results of a traffic survey of colour and type of car are given in the table shown.

   One car is selected at random from this group.
   Find the probability that the car selected is
      (i)   a green estate car
      (ii) a saloon car
      (iii) a black car or an estate car.

	Saloon	Estate
White	68	62
Green	26	32
Black	6	6

9. In a fairground game, players each choose a number on this board.
   An electronic device lights up and turns off the numbers
   in a random way. When it stops, one number is lit up.
   What is the probability that the lit-up number is

1	2	3	4
5	6	7	8
9	10	11	12
13	14	15	16

      (i)   in the first row
      (ii) in the first column
      (iii) either in the first row or the first column
      (iv) on the edge of the board
      (v)   on the diagonal from top left to bottom right
      (vi) either on the edge or on the diagonal from top left to bottom right
      (vii) either a square number or an odd number?

10. A bag contained 8 red, 12 blue and an unknown number of green beads.
    In a random draw, the probability of drawing a green bead was $\frac{1}{5}$.
    How many green beads were in the bag at the start?

11. Of 100 tickets sold in a raffle, 40 were red, 30 were blue and 30 were green.
If the winning ticket was drawn at random, find the probability that it was
   (i) red   (ii) not blue.

Every red ticket is even-numbered and every blue ticket is odd-numbered.
Of the green tickets, 20 are even-numbered and 10 are odd-numbered.
Find the probability that the winning ticket was
(iii) green or even-numbered.

12. Of one hundred people in a sports club, 40% are male. A recent survey showed that 10% of the males and 15% of the females play tennis.
   (i) Find the probability that a person chosen at random from the group is male and plays tennis.
   (ii) Find the probability that a person chosen at random from the group plays tennis.
   (iii) Find the probability that the person chosen is female **or** plays tennis.

13. These cards are turned over and shuffled.
   A card is picked at random.

   | 20 | 21 | 22 | 23 | 24 | 25 | 26 | 27 | 28 | 29 |

   The event A is 'The number picked is less than 24'.
   The event B is 'The number picked is a multiple of 5'.
   The event C is 'The number picked is prime'.
   The event D is 'The number picked is a multiple of 3'.
   (i) Are these pairs of events mutually exclusive?
       (a) A, B   (b) A, C   (c) A, D   (d) B, C   (e) B, D
   (ii) What is the probability that the number picked is either prime or a multiple of 3?
   (iii) Jeff said:
       'The probability of picking a number less than 24 is $\frac{4}{10}$.
       The probability of picking an even number is $\frac{5}{10}$.
       So the probability of picking either a number less than 24 or an even number is $\frac{9}{10}$.'
       Is he right? If not, why not?

14. The Venn diagram on the right shows the number of elements in each region.

   Write down   (i) $P(A)$ (ii) $P(B)$ (iii) $P(A \cup B)$.
   Now verify that $P(A \cup B) = P(A) + P(B) - P(A \cap B)$.

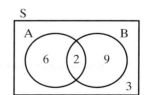

15. The given Venn diagram shows the probabilities of events C and D in the universal set S.

   Find   (i) $P(C)$ (ii) $P(D)$
         (iii) $P(C \cup D)$ (iv) $P(C \cap D)$
   Verify that $P(C \cup D) = P(C) + P(D) - P(C \cap D)$

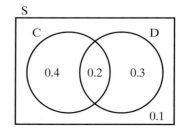

16. The given Venn diagram shows the languages taken by a group of 50 students.
    (i) Find the value of x.
    If a student is selected at random, find the probability that the student takes
    (ii) French
    (iii) both French and Spanish
    (iv) French or Spanish
    (v) one of these languages only.

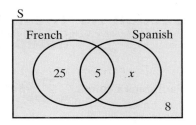

17. The Venn diagram shows the hobbies of a group of girls.
    (i) Write down the total number of girls.
    (ii) A girl is chosen at random. Find the probability that she does both Drama and Art.
    (iii) A girl is chosen at random. She does Drama. Find the probability that she does Art.
    (iv) A girl is chosen at random. She does Sport. Find the probability that she does Drama.
    (v) A girl is chosen at random. She does both Drama and Art. Find the probability that she does all three.

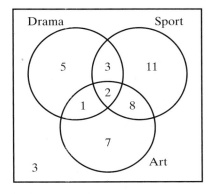

18. A town council gets a grant to build two sports centres. During the first year the centres were open, it was found that 36% of the population had been to centre A, 22% had been to centre B and 10% had been to both.
    (i) Draw a Venn diagram to represent this data.
    (ii) What percentage of the population had been to neither centre?
    (iii) What percentage had been to centre A only?

19. For events A and B, it is known that $P(A) = \frac{2}{3}$, $P(A \cup B) = \frac{3}{4}$ and $P(A \cap B) = \frac{5}{12}$. Find $P(B)$.

20. For events X and Y, it is known that $P(X) = \frac{1}{2}$, $P(Y) = \frac{3}{5}$ and $P(X \cup Y) = \frac{9}{10}$. Find $P(X \cap Y)$.

21. For events C and D, $P(C) = 0.7$, $P(C \cup D) = 0.9$ and $P(C \cap D) = 0.3$. Find $P(D)$.

22. A and B are two events such that $P(A) = 0.8$, $P(B) = 0.5$ and $P(A \cap B) = 0.3$.
    (i) Find $P(A \cup B)$.
    (ii) Verify that $P(A \cup B) = P(A) + P(B) - P(A \cap B)$.

23. A and B are two events such that $P(A) = \frac{8}{15}$, $P(B) = \frac{2}{3}$ and $P(A \cap B) = \frac{1}{3}$.
    (i) Find $P(A \cup B)$.
    (ii) Are A and B mutually exclusive? Explain your answer.

24. A and B are mutually exclusive events.
    If $P(A) = \frac{3}{7}$ and $P(B) = \frac{1}{5}$, find $P(A \cup B)$.

Section 1.6 The multiplication law for independent events

Paul spins a coin and rolls a dice.

His results are shown on the right.

The coin and the dice do not affect each other, so their outcomes are **independent**.

There are 12 equally likely outcomes of the coin and dice, as shown in the diagram on the right.

From the sample space, we can see that the probability of a head and a 5 is $\frac{1}{12}$.

Dice	H(ead)	T(ail)
6	H, 6	T, 6
5	H, 5	T, 5
4	H, 4	T, 4
3	H, 3	T, 3
2	H, 2	T, 2
1	H, 1	T, 1

Coin

The probability of each outcome can also be found by multiplying the separate probabilities, as shown above.

This illustrates the **multiplication law** of probability which states that for independent events A and B,

$$P(A \text{ and } B) = P(A) \times P(B)$$

This law is sometimes called the AND Rule.

The multiplication law applies to any number of independent events. If the events are A, B, C, ..., then

$$P(A \text{ and } B \text{ and } C \dots) = P(A) \times P(B) \times P(C) \times \dots$$

The multiplication law is particularly useful when dealing with problems where one event is followed by another event such as throwing two dice or selecting two or more cards from a pack. The use of the multiplication law eliminates the need to construct a sample space and so significantly reduces the work involved in solving certain problems.

Example 1

When two dice are thrown, what is the probability of getting
(i) two sixes
(ii) 4 or more on each die?

(i) The probability of getting 6 on the first dice is $\frac{1}{6}$.

The probability of getting 6 on the second dice is also $\frac{1}{6}$.

∴ $P(6, 6) = \frac{1}{6} \times \frac{1}{6} = \frac{1}{36}$

(ii) The probability of getting 4 or more on any dice is $\frac{1}{2}$.

∴ $P(4 \text{ or more on each dice}) = \frac{1}{2} \times \frac{1}{2} = \frac{1}{4}$

(Both of these answers could be found by using the sample space for throwing two dice.)

Example 2

These two spinners are spun.
What is the probability that
   (i)   spinner A shows red
   (ii) spinner B shows red
   (iii) both spinners show red
   (iv) A shows red and B shows blue
   (v)   both show blue
   (vi) both show white
   (vii) neither shows white?

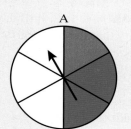 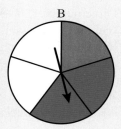

   (i) $P(\text{A shows red}) = \frac{1}{6}$

   (ii) $P(\text{B shows red}) = \frac{1}{5}$

   (iii) $P(\text{both show red}) = P(\text{A red}) \times P(\text{B red})$
   $$= \frac{1}{6} \times \frac{1}{5} = \frac{1}{30}$$

   (iv) $P(\text{A red and B blue}) = P(\text{A red}) \times P(\text{B blue})$
   $$= \frac{1}{6} \times \frac{2}{5} = \frac{2}{30} = \frac{1}{15}$$

   (v) $P(\text{both blue}) = P(\text{A blue}) \times P(\text{B blue})$
   $$= \frac{2}{6} \times \frac{2}{5} = \frac{4}{30} = \frac{2}{15}$$

   (vi) $P(\text{both white}) = P(\text{A white}) \times P(\text{B white})$
   $$= \frac{1}{2} \times \frac{2}{5} = \frac{2}{10} = \frac{1}{5}$$

   (vii) $P(\text{neither shows white}) = P(\text{A not white}) \times P(\text{B not white})$
   $$= \frac{1}{2} \times \frac{3}{5} = \frac{3}{10}$$

Example 3

A gambler must throw a 6 with a single dice to win a prize.
Find the probability that he wins at his third attempt.

To win at his third attempt, he must fail at the first, fail at the second and win at the third attempt.

$P(\text{not throwing a 6 at his first attempt}) = \frac{5}{6}$

$P(\text{not throwing a 6 at his second attempt}) = \frac{5}{6}$

$P(\text{throwing a 6 at his third attempt}) = \frac{1}{6}$

$\Rightarrow P(\text{winning at his third attempt}) = \frac{5}{6} \times \frac{5}{6} \times \frac{1}{6} = \frac{25}{216}$

Example 4

Three pupils A, B and C have their birthdays in the same week.
What is the probability that the three birthdays
   (i) fall on a Monday
   (ii) fall on the same day
   (iii) fall on three different days?

   (i) $P(A$'s birthday falls on a Monday$) = \frac{1}{7}$

   $P(\text{all three on Monday}) = \frac{1}{7} \times \frac{1}{7} \times \frac{1}{7} = \frac{1}{343}$

   (ii) $P(A$ has birthday on some day of week$) = 1$ ... a certainty

   $P(B$ has birthday on the same day$) = \frac{1}{7}$

   $P(C$ has birthday on the same day$) = \frac{1}{7}$

   $\therefore P(\text{all have birthday on the same day}) = 1 \times \frac{1}{7} \times \frac{1}{7} = \frac{1}{49}$

   (iii) $P(A$ has birthday on some day of the week$) = 1$ ... a certainty

   $P(B$ has birthday on a different day$) = \frac{6}{7}$

   $P(C$ has birthday on different day from A and $B) = \frac{5}{7}$

   $\Rightarrow P(\text{all have birthday on different days}) = 1 \times \frac{6}{7} \times \frac{5}{7} = \frac{30}{49}$

Exercise 1.6

1. This spinner is spun twice.
   Find the probability of getting
      (i)   2 reds
      (ii) 2 greens
      (iii) 2 yellows
      (iv) a red and a green in that order.

2. A dice is thrown twice. What is the probability of getting
      (i)   two sixes
      (ii) a six on the first throw and an even number on the second
      (iii) an odd number on the first throw and a multiple of 3 on the second?

3. A coin is tossed and a dice is thrown. Find the probability of obtaining
      (i) a head and a six
      (ii) a head and an even number.

4. A card is drawn from a pack of 52 and then replaced. A second card is then drawn.
   What is the probability that
      (i)   both cards are black
      (ii) both cards are kings
      (iii) the first card is a black ace and the second card is a diamond?

5. A bag contains 4 red discs and 6 blue discs. A disc is drawn at random and then replaced. A second disc is then drawn. Find the probability that
   (i) both discs are red
   (ii) the first is blue and the second is red
   (iii) the first is red and the second is blue
   (iv) both discs are blue
   (v) both discs are of the same colour.

6. The probability that it will rain tomorrow is $\frac{2}{3}$.
   The probability that Jean will forget her umbrella tomorrow is $\frac{3}{4}$.
   Work out the probability that it will rain tomorrow and Jean will forget her umbrella.

7. A card is taken at random from each of two ordinary packs of cards, pack A and pack B. Work out the probability of getting:
   (i) a red card from pack A and a red card from pack B
   (ii) a diamond from pack A and a club from pack B
   (iii) a King from pack A and a picture card (King, Queen, Jack) from pack B
   (iv) a 10 from pack A and the 10 of clubs from pack B
   (v) an ace of hearts from each pack.

8. A fruit machine has three independent reels and pays out a Jackpot of €50 when three raspberries are obtained. Each reel has 12 pictures. The first reel has four raspberries, the second has three raspberries and the third has two raspberries.
   Find the probability of winning the Jackpot.

9. An archer shoots at a target. The probability of hitting the gold area is 0.2.
   He fires two shots at the target.
   (i) What is the probability that both arrows hit the gold area?
   (ii) What is the probability that exactly one arrow hits the gold area?

10. Three children take a test. The probability that Chris passes is 0.8, the probability that Georgie passes is 0.9 and the probability that Phil passes is 0.7.
    (i) What is the probability that all three pass?
    (ii) What is the probability that all three fail?
    (iii) What is the probability that at least one passes?

11. Two men, Alan and Shane, each have one shot at a target. The probability that Alan hits the target is $\frac{1}{2}$ and the probability that Shane hits the target is $\frac{2}{3}$.
    Find the probability that
    (i) both men hit the target
    (ii) neither hits the target
    (iii) only one of them hits the target.

12. John drives to work and passes three sets of traffic lights.
    The probability that he has to stop at the first is 0.6.
    The probability that he has to stop at the second is 0.7.
    The probability that he has to stop at the third is 0.8.

(i) Calculate the probability that he stops at all three sets of traffic lights.

He arrives late if he has to stop at any two sets of traffic lights.
 (ii) Calculate the probability that he is late.

13. A fair dice is thrown 3 times. Find the probability that there will be
    (i) no sixes   (ii) at least one six   (iii) exactly one six.
    Find also the probability that the three throws all show the same number.

14. The birthdays of Jack and Jill fall on the same week. Find the probability that
    (i)   both have their birthdays on Monday
    (ii) both have their birthdays on the same day
    (iii) they have their birthdays on different days
    (iv) Monday is the birthday of one or both.

15. Three people were selected at random and asked on which day of the week their next
    birthday was falling.
    What is the probability that
    (i)   none of the birthdays falls on a Sunday
    (ii) only one of the birthdays falls on a Sunday
    (iii) at least one of the birthdays falls on a Sunday?

Section 1.7 Conditional probability

A box contains 2 red counters and 4 yellow counters,
as shown.

One counter is picked at random.

$P(\text{red}) = \frac{2}{6}$ and $P(\text{yellow}) = \frac{4}{6}$

Suppose the counter is **not** put back in the box.
The contents of the box will be different, depending on whether the counter taken out was
red or yellow.

If it was red, the box would now contain 1 red and
4 yellow counters, as shown.

If another counter is now taken out at random, the probability that it is red is **dependent** on
the colour of the first counter.

This is called **conditional probability**.

Returning to the second box above, $P(\text{red})$ is now $\frac{1}{5}$.

This probability is calculated on the assumption that a red was got on the first draw.

The box and counters discussed above is an example of a situation where the probability of
the second event depends on the outcome of the first event.

If A and B are two events, the **conditional probability** that A occurs, **given that B has already
occurred**, is written $P(A \mid B)$.
$P(A \mid B)$ is read as "the probability of A given B".

The conditional probability (A | B) is illustrated in the given Venn diagram.

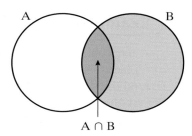

A ∩ B

To find $P(A \mid B)$, the sample space is reduced to B only, since B has already occurred.

Thus $P(A \mid B) = \dfrac{\#(A \cap B)}{\#B} = \dfrac{P(A \cap B)}{P(B)}$.

The part of B in which A also occurs is the part denoted by A ∩ B.

Thus $P(A \mid B) = \dfrac{\#(A \cap B)}{\#B} = \dfrac{P(A \cap B)}{P(B)}$

This result should be memorised as it will be used later in our study of probability.

This result can be described in words as follows:

"The probability of A given B is the probability of A and B divided by the probability of B".

The result $P(A \mid B) = \dfrac{P(A \cap B)}{P(B)}$ can be rearranged as follows:

$P(A \mid B) \times P(B) = P(A \cap B)$ ... multiply both sides by $P(B)$.

$\therefore \quad P(A \cap B) = P(A \mid B) \times P(B)$

Also $P(B \cap A) = P(B \mid A) \times P(A)$

Thus $P(A \cap B) = P(A) \times P(B \mid A)$ ... since $P(A \cap B) = P(B \cap A)$.

The General Multiplication law

$P(A \text{ and } B) = P(A) \times P(B \mid A)$

Example 1

The numbers 1 to 9 are written on cards and placed in a box.
A card is drawn at random from the box.
Find the probability that the number is prime, given that the number is odd.

The prime numbers up to 9 are 2, 3, 5, 7.

$P(\text{prime, given odd number}) = \dfrac{\text{number of odd primes}}{\text{number of odd numbers}}$

$= \dfrac{3}{5}$

Example 2

A bag contains 6 red and 4 blue discs. A disc is drawn from the bag and not replaced. A second disc is then drawn.

Find the probability that

  (i) the first two discs are blue

 (ii) the second disc drawn is red

(iii) one disc is red and the other disc is blue

(iv) both discs are the same colour.

[The notation $P(R, B)$ represents the probability of red first and blue second.]

  (i) $P(\text{1st disc is blue}) = \frac{4}{10}$

      $P(\text{2nd disc is blue}) = \frac{3}{9}$

      $\Rightarrow P(B, B) = \frac{4}{10} \times \frac{3}{9} = \frac{12}{90} = \frac{2}{15}$

 (ii) For the 2nd disc to be red, we could have

      (a) 1st red and 2nd red **or** (b) 1st blue and 2nd red

      $P(\text{1st red and 2nd red}) = \frac{6}{10} \times \frac{5}{9} = \frac{30}{90}$

      $P(\text{1st blue and 2nd red}) = \frac{4}{10} \times \frac{6}{90} = \frac{24}{90}$

      $\Rightarrow P(\text{2nd disc red}) = \text{sum of probabilities } \frac{30}{90} \text{ and} \frac{24}{90}$

                    $\frac{30}{90} + \frac{24}{90} = \frac{54}{90} = \frac{6}{10} = \frac{3}{5}$

(iii) $P(\text{one disc is red and the other blue})$ is

      $P(\text{1st red and 2nd blue or 1st blue and 2nd red})$

      $= P(R, B) + P(B, R)$

      $= \left(\frac{6}{10} \times \frac{4}{9}\right) + \left(\frac{4}{10} \times \frac{6}{9}\right)$

      $= \frac{24}{90} + \frac{24}{90} = \frac{48}{90} = \frac{8}{15}$

      $\therefore P(\text{one red, one blue}) = \frac{8}{15}$

(iv) $P(\text{both discs the same colour}) = P(R, R) + P(B, B)$

      $P(R, R) = \frac{6}{10} \times \frac{5}{9} = \frac{30}{90}$

      $P(B, B) = \frac{2}{15} \ldots$ from (i) above

      $\Rightarrow P(\text{both discs the same colour}) = \frac{30}{90} + \frac{2}{15} = \frac{7}{15}$

Example 3

Use the given Venn diagram to write down
(i) $P(A \mid B)$ (ii) $P(B \mid A)$

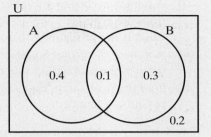

(i) $P(A \mid B) = \dfrac{P(A \cap B)}{P(B)} = \dfrac{0.1}{0.4} = 0.25$

(ii) $P(B \mid A) = \dfrac{P(B \cap A)}{P(A)} = \dfrac{0.1}{0.5} = 0.2$

[These probabilities could be written
down directly from the Venn diagram.]

Example 4

Two events A and B are such that $P(A) = 0.7$, $P(B) = 0.4$ and $P(A \mid B) = 0.3$.
Determine the probability that neither A nor B occurs.

The shaded region is the part of the diagram
where **neither A nor B** occurs.

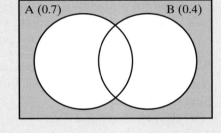

We use the formula $P(A \mid B) = \dfrac{P(A \cap B)}{P(B)}$

to find the probability of $A \cap B$.

$P(A \mid B) = \dfrac{P(A \cap B)}{P(B)} \Rightarrow 0.3 = \dfrac{P(A \cap B)}{0.4}$

$$\Rightarrow P(A \cap B) = 0.3 \times 0.4 = 0.12$$

We now fill in the other probabilities
in the Venn diagram.

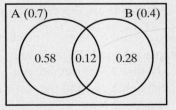

$P(\text{neither A nor B}) = 1 - P(A \cup B)$
$= 1 - [0.58 + 0.12 + 0.28]$
$= 1 - 0.98 = 0.02$

Exercise 1.7

1. A card is drawn at random from a pack of 52 playing cards.
    (i) Given that the card is black, find the probability that it is a spade.
    (ii) Given that the card is red, find the probability that it is a queen.
    (iii) Given that the card is a picture card, find the probability that it is a king.

2. The table shows information about a group of adults.

	Can drive	Cannot drive
Male	32	8
Female	38	12

   (i) A person is chosen at random from the group.
      What is the probability that the person can drive?
   (ii) A man in the group is chosen at random.
      What is the probability that he can drive?
   (iii) Find the probability that a person chosen at random can drive, given that the person is a female.

3. Two fair dice are thrown and the product of the numbers showing is recorded.
   Given that one dice shows a 2, find the probability that the product of the two numbers showing is
   (i) exactly 6   (ii) 6 or more.

4. A school enters 120 pupils for the Junior Certificate maths exam.
   The given table shows the details of the entries.

	Ordinary	Higher
Girls	20	35
Boys	25	40

   (i) Write down the probability that a pupil chosen at random is entered for Ordinary level.
   (ii) A pupil is chosen at random. This pupil is a girl.
      Find the probability that the girl was entered for Higher level.
   (iii) A pupil is chosen at random. The pupil was entered for Ordinary level.
      Find the probability that the pupil was a boy.

5. A bag contains 5 red discs and 3 blue discs.
   A disc is taken from the bag and not replaced. A second disc is then taken from the bag.
   Find the probability that
   (i) the first disc is red
   (ii) the first 2 discs are red
   (iii) the first two discs are blue
   (iv) both discs are the same colour.

6. A bag contains 5 red and 6 black marbles. The marbles are removed, one at a time, and not replaced. Find the probability that
   (i) the first 2 removed are red
   (ii) the first is red and the second is black
   (iii) the first 2 removed are black
   (iv) the first 2 removed are of the same colour
   (v) the second marble removed is red.

7. Five cards, labelled E, V, E, N, T, are thoroughly shuffled and then dealt out, face upwards, on a table.
   Find the probability that
   (i) the first two cards to appear are labelled T, N, in that order
   (ii) the first two cards to appear are labelled E, V, in that order
   (iii) the second card to appear is labelled E.

8. If two letters are selected at random from the word SWIMMING, what is the probability that both letters are the same?

9. This table gives information about the children in a primary school class.

	Left-handed	Right-handed
Girls	5	15
Boys	4	9

   (i)   One of the children is picked at random from the class.
         What is the probability that the child is a girl?
   (ii) One of the boys in the class is picked at random.
         What is the probability that he is left-handed?
   (iii) A boy in the class is picked at random, and a girl is picked at random.
         What is the probability that they are both left-handed?
   (iv) One of the right-handed children is picked at random.
         What is the probability that the child is a boy?

10. In a TV game show, contestants are given two tasks.
    In each task, they either succeed or fail.

    The probability of succeeding in the first task is 0.8.

    If a contestant succeeds in the first task, the probability of succeeding in the second is 0.6.
    If a contestant fails in the first task, the probability of succeeding in the second is 0.3.

    What is the probability that a contestant
    (i) succeeds in both tasks   (ii) fails in at least one task?

11. Josie takes a card at random from this pack and keeps it.
    Then she takes a second card at random.
    Find the probability that she takes one odd number
    and one even number (in either order).

12. Based on the probabilities shown in the given Venn diagram, find each of the following:

    (i) $P(A)$
    (ii) $P(A \cap B)$
    (iii) $P(A \cup B)$
    (iv) $P(A \mid B)$
    (v) $P(B \mid A)$.

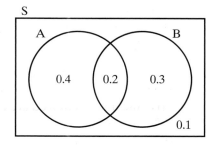

13. The given Venn diagram shows the numbers of elements in the sets A, B and the universal set S.
    Use the diagram to write down

    (i) $P(A)$
    (ii) $P(A \cap B)$
    (iii) $P(A \cup B)$
    (iv) $P(A \mid B)$.

    Is $P(A \mid B) = P(B \mid A)$?

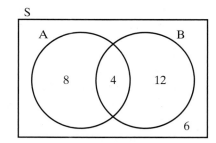

14. X and Y are two events such that $P(X) = 0.2$, $P(Y) = 0.25$ and $P(X \cap Y) = 0.1$.
    Illustrate this information on a Venn diagram.
    Use the diagram to find
    (i) $P(X \cup Y)$ (ii) $P(X|Y)$ (iii) $P(Y|X)$.

15. Use the given Venn diagram to find these
    probabilities:

    (i) $P(A)$ (ii) $P(A \cup B)$
    (iii) $P(A')$ (iv) $P(A \cup B)'$
    (v) $P(A' \cap B)$ (vi) $P(B|A)$.

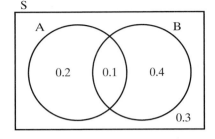

16. Two events A and B are such that
    $P(A) = 0.2$, $P(A \cap B) = 0.15$ and $P(A' \cap B) = 0.6$.

    (i)   Copy and complete this Venn diagram.
    (ii) Find the probability that neither A nor B
          occurs.
    (iii) Find $P(A|B)$.
    (iv) Is $P(A|B) = P(B|A)$?

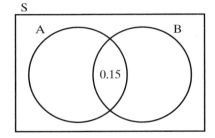

17. In a group of 100 people, 40 own a cat, 25 own a dog and 15 own a cat and a dog.
    Draw a Venn diagram to illustrate this information.
    Now write down the probability that a person chosen at random
    (i)   owns a dog or a cat
    (ii) owns a dog or a cat but not both
    (iii) owns a dog, given that (s)he owns a cat
    (iv) does not own a cat, given that (s)he owns a dog.

18. A and B are two events such that $P(A) = 0.6$, $P(B) = 0.5$ and $P(A \cap B) = 0.4$.
    Represent this information on a Venn diagram.
    Use the diagram to find
    (i) $P(A \cup B)$
    (ii) $P(B|A)$
    (iii) $P(A|B)$
    (iv) $P(B \cap A')$.

19. A and B are two events such that $P(A) = \frac{1}{3}$, $P(B) = \frac{1}{4}$ and $P(A|B) = \frac{1}{5}$.
    Draw a Venn diagram to show the probability of each region.
    Use the diagram to find
    (i) $P(A \cap B)$
    (ii) $P(B|A)$.

20. The probabilities of events A, B and C are shown in the given Venn diagram.

Use the Venn diagram to find
  (i) $P(B)$
  (ii) $P(A \cap C)$
  (iii) $P(A \mid B)$
  (iv) $P(C \mid B)$
  (v) $P(A \cap C')$
  (vi) $P(B \mid A \cap C)$.

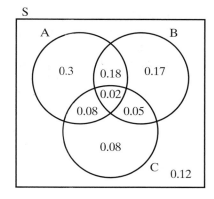

Test yourself 1

A – questions

1. How many different 3-digit numbers can be formed using the digits 1, 2, 3, 4, 5 if no digit is repeated in the number?
   (i) How many of these numbers begin with 3?
   (ii) How many of these numbers are greater than 300?

2. (i) How many different groups of four can be selected from five boys and six girls?
   (ii) How many of these groups consist of two boys and two girls?

3. A pair of dice are thrown and the numbers are added. What is the probability of getting
   (i) a total of 12
   (ii) the same number on both dice
   (iii) a total of 12 or the same number on both dice?

4. This spinner is biased.
   The probability that the spinner will land on each of the numbers 1 to 4 is given in the table below.

   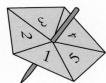

Number	1	2	3	4	5
Probability	0.35	0.1	0.25	0.15	

   The spinner is spun once.
   (i) Work out the probability that the spinner will land on 5.
   (ii) Write down the number on which the spinner is most likely to land.
   (iii) If the spinner is spun 200 times, how many times would you expect it to land on 3?

5. Six people, including Mary and John, sit in a row.
   (i) How many different arrangements of the six people are possible?
   (ii) In how many of these arrangements are Mary and John next to each other?

6. Thirty students were asked to state the activities they enjoyed from swimming (S), tennis (T) and hockey (H).
   The numbers in each set are shown.
   One student is randomly selected.
   (i) Which of these pairs of events are mutually exclusive?
      (a) 'selecting a student from S', 'selecting a student from H'
      (b) 'selecting a student from S', 'selecting a student from T'
   (ii) What is the probability of selecting a student who enjoyed either hockey or tennis?

7. A dice has the numbers 1, 1, 1, 2, 2, 3 on its faces.
   (i) What is the probability of scoring 2?

   The dice is thrown three times.
   (ii) What is the probability of getting a 2 on each of the first two throws?
   (iii) What is the probability of getting the first 2 on the third throw?

8. There are thirteen tickets in a draw. Six of the tickets are blue, four are red and three are green. Three tickets are drawn at random, one at a time, without replacement. Find the probability that the first ticket drawn is blue, the second is red and the third is red or green.

9. A **possibility space** consists of integers from 1 to 20 inclusive.

   A is the event: The number is a multiple of 3
   B is the event: The number is a multiple of 4.

   If an integer is picked at random, find
   (i) $P(A)$ (ii) $P(A \cup B)$ (iii) $P(A \cap B)'$.

10. The following table gives the age and gender of twenty five pupils in a class.

	Boys	Girls
16-year-olds	5	7
17-year-olds	7	6

    (i)   If a pupil is picked at random, what is the probability that the pupil picked is a girl aged seventeen or a boy aged sixteen?
    (ii) Find the probability of selecting a pupil aged 16, given that the pupil chosen was a girl.
    (iii) If two pupils are picked at random, find the probability that both are 16-year-old boys.

B – questions

1. To start a game, a player has to throw a 6 with a dice.
   Find the probability that a player starts at
   (i)   his first throw   (ii)   his second throw
   (iii) either his first or his second throw.

2. Four delegates are to be chosen from eight members of a club.
   (i)   How many choices are possible?
   (ii) How many contain a certain member A?
   (iii) How many contain A or B but not both?

3. (i)   How many arrangements can be made with the letters of the word SOLDIER if all the letters are taken at a time?
   (ii) How many of these arrangements begin with the letters SO in that order?
   (iii) How many of the arrangements begin and end with a consonant?

4. A game is played by spinning each of 3 arrows which are freely pivoted at the centres of 3 circles as shown below. Each arrow may score either 2 or 3 points according to the sector to which it points on stopping, and it is equally likely to face in either direction. The sectors scoring 2 points are of 240°, 180° and 240° respectively.

 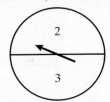 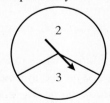

   Given that the game score is the sum of the points scored by the 3 arrows, calculate the probability of getting a game score of
   (i)   6   (ii)   9   (iii)   7.

5. (i)   Give an equation involving probabilities which represents the statement 'the events L and M are mutually exclusive'. Explain what is meant by 'mutually exclusive events'.
    (ii) Janelle's mathematics class has 22 students.
          Four students are selected at random to enter a mathematics competition.
          (a) In how many ways can the four students be selected?
          (b) In how many of the selections is Janelle included?
          (c) Now find the probability that Janelle is included to enter the competition.

6. Karen has two 5c and four 10c coins in her purse. At random, she takes out one coin and then a second coin (without replacing the first). Find the probability that
    (i)   the first coin is a 10c and the second coin a 5c
    (ii) the two coins are worth 15c
    (iii) the two coins are worth 20c.

7. Use the given Venn diagram to answer these questions.

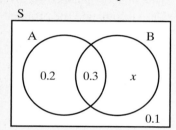

    (i)   Find the value of x (ii) Find $P(A)$
    (iii) Find $P(A \cup B)$ (iv) Find $P(A|B)$
    (v)   Verify that $P(A|B) = \dfrac{P(A \cap B)}{P(B)}$

8. There are 15 male and 20 female passengers on a train.
    10 of the males and 16 of the females are over 25 years old.
    A ticket inspector selects one of the passengers at random.

    A is the event: The person selected is female
    B is the event: The person selected is over 25 years old.

    Write down each of these:
    (i) $P(A)$ (ii) $P(B)$ (iii) $P(A|B)$ (iv) $P(A \cap B)$ (v) $P(A \cup B)$.
    Hence verify that $P(A \cap B) = P(B) \cdot P(A|B)$
    Why is it not possible to apply the result $P(A \cup B) = P(A) + P(B)$ in this case?

9. A box contains 4 white discs, 2 red discs and x green discs.
    Two discs are picked at random, without replacement, from the box.
    (i)   Write down an expression in x for the probability that the two discs are green.

    If it is known that the probability of picking two green discs is $\frac{4}{13}$,
    (ii) how many discs are in the box?
    (iii) what is the probability that neither of the two discs picked is green?

10.

SWEET SIXTEEN

START ⇒	1	2	3	
○ counter	8	7		5
	9		11	12
	16	15	14	13

'Sweet Sixteen' is a game for any number of players. To play the game, players take it in turns to throw a fair dice and then move their counter the number of places shown uppermost on the dice. If a player lands on one of the shaded squares, the player must start again. The first player to finish on square 16 is the winner. If a player would move past square 16 on a throw, the player is not allowed to move and misses that turn.

(i)   What is the probability that a player lands on a shaded square on the first throw?

(ii)   A player moves to square 3 on the first throw. What is the probability that the player lands on a shaded square on the second throw?

(iii) (a)   A player is on square 12 after three throws.
          Write, in the order thrown, three scores the player could have had.

       (b)   In how many different ways could a player have reached square 12 with three throws? Show your working to support your answer.

(iv) (a)   What is the minimum number of throws necessary to complete the game?

       (b)   What is the probability of this happening?

C – questions

1.   A bag contains 5 red and 4 green discs, identical in all but colour.
     Three discs are drawn at random from the bag without replacement.
     Find the probability that
     (i)   they are all the same colour
     (ii)   at least one is red
     (iii) at most one is green.

2.   8% of a population is known to have a certain virus which can be detected by a medical test. However this test is only 90% effective, meaning that it gives a correct reading only 90% of the time. If Sam is tested for the virus, what is the probability that
     (i)   he has the virus but it is not detected
     (ii)   he has the virus and it is detected
     (iii) he does not have the virus but it is falsely detected?

3.   (i)   What do you call outcomes that have the same chance of happening?
     (ii)   Explain conditional probability.
            Complete the following formula: $P(A|B) = \dfrac{P...}{P...}$

     (iii) Two events C and D are such that $P(C) = \frac{8}{15}$, $P(D) = \frac{1}{3}$ and $P(C|D) = \frac{1}{5}$.
            Find   (a) $P(C \cap D)$ (b) $P(C \cup D)$ (c) $P[(C \cup D)']$

4. The probability that a person has blue eyes is $\frac{2}{5}$ and the probability that a person is left-handed is $\frac{1}{5}$.
   Find the probability that a person
   (i) is not left-handed
   (ii) has blue eyes and is left-handed.

   Given that two people are chosen at random, find the probability that one of them has blue eyes and is left-handed and the other has blue eyes and is not left-handed.

5. To drive legally on Irish roads, all drivers are required to have both a driving licence and an insurance disc. At a checkpoint, a garda officer found that 14% had no insurance, 8% had no driving licence and 2% had neither a driving licence nor insurance.
   (i) Represent this information on a Venn diagram.
   (ii) Find the probability, as a fraction, that a driver checked in this survey was driving illegally.
   (iii) The following day, 300 drivers were stopped and checked.
   How many of these drivers can the gardaí expect to find who have a driving licence but no insurance?

6. A game is played using a regular 12-sided spinner numbered 1 to 12, a coin and a simple board with 9 rectangles, as shown in the diagram below.

L								R

   Initially the coin is placed on the shaded rectangle.
   The game consists of spinning the spinner and then moving the coin one rectangle towards L or R. If the outcome is a prime number (2, 3, 5, 7 or 11), the move is towards R; otherwise it is towards L.
   The game stops when the coin reaches either L or R.
   Find, correct to three decimal places, the probability that the game
   (i) ends on the fourth move at R
   (ii) ends on the fourth move
   (iii) ends on the fifth move.

7. In a multiple-choice test, each question offers a choice of 5 answers, only one of which is correct. The probability that a student knows the correct answer is $\frac{5}{8}$. If he does not know which answer is correct, he selects one of the 5 answers at random.
   Find the probability that he selects the correct answer to a question.

8. The given Venn diagram shows the probabilities of the events A, B and C happening.
   (i) Given that $P(B) = 0.4$ and $P(C) = 0.35$, find the values of x, y and z.

   Now find each of these probabilities
   (ii) $P(A|B)$
   (iii) $P(B|C)$
   (iv) $P[(A \cup B)']$
   (v) $P(A \cup B \cup C)$
   Now show that $P(A|B) = \dfrac{P(A \cap B)}{P(B)}$

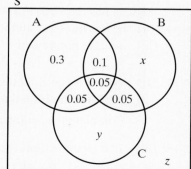

9. Two dice are thrown. Find the probability that
   (i) there is at least one 6
   (ii) the sum is 8
   (iii) there is at least one 6 *and* the total score is 8
   (iv) there is at least one 6 *or* the total score is 8 (or both)
   (v) there is at least one 6, given that the total score is 8.

10. A high-jumper training for the Olympic games estimates the probabilities that she will be able to clear the bar at various heights, based on her experience in training. These probabilities are given in the table below:

Height	Probability of success at each attempt
1.60 m	1
1.65 m	0.6
1.70 m	0.2
1.75 m	0

In a competition, she is allowed up to three attempts to clear the bar at each height. If she succeeds, the bar is raised by 5 cm and she is allowed three attempts at the new height, and so on.
If it is assumed that the result of each attempt is independent of all her previous results,
   (i) show that the probability that she will be successful at 1.65 m is 0.936.
   (ii) calculate the probability that if she is successful at 1.65 m, she will not be successful at 1.70 m.

Hence find the probabilities that, in the competition, the height she jumps will be recorded as
(iii) 1.60 m   (iv) 1.65 m.

Statistics 1

Key words

discrete data   continuous data   categorical data   primary data
secondary data   univariate   bivariate   surveys   questionnaires
control group   population   sample   stratified   systematic   quota
cluster   convenience   mode   mean   median   outlier
interquartile range   standard deviation   percentile   stem and leaf diagram
histogram   positive skew   negative skew   explanatory variable
response variable

Introduction to statistics

The aim of statistics is to help us make sense of large amounts of information or data.
In pursuit of this aim, statistics divides the study of data into three parts:
  (i)   Collecting data
 (ii)   Describing and presenting data
(iii)   Drawing conclusions from data.

In this chapter, we will discuss the variety of ways that information or data can be collected.
These include questionnaires, experiments and observations. Once data has been gathered,
we must then concern ourselves with the **description** of data so that ordinary people can
understand it. We can do this by representing the data graphically. You will meet a variety of
graphical methods in this chapter, as shown below. These are known as **descriptive statistics**.

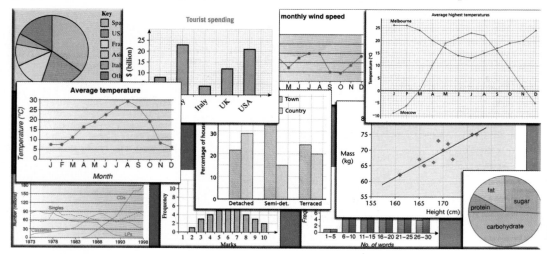

Another way of making a large amount of data easily understood is by **summarising** the data. Data may be summarised by simply finding an average or some other number that could be representative of the data as a whole. These numbers are known as **summary statistics**.

One of the most widely-used and important statistical processes is concerned with gathering information from a small group of people (or items) and using this data to draw conclusions about a much larger group of people. A good example of this is provided by the opinion poll. A poll is taken of a few thousand people. From the information that these people provide, remarkably accurate conclusions can be drawn that refer to the whole population, which is many times greater in number. Collecting information from a small group to draw conclusions about a large group is know as **inferential statistics**.

Section 2.1 Types of data

When we observe, count or measure something, we end up with a collection of numbers. These numbers are called **data**. Data is the plural of **datum** which means a piece of information.

1. Numerical data

Data which can be counted or measured is called **numerical** data because the answer is a number. Numerical data can be either **discrete** or **continuous**.

Discrete data	Continuous data
Data which can take only certain individual values is called **discrete data**. Here are some examples of **discrete data**: > The number of goals scored by football teams on a Saturday > The number of desks in the classrooms of the school > The marks achieved in a test	Continuous data is measured on some scale and can take any value on that scale. Here are some examples of **continuous data**: > The heights of students in your class > The speed of cars passing a certain point on a road > The time taken to complete a 100-metre sprint

---

Example 1

For each of these types of data, write down whether it is discrete or continuous.
  (i)   the number of coins in your pocket
  (ii) the number of tickets sold for a concert
  (iii) the time taken to complete a puzzle
  (iv) the weights of students in your class
  (v)   dress sizes

  (i)   discrete   (ii) discrete   (iii) continuous
  (iv) continuous   (v)   discrete

---

2. Categorical data

The answer to the question, 'What colour is your car?' will not be a numerical value. Rather, it will fit into a group or category such as blue, red, black, white, …
Data which fits into a group or category is called **categorical data**.

Here are some examples of categorical data:

> gender (male, female)
> country of birth (Ireland, France, Spain, Nigeria …)
> favourite sport (soccer, hurling, tennis, basketball …)

The three examples of data above are generally referred to as **nominal categorical data**.

Categorical data in which the categories have an obvious order such as first division, second division, third division, etc, is called **ordinal data**.

Other examples of ordinal data are:

> type of house (1-bedroomed, 2-bedroomed, 3-bedroomed)
> attendance at football matches (never, sometimes, very often)
> opinion scales (strongly disagree, disagree, neutral, agree, strongly agree).

The data you collect can be divided into two broad categories, namely, **primary data** and **secondary data**.

3. Primary data

Data that is collected by an organisation or an individual who is going to use it is called **primary data**.

Primary data is generally obtained

> by using a questionnaire
> by carrying out an expeirment
> by investigations
> by making observations and recording the results.

4. Secondary data

Data which is already available, or has been collected by somebody else for a different purpose, is called secondary data.

Secondary data is obtained

> from the internet, e.g., the National Census
> from published statistics and databases
> from tables and charts in newspapers and magazines.

5. Univariate data

When one item of information is collected, for example, from each member of a group of people, the data collected is called univariate data.

Examples of univariate data include:

> colour of eyes
> distance from school
> height in centimetres.

6. Bivariate data

Data that contains **two items** of information, such as the height and weight of a person, is generally called **paired data** or **bivariate data**.

Examples of bivariate data are:

> hours of study per week and marks scored in an examination
> the age of a car and the price of that car
> the engine sizes of cars and the number of kilometres travelled on a litre of petrol.

Colour of hair and gender is an example of **bivariate categorical data**.

The number of rooms in a house and the number of children in the house is an example of **bivariate discrete data**.

Example 2

For each of these sets of data, write down whether it is numerical or categorical:
  (i)   the sizes of shoes sold in a shop
  (ii) the colours of socks sold in a shop
  (iii) the subjects offered to Leaving Certificate students
  (iv) the marks given by judges in a debating competition
  (v)   the crops grown on a village farm
  (vi) the area of your classroom.

(i) numerical	(ii) categorical	(iii) categorical
(iv) numerical	(v) categorical	(vi) numerical

Exercise 2.1

1. State whether each of the following is categorical or numerical data:
    (i)   The number of bicycles sold by a shop in a particular week
    (ii) The colours of cars sold by a garage last month
    (iii) The number of horses in the six races at a meeting
    (iv) The favourite sports of all the students in a school.

2. State if each of the following data is discrete or continuous:
    (i)   The number of rooms in each of the houses on a road
    (ii) The number of CDs that have been sold
    (iii) The weights of the eggs in a carton
    (iv) Shoe sizes

    (v) The time taken to complete a crossword puzzle

    (vi) The score obtained when a dice is thrown

    (vii) The number of spanners in a toolbox

    (viii) The marks given by judges in a competition

3. Imelda bought a new dress.
    She wrote down (i) the colour of the dress
                         (ii) the number of buttons on the dress
                         (iii) the length of the dress.
    For each of these data types, write down whether it is numerical or categorical.
    Which of the three is discrete data?

4. Sonia recorded how long it took her to run a cross-country race and the race-number on her bib.
    Say if each of these variables is discrete or continuous.

5. State if each of the following is paired data:
    (i) The colours of shirts on a stand
    (ii) The ages and the heights of a group of students
    (iii) The number of brothers and their ages that each pupil in a class has
    (iv) The ages of all the people living on my street

6. *The amount of flour and the number of eggs needed to make a cake.*
    (i) Explain why this is paired data.
    (ii) Which part of the data is discrete?
    (iii) Which part of the data is continuous?

7. A doctor records information about her patients.
    The variables that she uses are described below:
    (i) the colour of the patient's eyes
    (ii) the patient's waist-size and height
    (iii) the patient's shoe size
    (iv) the patient's blood group.
    State if each variable is (a) categorical (b) numerical.
    Which of the four data types is discrete?
    Describe in full the data type given in part (ii).

8. State whether each of the following statements is true or false.
    Give a reason for your answer in each case.
    (i) The number of pockets on a jacket is discrete data.
    (ii) The types of trees in a forest is categorical data.
    (iii) The countries in which people like to holiday is numerical data.
    (iv) The number of bedrooms in each house on my street is categorical data.
    (v) The age of a tree and the circumference of the tree is bivariate data.
    (vi) The birth month of the students in your class is categorical data.

(vii) The number of matches played and the number of goals scored is bivariate and discrete data.

(viii) The weights of horses in a race and the times taken by the horses to complete the race is bivariate and continuous data.

9. Cars are often categorised as small, economy, family, executive and luxury.
   This is an example of **ordinal data**.
   Give three more examples of ordinal data.

10. Write down whether each of the following is an example of primary data or secondary data:
    (i) Alan counted the number of red vans passing the school gate.
    (ii) Helen examined records at a maternity hospital to find out how many babies were born each day in December.
    (iii) Robbie threw a dice 100 times and recorded the results to investigate if the dice was fair.
    (iv) Niamh used the internet to check the number of gold medals won by each competing country at the Beijing Olympics.

11. Roy and Damien want to predict next season's football league champions.
    Roy looks at the results for the last 5 years.
    Damien looks at the results for the 5 years before that.
    (i) What type of data are they using?
    (ii) Whose data is likely to be the more reliable and why?

12. Give one example of bivariate data which will be
    (i) discrete
    (ii) continuous.

Section 2.2 Collecting data

Data is collected for a variety of reasons and from a variety of sources.

Companies do market research to find out what customers like or dislike about their products and to see whether or not they would like new products. The government carries out a **census** of every person in the country every five years. Local government, education authorities and other organisations use the information obtained for further planning.

Data can be collected through direct observation such as a naturalist observing animal behaviour. In an observational study, the observer wishes to record data without interfering with the process being observed.

Apart from observational studies, data may also be collected by
> carrying out a survey
> doing an experiment
> conducting interviews or completing questionnaires
> using a data logger which records data or readings over a period of time, using a sensor.

1. Surveys

Surveys are particularly useful for collecting data that is likely to be personal.

The main survey methods are:
> postal surveys in which people are asked questions
> personal interviews in which people are asked questions; this type of survey is very widely-used in market research
> telephone surveys; here the interview is conducted by phone
> **observation**, which involves monitoring behaviour or information.

Survey method	Advantages	Disadvantages
Observation	> Systematic and mechanical	> Results are prone to chance
Personal interview and telephone survey	> Many questions can be asked > High response rate	> Expensive > Interviewer may influence responses
Postal survey	> Relatively cheap > Large amounts of data can be collected	> Limited in the type of data that can be collected > Poor response rate

2. Questionnaires

One of the most commonly-used methods of conducting a survey is by means of a questionnaire.

A **questionnaire** is a set of questions designed to obtain data from individuals.

People who answer questionnaires are called **respondents**.

There are two ways in which the questions can be asked.
> An interviewer asks the questions and fills in the questionnaire.
> People are given a questionnaire and asked to fill in the responses themselves.

When you are writing questions for a questionnaire,
> be clear on what you want to find out and what data you need
> ask short, concise questions
> start with simple questions to encourage the person who is giving the responses
> provide response boxes where possible: Yes ☐   No ☐
> avoid leading questions such as
> > 'Don't you agree that there is too much sport on television?'
> or   'Do you think that professional footballers are overpaid?'
> avoid personal questions such as,
> > 'Do you live in an affluent area?'
> or   'Are you well educated?'
> or   'Are you overweight?'

A choice of responses can be very useful in replying to the question, 'What age are you?'

Here is an example: Tick your age in one of the boxes below:

☐   ☐   ☐   ☐

Under 18 years   18–30   31–50   Over 50

Notice that there are no gaps in the ages and that only one response applies to each person.

When you are collecting data, you need to make sure that your survey or experiment is **fair** and avoids **bias**. If bias exists, the data collected might be unrepresentative.

The boxes given below contain questions that should be avoided because they either are too **vague**, too **personal**, or may **influence** the answer.

How often do you play tennis?

Sometimes ☐   Occasionally ☐   Often ☐

The three words *sometimes*, *occasionally* and *often* mean different things to different people.

Normal people enjoy swimming.
Do you enjoy swimming?

Yes ☐   No ☐

This is a leading question and may cause the result to be biased.
The first sentence should not be there.

Have you ever stolen goods from a supermarket?

Yes ☐   No ☐

Few people are likely to answer this question honestly if they have already stolen.

Whenever you undertake a survey or experiment, it is advisable to do a pilot survey. A pilot survey is one that is carried out on a very small scale to make sure the design and methods of the survey are likely to produce the information required. It should identify any problems with the wording of the questions and likely responses.

3. Control group

If we wish to investigate whether a new drug has any effect on those who take it, we select a group of patients, chosen at random, to form a sample. The sample is then divided randomly into two groups. Both groups think that they are taking the new drug, but only the first group actually take it.

The second group are given an inactive substance (or placebo) but they think they have taken the drug. This second group is called a **control group**. If more patients get better in the first group, then the drug has an effect.

4. Designed experiments

In statistics, the word 'experiment' generally refers to a situation where the experimentor carries out some controlled activity and records the results by counting or measuring or simply observing.

Thus an experiment may consist of
> tossing three coins and recording the number of times two heads show
> measuring the circumference of oak trees in a wood
> throwing a dice several times to determine if it is biased
> recording the side-effects of a new drug
> investigating whether people are better at remembering words, numbers or pictures.

Explanatory and response variables

In a statistical experiment, one of the variables will be controlled while its effect on the other variable is observed.

The controlled variable is called the **explanatory variable**.
The effect being observed is called the **response variable**.

Example 1

A research team is investigating whether the adding of fish oil to the daily diet of school students increases their IQ. A school of 500 students is selected. Two groups, each of 50 students, are selected at random.
Group A is given a daily ration of fish oil.
Group B is given the same food as Group A, but no fish oil.
  (i)   Which group is the control group?
  (ii) What is the explanatory variable in this experiment?
  (iii) What is the response variable?

  (i)   Group B is the control group.
  (ii) The explanatory variable is the fish oil; that is, the variable whose effect on the response variable we wish to study.
  (iii) The response variable is the IQ of the student; that is, the variable whose changes we wish to study.

Exercise 2.2

1. Jack wants to find out what students think about the library service at his college. Part of the questionnaire he has written is shown.

    Q1. What is your full name? ....

    Q2. How many times a week do you go to the library?
    ☐ Often   ☐ Sometimes   ☐ Never

    (i)   Why should Q1 not be asked?
    (ii) What is wrong with the choices offered in Q2?

2. Carol wants to find out what people think of the HSE. Part of the questionnaire she has written is shown.

    Q1. What is your date of birth? ....

    Q2. Don't you agree that waiting times for operations are too long?
    Yes ☐   No ☐

    Q3. How many times did you visit your doctor last year?
    ☐ less than 5   ☐ 5–10   ☐ 10 or more

(i) Why should Q1 not be asked?

(ii) Give a reason why Q2 is unsuitable.

(iii) (a) Explain why the responses to Q3 are unsuitable in their present form.

     (b) Rewrite a more suitable question to be included in the questionnaire.

3. Give a reason why questions A and B below should be re-worded before being included in a questionnaire.

Rewrite each one showing exactly how you would present it in a questionnaire.

Question A: Do you live in a working-class or middle-class area?

Question B: The new supermarket seems to be a great success. Do you agree?

4. Decide if the given question is suitable for use in a questionnaire. If it is not, give a reason why and rewrite the question to improve it.

How much pocket money do you get?

a little ☐   some ☐   a lot ☐

5. A market research company is conducting a survey to find out whether, last year, most people had a holiday in Ireland, elsewhere in Europe or in the rest of the world.

It also wants to know if they stayed in self-catering accommodation, hotels or went camping.

Design **two** questions that could be used in a questionnaire to efficiently find out all this information.

6. Which of the following questions do you think are biased?

Write down their letters and explain what makes them biased.

A: Did you go to a cinema in the last month?

B: It is important to eat fruit. Do you eat fruit?

C: How many hours of television do you watch each week?

D: In view of the huge number of road accidents outside this school, do you think the speed limit should be reduced?

7. Megan has to carry out a survey into the part-time jobs of all the 16-year-olds in her school.

She has to find out:

  ❯ what proportion of these 16-year-olds have part-time jobs

  ❯ whether more girls than boys have part-time jobs.

Design **two** questions which she could include in her questionnaire.

8. Richie is convinced that people with longer legs run faster in sprint races. He conducts an experiment to test his theory.

What are the explanatory and response variables he should measure?

9. The HSE has the following data on operations carried out in a large Dublin hospital.

Number of operating theatres	3	4	5	6	7
Number of operations per day	15	21	24	28	37

(i) What is the explanatory variable?

(ii) What is the response variable?

10. A medical research company wishes to investigate whether a new drug is effective in controlling blood-pressure.

They select 80 people who suffer from high blood-pressure and divide them randomly into two groups of 40.

Group A is given the drug. Group B is not given the drug, but they believe that they are taking it.

At the end of the study, the blood pressures of both groups are taken to see if the drug is effective.

    (i)   Which group is the control group?

   (ii)   What is the explanatory variable in the experiment?

  (iii)   What is the response variable?

  (iv)   Which of these would best describe the research?

        (a)   a designed experiment

        (b)   an observational study.

Section 2.3 Populations and sampling

In a statistical enquiry, you often need information about a particular group. This group is known as the population and it could be small, large or even infinite.

Examples of populations include

  (i)   all second-level pupils in Ireland

 (ii)   paid-up members of golf clubs

(iii)   people entitled to vote in a general election.

If information is obtained from all members of a population, the survey is called a census.

Sample survey

When a population is large, taking a census can be very time-consuming and difficult to do with accuracy. So when a census is ruled out as being impractical, information is normally taken from a small part of the population. The chosen members of the population are called a **sample** and an investigation using a sample is called a **sample survey**. Data from a sample can be obtained relatively cheaply and quickly. If the data is representative of the population, a sample survey can give an accurate indication of the population characteristic that is being studied.

The **size** of a sample is important. If the sample is too small, the results may not be very reliable.

If the sample is too large, the data may take a long time to collect and analyse.

However, large samples are more likely to give reliable information than small ones.

Bias in sampling

The sample you select for your study is very important. If the sample is not properly selected, the results may be **biased**. If **bias** exists, the results will be distorted and so may not be representative of the population as a whole.

Bias in a sample may arise from any of the following:

> **Choosing a sample which is not representative**
>   Example   Cara is doing a survey on people's attitude towards gambling. If she stands
>   outside a casino and questions people as they enter or leave, the results will
>   be biased as these people are already involved in gambling.

> **Not identifying the correct population**
>   Example   The school principal wants to find out about students' attitudes to school
>   uniforms. She questions ten Leaving Certificate students only. This may lead
>   to biased results as the opinions of the younger students (from 1st year to 5th
>   year) are not included.

> **Failure to respond to a survey**
>   Many people do not fill in responses to questionnaires sent through the post. Those who
>   do respond may not be representative of the population being surveyed.

> **Dishonest answers to questions**

Sampling methods

The purpose of sampling is to gain information about the whole population by selecting a
sample from that population. If you want the sample to be representative of the population,
you must give every member of the population an equal chance of being included in the
sample. This is known as **random sampling**. Before a random sample is selected, a **sampling
frame** must be used to identify the population. A sampling frame consists of all the items in
the population to ensure that every item has a chance of being selected in the sample.

Some of the most commonly-used sampling methods are given below.

1. Simple random sampling

A sample of size n is called a **simple random sample** if every possible sample of size n has an
equal chance of being selected. In practice, this means that each member of the population
has an equal chance of being selected.

There are many ways of doing this.

Methods for choosing a **simple random sample** could involve giving each member of the
population a number and then selecting the numbers for the sample in one of these ways:

> putting the numbers into a hat and then selecting however many you need for the sample
> using a random number table
> using a random number generator on your calculator or computer

Any of these methods are suitable only if the population is relatively small and the sampling
frame is clearly identified.

2. Stratified sampling

Stratified sampling is used when the population can be split into separate groups or strata that
are quite different from each other. The number selected from each group is proportional to
the size of the group. Separate random samples are then taken from each group.

Example 1

A survey to estimate the number of vegetarians in a mixed college with 660 boys and 540 girls is carried out.
A sample of 40 students is required.
How many boys and girls should be included?

The total number of students is $660 + 540 = 1200$.

Boys: $\dfrac{660}{1200} \times \dfrac{40}{1} = 22$ boys

Girls: $\dfrac{540}{1200} \times \dfrac{40}{1} = 18$ girls

So 22 boys and 18 girls should be chosen.

3. Systematic sampling

A sample which is obtained by choosing items at regular intervals from an unordered list is called a **systematic sample**. For example, if you wish to choose 20 students from 200 students, you could take every tenth student from the register. Select a random number between 1 and 10, e.g., 4. Thus you could select the 4th, 14th, 24th, 34th … until you get 20 students

4. Quota sampling

Quota sampling is widely used in market research and in opinion polls. First the population is divided into groups in terms of age, general education levels, social class, etc. The interviewer is then told how many people (the quota) to interview in each of these groups, but the interviewer makes the choice of who exactly is asked. A disadvantage of quota sampling is that the actual people or items chosen are left to the discretion of the interviewer which could lead to bias. An advantage of quota sampling is that no sampling frame is required.

5. Cluster sampling

In **cluster sampling**, the population being sampled is split into groups or clusters. The clusters are then randomly chosen and every item in the cluster is looked at. It is best if a large number of small clusters is formed as this minimises the chances of the sample being unrepresentative. Cluster sampling is very popular with scientists.

6. Convenience sampling

Convenience sampling involves selecting a group of people because it is easy for us to contact them and they are willing to answer our questions. For example, a sample of 40 students in a school could be selected by simply taking the first 40 names on the school register. Convenience sampling is very quick and easy to organise but it can lead to high levels of bias and so is very likely to be unrepresentative.

Example 2

Simon wanted to investigate whether people in Ireland measured their height in metric or imperial units. He went to his local supermarket and asked the first twenty people he met how tall they were.
   (i)   For this survey, state the sampling frame, the sampling method used and why it might be biased.
  (ii)   Outline a better method of choosing a sample.

   (i)   The sampling frame could be the whole population of Ireland.
         The sampling method used is convenience sampling.
         It may be biased as everyone chosen most likely lives in the same area and so may not provide a cross-section of social class and age-groups. Also, the sample is too small.
  (ii)   A better method would be to use stratified sampling. In this way, you could ensure that men and women across all age-groups, different ethnic groups and different social classes were represented in the sample.

Exercise 2.3

1. Explain briefly the difference between a **census** and a **sample**.
    Give two reasons why a sample may be preferred to a census.

2. There are 100 students in Transition Year.
    Generate random numbers on your calculator to select a sample of 10 students from Transition Year.
    Describe briefly what is meant by a simple random sample.

3. For each of the following methods, say whether it would give a random sample or whether it is likely to be biased:
    (i)   Interview all the people in a local supermarket.
    (ii)   Take every tenth person from a list.
    (iii) Put all the names in a hat and pick without looking.
    (iv)   Test the first article produced each hour by a machine.
    (v)   Number all the items and then select by using random number tables.

4. Describe briefly what is meant by convenience sampling.

    Jack is doing a statistical project. He decides to take a sample of 20 people.
    The sample he chooses is the first 20 names on a register.
    (i)   What sort of sample is he choosing?
    (ii)   Give two major problems with this method of taking a sample.

5. What type of sampling is being used in each of the following surveys?
   (i) Kate is doing a survey to find out how often people go to the cinema and how they travel to get there. She stands outside her local cinema and questions 20 people as they go in.
   (ii) Enda wants to know people's voting intentions as they enter the polling station on election day. He questions every 5th person as they enter the polling station.
   (iii) There are 60 girls and 40 boys in 5th year.
   The school principal wants to interview a sample of 20 students from 5th year.
   She randomly selects 12 girls and 8 boys.

6. After plans for a bypass to a large town were announced, the local newspaper received twelve letters on the subject. Eleven were opposed to it.
   The newspaper claimed

   ### OVER 90% ARE AGAINST NEW BYPASS

   (i) Give two reasons why the newspaper could be criticised for making this claim.
   (ii) The local council is to carry out a survey to find the true nature of local opinion. Give two factors that should be taken into account when selecting the sample.

7. Gillian wanted to find out how much people in Ireland were prepared to spend on holidays abroad. She asked people in the street where she lived.
   (i) What sampling method was Gillian using?
   (ii) Explain why the sample may be biased.
   (iii) Describe a better method of choosing the sample.

8. There are 1000 students in Nigel and Sonia's school.
   Nigel is carrying out a survey of the types of food eaten at lunchtime.
   (i) Explain how Nigel could take a random sample of students to carry out this survey.

   This table shows the gender and the number of students in each year group.

Year group	Number of boys	Number of girls	Total
1	100	100	200
2	90	80	170
3	120	110	230
4	80	120	200
5	100	100	200

   Sonia is carrying out a survey about how much homework students are given.
   She decides to take a stratified sample of 100 students from the whole school.
   (ii) Calculate how many in the stratified sample should be
      (a) students from year group 3
      (b) boys from year group 4.

9. A research company was asked to do a survey on people's attitudes to the HSE. They divided the population into ten groups of roughly equal size, based on gender, age and

annual income. They then asked fifty interviewers to question twenty people from each group and record their responses.

    (i)   What sampling method did the research company use?

    (ii) Give one advantage and one disadvantage of this method.

10. Explain briefly

    (i)   Why it is often desirable to take a sample rather than a census

    (ii) What you understand by the term 'sampling frame'.

11. In a school, there are 460 pupils in Junior Cycle and 420 pupils in Senior Cycle.

    (i)   How many pupils from each cycle of the school should be included in a stratified random sample of size 100?

    (ii) Explain briefly in what circumstances a stratified random sample might be taken rather than a simple random sample.

12. Julia and her friends are investigating the part-time jobs of the Senior Cycle students in their school. There are eight Senior Cycle classes.

    (i)   Julia chooses one class at random and questions every pupil in this class. What sampling method is she using?

    (ii) Brian goes into the school hall at morning break and chooses ten girls and ten boys. What sampling method is he using?

    (iii) Leah has a list of all the pupils in Senior Cycle, arranged in alphabetical order. For her sample, she chooses the third pupil on the list and then every tenth pupil after that. What sampling method is she using?

Section 2.4 Measures of location

When we are presented with a huge mass of numbers (data), we need just one or two numbers that would convey most of the essential information. These numbers are generally referred to as **summary statistics**.

There are two main types of summary statistic, namely, **measures of location** and **measures of spread**. Measures of location answer the question 'What value is typical of the values in the data?' Measures of spread answer the questions 'How much do the values vary?' or 'How spread out are the values?'

In this section, we will deal with measures of location or averages.
There are three different types of average in statistics.
These are the **mode**, the **mean** and the **median**.

1. The Mode

The **mode** is the most common value in a set of data. The mode is very useful when one value appears much more often than any other. It is easy to find and can be used for non-numerical data such as the colours of cars sold by a car dealership.

The following numbers represent the ages of students on a school bus.

10, 11, 12, 12, 12, 13, 13, 14, 14, 15, 15, 15, 15, 16, 16, 16, 17, 17

The number in this list with the greatest frequency is 15.

∴ the mode = 15 years.

2. The Mean

To find the mean of a set of numbers,

1. Find the sum of all the numbers.
2. Divide this sum by the number of numbers.

The mean is the most frequently-used 'average'.

It is important because it considers every piece of data. However, it can be affected by extreme values.

$$\text{The mean is} = \frac{\text{sum of the numbers}}{\text{number of numbers}}$$

The mean of the numbers 12, 14, 10, 17, 21 and 22 is:

$$\text{Mean} = \frac{12 + 14 + 10 + 17 + 21 + 22}{6} = \frac{96}{6} = 16$$

The mean of a frequency distribution

The table below shows the marks (from 1 to 10) scored by the twenty pupils in a class.

Marks	1	2	3	4	5	6	7	8	9	10
No. of pupils	1	1	1	3	5	3	2	2	1	1

The average or mean mark of this distribution is found by dividing the total number of marks by the total number of pupils.

To find the total number of marks, we multiply each mark (or *ariable*) by the number of pupils (*frequency*) who received that mark.

$$\therefore \quad \text{the mean} = \frac{1(1) + 2(1) + 3(1) + 4(3) + 5(5) + 6(3) + 7(2) + 8(2) + 9(1) + 10(1)}{1 + 1 + 1 + 3 + 5 + 3 + 2 + 2 + 1 + 1}$$

$$= \frac{110}{20} = 5.5 \text{ marks}$$

If x stands for the variable and f stands for the frequency, then

$$\text{mean} = \frac{\Sigma fx}{\Sigma f}$$

$$\text{Mean} = \frac{\Sigma fx}{\Sigma f}$$

where Σfx is the sum of all the variables multiplied by the corresponding frequencies and Σf is the sum of the frequencies.

Grouped frequency distributions

The grouped frequency distribution table below shows the marks (out of 25) achieved by fifty students in a test.

Marks achieved	1–5	6–10	11–15	16–20	21–25
No. of students	11	12	15	9	3

While it is not possible to find the exact mean of a grouped frequency distribution, we can find an estimate of the mean by taking the **mid-interval value** of each class.
The mid-interval value in the (1–5) class is found by adding 1 and 5 and dividing by 2,

i.e., $\dfrac{1+5}{2} = 3$

Similarly, the mid-interval value of the (6–10) class is $\dfrac{6+10}{2} = 8$.

The table given on the previous page is reproduced, with the mid-interval values written in smaller size over each class interval.

	3	8	13	18	23
Marks achieved	1–5	6–10	11–15	16–20	21–25
No. of students	11	12	15	9	3

$$\text{Mean} = \frac{\Sigma fx}{\Sigma f} = \frac{11(3) + 12(8) + 15(13) + 9(18) + 3(23)}{11 + 12 + 15 + 9 + 3} = \frac{555}{50} = 11.1$$

3. The Median

To find the median of a list of numbers, put the numbers in order of size, starting with the smallest. The **median** is the middle number.

If there are 11 numbers in the list, the middle value is $\frac{1}{2}(11 + 1)$, i.e., the 6th value.

If there are 10 numbers in the list, the middle number is $\frac{1}{2}(10 + 1)$, i.e., the $5\frac{1}{2}$th value.

This value is half the sum of the 5th and 6th values.

> If there are n numbers in a list, the middle value is $\frac{1}{2}(n + 1)$.
>
> If $\frac{1}{2}(n + 1) = 4$, then the 4th value is the median.

Example 1

Find the median of these numbers: 5, 8, 12, 4, 9, 3, 7, 2.

Writing the numbers in order of size, we get:

$$2, \ 3, \ 4, \ \boxed{5, \ 7,} \ 8, \ 9, \ 12$$

The median is $\frac{1}{2}(5 + 7) = \dfrac{5+7}{2} = \dfrac{12}{2} = 6$

∴ the median = 6

> Write the numbers in order of size to find the median.

The mode and median of a frequency distribution

The frequency table below shows the number of letters in the answers to a crossword.

No. of letters in word	3	4	5	6	7
Frequency	3	4	9	5	2

The **mode** is the number of letters (in the word) that occurs most frequently.
Thus the mode is 5 as it occurs more often than any other number.

The **median** is the middle number in the distribution.

The total frequency is $3 + 4 + 9 + 5 + 2$, i.e., 23.

The middle value of the 23 values is $\frac{1}{2}(23 + 1)$, i.e., the 12th value.

We take the frequency row and find the column that contains the 12th number.
The sum of the first two frequencies is $3 + 4 = 7$.
The sum of the first three frequencies is $3 + 4 + 9 = 16$.
Thus the 12th value occurs in the third column, where the number of letters in the word is 5.
$\therefore$ the median $= 5$

When dealing with grouped frequency distributions, we use the same procedure to find the **class interval** in which the median lies.

Deciding which average to use

The three averages, the **mean**, the **mode** and the **median**, are all useful but one may be more appropriate than the others in different situations.

The **mode** is useful when you want to know, for example, which shoe size is the most common.

The **mean** is useful for finding a 'typical' value when most of the data is closely grouped. The mean may not give a typical value if the data is very spread out or if it includes a few values that are very different from the rest. These values are known as **outliers**.

Take, for example, a small company where the chief executive earns €12 100 a month and the other eleven employees each earn €2500 a month.

Here the mean monthly salary is €3300 which is not typical of the monthly salaries.

In situations like this, the **median** or middle value may be more typical.

The table below, which compares the advantages and disadvantages of each type of average, should help you make the correct decision.

Average	Advantages	Disadvantages
Mode	› Easy to find › Not influenced by extreme values	› May not exist › Not very useful for further analysis
Median	› Unaffected by extremes › Easy to calculate if data is ordered	› Not always a given data value › Not very useful for further analysis
Mean	› Uses all the data › Easy to calculate › Very useful for further analysis	› Distorted by extreme results › Mean is not always a given data value

Example 2

There are 10 apartments in a block.
On a particular day, the number of letters delivered to each of the apartments is

$$2, 0, 5, 3, 4, 0, 1, 0, 3, 15$$

Calculate the mean, mode and median number of letters.
Which of these averages is the most suitable to represent this data?
Give a reason for your answer.

$$\text{Mean} = \frac{2 + 0 + 5 + 3 + 4 + 0 + 1 + 0 + 3 + 15}{10} = \frac{33}{10} = 3.3$$

Mode = 0

Median: 0, 0, 0, 1, $\boxed{2, 3,}$ 3, 4, 5, 15

$$\text{Median} = \frac{2 + 3}{2} = \frac{5}{2} = 2\frac{1}{2}$$

Here the mean has been distorted by the large number of letters delivered to one apartment. It is, therefore, not a good measure of the 'typical' number of letters delivered.
Neither is the mode a good measure of the 'typical' number of letters, since seven out of ten apartments do receive some letters.
The median is the best measure of the 'typical' number of letters delivered since half of the apartments receive more than the median and half receive less than the median.

Outliers

An outlier is a very high or very low value that is not typical of the other values in a data set.
If the data set is small, an outlier can have a significant effect on the mean.

Exercise 2.4

1. Rewrite each of the following arrays of numbers in order of size and then write down
   (i) the mode   (ii) the median.
      (a) 8, 11, 2, 5, 8, 7, 8, 2, 5   (b) 3, 3, 7, 8, 7, 9, 8, 5, 7, 11, 12

2. The speeds, in kilometres per hour, of 11 cars travelling on a road are shown:
      41, 42, 31, 36, 42, 43, 42, 34, 41, 37, 45
   (i) Find the median speed.   (ii) Find the mean speed.

3. A rugby team played 10 games.
   Here are the numbers of points the team scored:
      12, 22, 14, 11, 7, 18, 22, 14, 36, 14
   (i) Write down the mode.
   (ii) What is the median number of points scored?
   (iii) Find the mean number of points scored.

4. The mean of four numbers is 19. Three of them are 21, 25 and 16.
   Find the fourth number.

5. Kate's marks in four tests were: 8, 4, 5, 3.
   What marks did she get in her fifth and sixth tests if her modal mark was 4 and her
   mean mark was 5 after the six tests?

6. Find (i) the mean (ii) the median of these numbers:

   $$9, \quad 11, \quad 11, \quad 15, \quad 17, \quad 18, \quad 100$$

   Which of these two averages would you choose to best describe these numbers?

7. The mean of five numbers is 39.
   Two of the numbers are 103 and 35 and each of the other three numbers is equal to x.
   Find   (i)   the total of the five numbers
           (ii)   the value of x.

8. There are 12 children in Phil's group. Their mean mark in a Maths test is 76%. In Paul's
   group, there are only 8 children.
   Their mean mark is 84%. Find the overall mean mark for the 20 children.

9. A teacher sets a test.
   He wants to choose a minimum mark for a distinction so that 50% of his students score
   higher than this mark.
   Should he use the modal mark, the median mark or the mean mark?
   Give a reason for your answer.

10. A class took a test.
    The mean mark of the 20 boys in the class was 17.4.
    The mean mark of the 10 girls in the class was 13.8.
     (i) Calculate the mean mark for the whole class.

    Five pupils in another class took a different test.
    Their marks, written in order, were 12, 18, 20, 25 and x.
    The mean of these 5 marks was 2 greater than the median of the 5 marks.
     (ii) Calculate the value of x.

11. A test consisted of ten questions, 1 mark per question, and 0 for an incorrect solution.
    The following table shows how a class of students scored in the test:

Marks	3	4	5	6	7	8	9
No. of students	3	2	6	10	0	3	1

     (i)   How many students were in the class?
     (ii) Write down the mode of the data.
     (iii) Calculate the mean mark per student.
     (iv) How many students scored better than the mean mark?
     (v)   Find the median mark.

12. Paula has 6 people in her family. She wonders how many people are in her friends' families. She asks each of her friends and records the information in a table.

Number in family	2	3	4	5	6	7	8
Frequency	2	4	6	5	2	0	1

   (i)   Write down the modal number of people in these families.
   (ii) Find the median number of persons per family.
   (iii) Calculate the mean of the distribution.

13. The ages of some people watching a film are given in this frequency table:

Age (in years)	10–20	20–30	30–40	40–50
No. of people	4	15	11	10

   (i) Use the mid-interval value of each class to estimate the mean of the distribution, giving your answer correct to the nearest year.
   (ii) In which interval does the median lie?

14. Joe collects six pieces of data x_1, x_2, x_3, x_4, x_5 and x_6. He works out that Σx is 256.2.
   (i) Calculate the mean for these data.

   He collects another piece of data. It is 52.
   (ii) Write down the effect this piece of data will have on the mean.

15. The frequency distribution table below shows the ratings of a disco by a random sample of 40 students.
   A capital A means they enjoyed it very much.
   A capital E means that they did not enjoy it at all.

Rating	A	B	C	D	E
Number of students	6	13	10	7	4

   (i) Work out (a) the mode, (b) the median for this distribution.
   (ii) Explain why you cannot write down the mean of this distribution.

16. The rainfall in a certain seaside holiday resort was measured, in millimetres, every week for ten weeks. The hours of sunshine were also recorded. The data is shown in the table.

Rainfall (mm)	0	1	2	3	3	26	3	2	3	0
Sunshine (hours)	70	15	10	15	18	0	15	21	21	80

   (i)   Calculate the mean rainfall per week.
   (ii) Calculate the mean number of hours of sunshine per week.
   (iii) Write down the modal amount of rainfall and the modal amount of sunshine per week.
   (iv) Work out the median rainfall and the median amount of sunshine per week.

The council plans to produce a brochure and in it they wish to promote the resort as having lots of sunshine and little rain.

    (v) Write down, with reasons, which of the mean, mode or median they should quote in their brochure as the average rainfall and hours of sunshine.

17. An ordinary dice was thrown 50 times and the resulting scores were summarised in a frequency table.

    The mean score was calculated to be 3.42.

    It was later found that the frequencies 12 and 9 of two consecutive scores had been swapped.

    What is the correct value of the mean?

Section 2.5 Measures of variability

When dealing with **averages** in the previous section, we were looking for a data value that was typical or representative of all the data values.

In this section, we will discuss the measure of the spread of the data about the mean to help us describe the data more fully.

The three most common ways of measuring the spread or **variability** of data are the **range**, the **interquartile range** and **standard deviation**.

1. The range

The **range** of a set of data is the highest value of the set minus the lowest value.

It shows the **spread** of the data.

It is very useful when comparing two sets of data.

> The range of a set of data is the largest value minus the smallest value.

The range is a crude measure of spread because it uses only the largest and smallest value of the data.

The range of the numbers 14, 18, 11, 27, 21, 19, 33, 24 is

      Range $= 33 - 11 = 22$

2. Quartiles and Interquartile range

When data is arranged in order of size, we have already learned that the median is the value halfway into the data. So we can say that the median divides the data into two halves. The data can also be divided into four quarters.

When the data is arranged in ascending order of size:

> the **lower quartile** is the value one quarter of the way into the data
> the **upper quartile** is the value three quarters of the way into the data
> the upper quartile minus the lower quartile is called the **interquartile range**.

The lower quartile is written Q_1; the median is Q_2; the upper quartile is Q_3.

Consider the following data which is arranged in order of size. It contains 15 numbers.

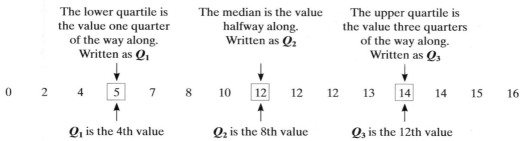

The lower quartile is the value one quarter of the way along. Written as Q_1

The median is the value halfway along. Written as Q_2

The upper quartile is the value three quarters of the way along. Written as Q_3

| 0 | 2 | 4 | 5 | 7 | 8 | 10 | 12 | 12 | 12 | 13 | 14 | 14 | 15 | 16 |

Q_1 is the 4th value Q_2 is the 8th value Q_3 is the 12th value

The lower quartile $Q_1 = 5$.
The median $Q_2 = 12$.
The upper quartile $Q_3 = 14$.
The interquartile range $= Q_3 - Q_1 = 14 - 5 = 9$.

> The interquartile range is
> upper quartile − lower quartile
> $= Q_3 - Q_1$

When n data values are written in order:

➤ the lower quartile, Q_1, is the $\frac{1}{4}(n + 1)$th value
➤ the median, Q_2, is the $\frac{1}{2}(n + 1)$th value
➤ the upper quartile, Q_3, is the $\frac{3}{4}(n + 1)$th value.

If you get a non-integer value for $\frac{1}{4}(n + 1)$ or $\frac{3}{4}(n + 1)$, e.g., $3\frac{3}{4}$, find the mean of the 3rd and 4th pieces of data.

If you get a non-integer for $\frac{1}{2}(n + 1)$, take the mean of the two data values on either side.
For example if $\frac{1}{2}(n + 1) = 3\frac{1}{2}$, find the mean of the 3rd and 4th data values.

Example 1

These are the test marks of 11 students:

$$52, 78, 61, 49, 79, 47, 54, 58, 72, 62, 73$$

Find   (i) the median   (ii) the lower quartile
         (iii) the upper quartile   (iv) the interquartile range.

We first rewrite the numbers in order, starting with the smallest:

$$47, 49, 52, 54, 58, 61, 62, 72, 73, 78, 79$$

(i) The median is the middle value of the list.
Since there are 11 values, the middle value is
$\frac{1}{2}(11 + 1)$ i.e. the 6th value.
The 6th value is 61 ⇒ the median = 61.

(ii) The lower quartile is the value that is $\frac{1}{4}$ way through the distribution.
This value is found by getting $\frac{1}{4}(11 + 1) =$ the 3rd value.
The 3rd value is 52 ⇒ the lower quartile $(Q_1) = 52$.

(iii) The upper quartile is the value that is $\frac{3}{4}$ way through the distribution.
This value is found by getting $\frac{3}{4}(11 + 1) =$ the 9th value.
This ninth value is 73 ⇒ the upper quartile $(Q_3) = 73$.

(iv) The interquartile range $= Q_3 - Q_1$
$$= 73 - 52 = 21$$

71

3. Standard deviation

One of the most important and frequently-used measures of spread is called **standard deviation**. It shows how much variation there is from the average (mean). It may be thought of as the average difference of the scores from the mean, that is, how far they are away from the mean. A low standard deviation indicates that the data points tend to be very close to the mean; a high standard deviation indicates that the data is spread out over a large range of values.

The Greek letter σ is used to denote standard deviation.

Take, for example, all adult men in Ireland. The average height is about 177 cm with a standard deviation of about 8 cm.

For this large population, about 68% of the men have a height within 8 cm of the mean.

> If the mean is $\bar{x}$ and σ is the standard deviation of a large sample, then 68% will lie between $\bar{x} + \sigma$ and $\bar{x} - \sigma$

Procedure for finding the standard deviation

The steps used to find the standard deviation of a set of numbers are as follows:

1. Calculate the mean of the numbers. This is written $\bar{x}$.

2. Find the deviation (or difference) of each variable, x, from the mean. This is denoted by $(x - \bar{x})$.

3. Square each of these deviations, i.e., find $(x - \bar{x})^2$.

4. Find the sum (Σ) of these values, i.e., find $\Sigma(x - \bar{x})^2$.

5. Divide this result by n, the number of numbers.
   This gives $\dfrac{\Sigma(x - \bar{x})^2}{n}$.

6. Finally, get the square root of the result in 5.

   There is no need to use this formula if you can remember the steps listed above.
   Alternatively, you may use a calculator.

> Standard deviation
> $$\sigma = \sqrt{\frac{\Sigma(x - \bar{x})^2}{n}}$$

Example 2

Find the standard deviation of the numbers 6, 9, 10, 12, 13.

The mean $= \dfrac{6 + 9 + 10 + 12 + 13}{5} = \dfrac{50}{5} = 10.$

$$\sigma = \sqrt{\frac{(6 - 10)^2 + (9 - 10)^2 + (10 - 10)^2 + (12 - 10)^2 + (13 - 10)^2}{5}}$$

$$= \sqrt{\frac{(-4)^2 + (-1)^2 + (0)^2 + (2)^2 + (3)^2}{5}}$$

$$= \sqrt{\frac{16 + 1 + 0 + 4 + 9}{5}} = \sqrt{\frac{30}{5}} = \sqrt{6} = 2.45$$

$\therefore$ the standard deviation is 2.45

Finding the Standard Deviation of a Frequency Distribution

When finding the standard deviation from a frequency distribution, the deviation of each variable from the mean is squared and then multiplied by the frequency (f) of that variable. The result is then divided by the sum of the frequencies.

Finally, we get the square root of the result.

This procedure can be represented by the formula

$$\sqrt{\frac{\Sigma f(x - \bar{x})^2}{\Sigma f}}$$ where $\Sigma f(x - \bar{x})^2$ is the sum of the $f(x - \bar{x})^2$ column and Σf is the sum of the frequencies.

The worked example below will show you how to lay out your work when finding the standard deviation of a frequency distribution.

Example 3

Find the standard deviation of the following frequency distribution:

Variable (x)	1	2	3	4	5	6
Frequency (f)	9	9	6	4	7	3

First find the mean of the distribution.

$$\text{The mean} = \frac{(9 \times 1) + (9 \times 2) + (6 \times 3) + (4 \times 4) + (7 \times 5) + (3 \times 6)}{9 + 9 + 6 + 4 + 7 + 3}$$

$$\Rightarrow \quad \bar{x} = \frac{114}{38} = 3$$

Now set out a table like this.

x	f	$x - \bar{x}$	$(x - \bar{x})^2$	$f(x - \bar{x})^2$
1	9	−2	4	36
2	9	−1	1	9
3	6	0	0	0
4	4	1	1	4
5	7	2	4	28
6	3	3	9	27
	↓			↓
	$\Sigma f = 38$			$\Sigma f(x - \bar{x})^2 = 104$

$$\sigma = \sqrt{\frac{\Sigma f(x - \bar{x})^2}{\Sigma f}} = \sqrt{\frac{104}{38}} = 1.65$$

Note: To calculate the standard deviation of a grouped frequency distribution, take the mid-interval values of the variables and proceed as in Example 3 above.

Use of calculator to find standard deviation

The tedious work involved in calculating the standard deviation of a large set of data can be substantially reduced by using a scientific calculator.

In the following examples, we will use the **Casio fx-83ES** calculator to illustrate the keys and steps involved in finding standard deviation.

Example 4

Find (a) the mean (b) the standard deviation of the following set of numbers:
(i) 5, 3, 1, 8, 2   (ii) 10, 6, 2, 16, 4

(i) Key in [MODE] and select [2] for statistics mode.

Then select [1] for 1 − VAR.

Now input the numbers [5] [=]
[3] [=]
[1] [=]
[8] [=]
[2] [=]

CASIO		fx-83ES
	X	FREQ
1	5	1
2	3	1
3	1	1
4	8	1
5	2	1

To get your answers, key in [AC] to clear, and [SHIFT] [1] to go to menu.

Now select [5] to get statistics on variables.

Then select [2] for $\bar{x}$ (the mean), then [=]

The mean $\bar{x}$ is 3.8.

To proceed to get the standard deviation, key in [AC] to clear.

Now key in [SHIFT] [1] to go to menu and select [5] to get statistics on variables.

Now key in [3] for $x\sigma n$ (standard deviation) [=]

The result is 2.4819… = 2.5
∴ standard deviation = 2.5

(ii) 10, 6, 2, 16, 4.
Here is the sequence of keys to find the mean and standard deviation.
[MODE] [2] [1]

[10] [=] [6] [=] [2] [=] [16] [=] [4] [=]

[AC] [SHIFT] [1] [5] [2] [=]   7.6 = mean

[AC] [SHIFT] [1] [5] [3] [=]   4.963869… = 5.0 = standard deviation

4. Percentiles

Percentiles divide data into 100 equal parts.

Percentiles give a measure of your position relative to others in a data set. If you are told that you are on the 70th percentile in a competitive test, this means that 70% of the competitors had scores lower than yours (or 30% higher than yours). It is important not to confuse percentiles with percentages. For example, you could achieve a score of 70% in a state examination but you could be at the 80th percentile.

Percentiles are denoted by $P_1, P_2, P_3, P_{40} \ldots$

How to find P_k of a data set

When asked to find the 40th percentile, P_{40}, we are required to find the value of the number that is 40% of the way into the data set.

Thus to find P_k of a data set:

1. Order the numbers in the data set from smallest to largest.

2. Now find $k\%$ of the total number of data points in the set.
    i.e. find $\dfrac{k}{100} \times n$, where n is the number of numbers in the set.

3. (i) If the answer in 2 is a whole number, for example 5, then the kth percentile is the mean of the 5th and 6th numbers in the data set.
    (ii) If the answer in 2 is not a whole number, for example $6\frac{1}{4}$, round up to 7.
    The 7th number in the data set will be the kth percentile.

Example 5

Here are the marks of 24 students in a science test:

| 48 | 54 | 76 | 34 | 82 | 67 | 76 | 92 | 54 | 72 | 86 | 47 |
| 80 | 73 | 64 | 57 | 68 | 36 | 82 | 74 | 71 | 62 | 46 | 52 |

(i)   Find P_{60}
(ii) Find P_{75}
(iii) If Sinead scored 74 in the test, find on what percentile is her score.

First we order the data, starting with the smallest:

| 34 | 36 | 46 | 47 | 48 | 52 | 54 | 54 | 57 | 62 | 64 | 67 |
| 68 | 71 | 72 | 73 | 74 | 76 | 76 | 80 | 82 | 82 | 86 | 92 |

(i) $P_{60} = \frac{60}{100} \times \frac{24}{1} = 14.4$

Since 14.4 is not a whole number, we go to the next whole number, i.e. 15.

P_{60} = the 15th number in the set.

This number is 72. Thus $P_{60} = 72$.

(ii) $P_{75} = \frac{75}{100} \times \frac{24}{1} = 18$

As this is a whole number, we find the mean of the 18th and 19th numbers in the data set.

These numbers are 76 and 76.

$$\therefore \quad P_{75} = \frac{76 + 76}{2} = 76$$

(iii) If Sinead scored 74, this means that 16 students scored lower than she did. We now find the percentile that corresponds to 16.

Percentile $= \frac{16}{24} \times \frac{100}{1} = 66.66$

Therefore Sinead is in the 67th percentile.

Example 6

Leah lives near the local bus stop. One day she recorded the number of people waiting in the queue for each bus. The table below shows her data.

Number of people	3	4	5	6	7	8	9	10	11
Frequency	4	6	3	8	0	7	5	9	8

(i) Find P_{40} (ii) Find P_{82}

(i) To find P_{40}, we find $\frac{40}{100}$ of the total frequency.

The total frequency is 50.

$$P_{40} = \frac{40}{100} \times \frac{50}{1} = 20 \Rightarrow P_{40} = \frac{20\text{th value} + 21\text{st value}}{2}$$

The 20th and 21st values lie in the fourth column, i.e., 6 people.

$$\therefore \quad P_{40} = 6 \text{ people}$$

(ii) $P_{82} = \frac{82}{100} \times \frac{50}{1} = 41 \Rightarrow P_{82} = \frac{41\text{st value} + 42\text{nd value}}{2}$

The 41st and 42nd values lie in the eight column, i.e., 10 people.

$$\therefore \quad P_{82} = 10 \text{ people}$$

Exercise 2.5

1. Find the range for each of the following sets of data:

   (i) 6, 3, 8, 2, 9, 5, 10   (ii) 21, 16, 72, 40, 67, 65, 55, 34, 17, 48, 32, 19, 44, 61, 73

2. Nine students submitted their assignments which were marked out of 40. The marks obtained were:

   37, 34, 34, 29, 27, 27, 10, 4, 34

   (i) Write down the range of marks.   (ii) Write down the median mark.

   (iii) Find (a) the lower quartile (b) the upper quartile (c) the interquartile range.

3. Here are the times, in minutes, for a bus journey:

    15, 7, 9, 12, 9, 19, 6, 11, 9, 16, 8

    (i) Find the range of these times.   (ii) Find the lower quartile.
    (iii) Find the upper quartile.   (iv) Write down the interquartile range.

4. A group of boys and girls took a French test. These are the marks which the boys got:

    13, 14, 14, 15, 14, 14, 15, 17, 16, 14, 16, 12

    (i) Find the range of the boys' marks.
    (ii) Calculate the mean mark of the boys.

    The mean mark for the girls in the class was 13.2 and the girls' marks had a range of 7.

    (iii) Make two statements about the differences between the boys' and girls' marks in the French test.

5. Conor played nine rounds of crazy golf. Here are his scores:

    51, 53, 50, 41, 59, 64, 66, 65, 50

    Find   (i) the range   (ii) the lower quartile
            (iii) the upper quartile   (iv) the interquartile range.

6. The blood glucose of 30 adults is recorded.
   The results, in mmol/litre, are given below:

    3.1 3.6 3.7 2.2 2.3 4.0 4.4 4.0 5.1 4.0 4.5 3.7 3.8 3.8 2.3
    4.6 4.8 3.8 3.9 2.5 3.8 2.7 3.9 3.9 5.5 2.2 4.7 3.2 3.7 4.0

    (i) Find Q_1 and Q_3 and hence find the interquartile range.
    (ii) If an outlier can be identified as being $1\frac{1}{2}$ times the interquartile range above the upper quartile or $1\frac{1}{2}$ times the interquartile range below the lower quartile, find any outliers in the distribution.

7. Calculate the standard deviation of each of the following arrays of numbers, giving your answer correct to one decimal place:
    (i) 1, 3, 7, 9, 10   (ii) 8, 12, 15, 9   (iii) 1, 3, 4, 6, 10, 12
    Use your calculator to verify your answer in each case.

8. Find the standard deviation of the numbers: 2, 3, 4, 5, 6.

    Now find the standard deviation of these numbers: 12, 13, 14, 15, 16.

    (i) What is the relationship between the two sets of numbers?
    (ii) What is the relationship between their standard deviations?
    (iii) What conclusion can you draw from the results?

9. Use your calculator, or otherwise, to show that the standard deviation of the numbers
    3   4   6   2   8   8   5   is 2.17.

10. There are two routes for a worker to get to his office.
Both the routes involve hold-ups due to traffic lights.
He records the time it takes over a series of six journeys for each route.
The results are shown in the table.

Route 1	15	15	11	17	14	12
Route 2	11	14	17	15	16	11

   (i) Work out the mean time taken for each route.
   (ii) Calculate the standard deviation of each of the two routes.
   (iii) Using your answers to (i) and (ii), suggest which route you would recommend.
       State your reason clearly.

11. Verify that 2 is the mean of this distribution.
Hence calculate the standard deviation, correct to 1 decimal place.

Variable	0	2	3	4
Frequency	4	3	2	3

12. Show that the mean of the given frequency distribution is 3 and hence find the standard deviation, correct to 2 decimal places.

Variable	1	2	3	4
Frequency	1	4	9	6

13. Use the mid-interval values to show that the mean of the grouped frequency distribution below is 5.
Hence find the standard deviation of the distribution.

Class	1–3	3–5	5–7	7–9
Frequency	4	3	9	2

14. Use the mid-interval values to find the mean and standard deviation of the given grouped frequency distribution:

Variable	0–4	4–8	8–12	12–16	16–20
Frequency	2	3	9	7	3

15. The number of letters delivered to a business premises on each day of the 5-day working week were as follows:

   18, 26, 22, 34, 25

   (i) Calculate the mean number of letters delivered.
   (ii) Calculate the standard deviation, correct to one decimal place.
   (iii) If $\bar{x}$ is the mean and σ is the standard deviation, find the values of $\bar{x} + \sigma$ and $\bar{x} - \sigma$.
   (iv) On how many days is the number of letters delivered within one standard deviation of the mean?

16. The mean of the numbers 1, 9, a and $3a - 2$ is $\bar{x}$ and the standard deviation is σ.
  (i) Express $\bar{x}$ in terms of a.
  (ii) If $\sigma = \sqrt{20}$, find the value of a, if $a \in Z$.

17. Jack is wondering if he is taller or smaller than other boys in his age-group.
  After investigating, he discovered that he is at the 80th percentile.
  What percentage of boys in his age-group are
  (i) smaller than Jack   (ii) taller than Jack?

18. (i) The scores in a test ranged from 1 to 100.
    If Elaine's score was 85, does this mean that her score is in the 85th percentile?
    Explain your answer.
  (ii) In a national examination, Tanya's mark was at the 40th percentile.
    If 800 people took the examination, how many people did better than Tanya?

19. Here are the marks, out of 100, of 20 students in a maths test:

> 38 43 44 44 52 55 58 63 65 66
> 68 69 71 72 72 77 79 79 84 85

  (i) What score indicates the 25th percentile?.
  (ii) What score indicates the 75th percentile?
  (iii) Find the difference between the 40th and 75th percentile.
  (iv) How many students have scores greater than or equal to the 80th percentile?
  (v) Eoin received 65 marks in the test. At what percentile is Eoin's mark?

20. Here are the prices (in €) of gents' T-shirts in a sports shop:

> 21 22 22 22 23 25 26 26 26 27 28 29
> 29 32 32 32 33 37 40 40 42 42 46 48
> 52 55 55 57 59 60 60 65 70 70 75 80

  (i) Calculate P_{70}, the 70th percentile.   (ii) Calculate P_{40}, the 40th percentile.
  (iii) How many of the T-shirts are lower in price than the 40th percentile.
  (iv) Find P_{80} and then find the number of T-shirts that are more expensive than the price at the 80th percentile.
  (v) If the price of a T-shirt is €40, find what percentile this price represents.

21. The numbers $a, b, 8, 5, 7$ have a mean of 6 and a standard deviation of $\sqrt{2}$.
  Express a in terms of b and hence find the values of a and b for $a > b$.

Section 2.6 Stem and leaf diagrams (stemplots) ⎯⎯⎯⎯⎯

A **stem and leaf diagram** is a very useful way of presenting data. It is useful because it shows all the original data and also gives you the overall picture or shape of the distribution.

It is similar to a horizontal bar chart, with the numbers themselves forming the bars.

Stem and leaf diagrams are suitable only for small amounts of data.

Often the stem shows the tens digit of the values and the leaves show the units digit.
If you put them together, you get the original value.

For example 4|2 represents 42.

A typical stem and leaf diagram is shown below.

0	6	9		
1	2	5	⑦	← This represents 17.
2	3	3	6	8
3	0	2	7	
4	1	2	6	
5	3			

You must always add a key to show how the stem and leaf combine.

Key: 3|2 = 32

The data represented above is:

6, 9, 12, 15, 17, 23, 23, 26, 28, 30, 32, 37, 41, 42, 46, 53

Example 1

Here are the marks gained by a class of students in a science test.

58 65 40 59 68 63 81 76 63 57 44 47 53 70 80
68 81 61 57 49 70 54 75 69 65 59 52 63 63 74

(i)   Construct a stem and leaf diagram to represent this data.
(ii) What is the mode of the data?
(iii) What is the median?
(iv) What is the range of the data?

(i)   First draw the stem of the diagram.
      The smallest value in the list is 40 and the largest value is 81.
      The stem of the diagram will be the tens digits from 4 to 8.
      Now work through the data values and put the second digit on the
      appropriate row.

4	0	4	7	9					
5	8	9	7	3	7	4	9	2	
6	5	8	3	3	8	1	9	5	3	3
7	6	0	0	5	4				
8	1	0	1						

For the first value, 58, the 8 will go on the 5 row.

The numbers on the right of the diagram are the leaves.

Finally, rewrite the diagram with all the leaves in order, with the smallest
nearest to the stem.

Remember to include a key.

4	0	4	7	9					
5	2	3	4	7	7	8	9	9	
6	1	3	3	3	3	5	5	8	8	9
7	0	0	4	5	6				
8	0	1	1						

Key: 6|3 = 63

(ii)   The mode is 63 as this is the value that occurs most often.
(iii) As there are 30 values, the median will be the mean of the 15th and 16th values.
       Count the values in the stem and leaf diagram to find the 15th and 16th values.
       Since these are both 63, the median is 63.

> If there are 30 values, the middle value is $\frac{1}{2}(30 + 1)$, i.e., $15\frac{1}{2}$.
> This will be half the sum of the 15th and 16th values.

(iv)   The range is the highest value minus the lowest value.
$$= 81 - 40 = 41$$

Different values for the stems

In a stem and leaf diagram, each leaf consists of one digit only.
The stem may have more than one digit.

Here are the times, in seconds, for the contestants in a 60-metre race.

| 6.6 | 4.9 | 5.7 | 7.6 | 8.2 | 6.3 | 6.5 | 7.4 | 5.1 | 5.3 | 6.2 | 7.8 |

This time we will use the units as the stems.

Step 1   Draw the first diagram.
The units are the stems.
The tenths are the leaves.

```
4 | 9
5 | 7  1  3
6 | 6  3  5  2
7 | 6  4  8
8 | 2
```
Key: 6|3 = 6.3 seconds

Step 2   Put the leaves in numerical order.

```
4 | 9
5 | 1  3  7
6 | 2  3  5  6
7 | 4  6  8
8 | 2
```

Back-to-back stem and leaf diagrams

Two stem and leaf diagrams can be drawn using the same stem.

These are known as **back-to-back stem and leaf diagrams**.

The leaves of one set of data are put to the right of the stem.

The leaves of the other set of data are put on the left.

A back-to-back stem and leaf diagram is very useful to compare two sets of data.

Jack and Ciara compared the length of time they spent each evening on their homework.

Their times are shown in this back-to-back stem and leaf diagram.

			Jack				Ciara			
6	5	5	3	2	2					
		8	6	5	3	6	7			
			3	2	4	4	6	6		
				1	5	2	3	4	5	
					6	4	8			

Key: 5|3 = 35 minutes   Key: 4|6 = 46 minutes

Sometimes the key is given as 5|3|6. This means 35 for Jack and 36 for Ciara.

We read Jack's times from the stem to the left.

Thus Jack's times are:

22, 23, 25, 25, 26, 35, 36, …

Ciara's times are:

36, 37, 44, 46, 46, 52, …

The following example shows how a back-to-back stem and leaf diagram can be used to compare two sets of data.

Example 2

Robert and Jane compared the lengths of time they spent each evening watching television.

Their times are shown in the following back-to-back stem and leaf diagram.

			Robert				Jane			
7	4	4	3	2	2					
		9	6	4	3	4	6			
			5	③	4	5	7	7		
				2	5	3	3	4	6	
				6	⑤	7				

Key: 3|4 = 43 minutes   Key: 6|5 = 65 minutes

(i)   What does the diagram show about the lengths of time Robert and Jane spent watching television?
(ii) What was Jane's median time spent watching television?
(iii) What was Robert's median time?
(iv) Do these median times support your conclusion in (i) above?

(i)   By looking at the diagram, we can see that most of Robert's times are between 22 and 39 minutes.
      Most of Jane's times are between 45 and 67 minutes.
      This shows that Jane spends more time watching television than Robert does.
(ii) For Jane, the value that is halfway through the distribution is 53.
      Thus her median time spent watching television is 53 minutes.
(iii) Robert's median time is 34 minutes.
(iv) Because Jane's median time is greater than Robert's, it supports the view, expressed in (i) above, that she spends more time than Robert watching television.

Finding the interquartile range from a stem and leaf diagram

In Section 2.5 of this chapter, we found that the lower quartile is the value in the data that is one quarter way through the distribution. The upper quartile is the value that is three quarters way through the distribution. The difference between the upper quartile and the lower quartile is the **interquartile range**.

We will now show how to find the two quartiles and the interquartile range of a distribution presented as a stem and leaf diagram.

Example 3

The stem and leaf diagram below shows the marks, out of 50, obtained in a maths test.

Marks obtained

1	2	8			
2	1	4	7	7	8
3	1	4	5	7	
4	1	2	8		
5	0				

Key: $2|1 = 21$

Find   (i)   the median mark   (ii)   the lower quartile
       (iii)   the upper quartile   (iv)   the interquartile range.

(i)   The median mark is the mark that is halfway through the distribution. There are 15 data values.

The halfway value is $\frac{1}{2}(15 + 1)$ i.e. the 8th value.

Starting at the lowest value, the 8th value is 31.

∴   the median = 31

(ii)   The lower quartile is the value that is one quarter way through the distribution.

This value is $\frac{1}{4}(15 + 1)$ i.e.   the 4th value

This value is 24.

∴   the lower quartile = 24

(iii)   The upper quartile is the value that is three quarters of the way through the distribution.

This value is $\frac{3}{4}(15 + 1)$ i.e. the 12th value.

This value is 41.

∴   the upper quartile = 41

(iv)   The interquartile range = upper quartile minus lower quartile
                        = 41 − 24
                        = 17

Exercise 2.6

1. The stem and leaf diagram below shows the ages, in years, of 25 people who wished to enter a 10 km walking competition.

1	4 4 6 9
2	1 3 7 7 7 8
3	3 6 6 7 9
4	0 2 3 3 8 8
5	1 3 4 7

Key: 1|6 means 16 years old

- (i) How many people were less than 20 years old?
- (ii) Write down the modal age.
- (iii) How many people were between 35 and 45 years old?
- (iv) What was the median age?

2. Twenty four pupils were asked how many CDs they had in their collection. The results are shown below:

23	2	18	14	7	4	25	21	32	26	31	6
17	6	18	19	31	21	12	1	0	8	14	15

- (i) Draw a stem and leaf diagram to represent this information.
- (ii) How many pupils had more than twenty CDs?
- (iii) What is the median number of CDs per pupil?

3. The times, in seconds, taken to answer 24 telephone calls are shown.

3.2	5.6	2.4	3.5	4.3	3.6	2.8	5.8	3.3	2.6	3.5	2.8
5.6	3.5	4.2	1.5	2.7	2.5	3.7	3.1	2.9	4.2	2.4	3.0

Copy and complete the stem and leaf diagram on the right to represent this information.

1	
2	
3	2
4	
5	

Key: 3|2 means 3.2 seconds

- (i) How many of the calls took longer than 4 seconds to answer?
- (ii) What is the difference, in seconds, between the shortest and the longest times to answer the calls?
- (iii) What is the median length of time taken to answer the calls?
- (iv) What is the modal length of time?

4. The stem and leaf diagram below shows the marks achieved by 19 students in a test.

stem	leaf
2	2
3	4 6
4	2 7 9
5	3 4 5 8 9
6	0 2 6 7
7	2 6
8	1 4

Key: 4|2 = 42 marks

- (i) Write down the range of the marks.
- (ii) Find the value of the lower quartile.
- (iii) What is the upper quartile?
- (iv) What is the interquartile range?

5. The number of laptops sold by a store was recorded each month for a period of 26 months. The results are shown in the stem and leaf diagram below.

stem	leaf
1	8
2	3 6 7 9 9
3	2 6 6 6 7 8 8
4	4 5 5 5 7 7 7 7 9
5	2 7 7 9

Key: 1|8 means 18 laptops

(i) Find the median. (ii) Find the lower quartile.
(iii) Find the upper quartile. (iv) Work out the interquartile range.
(v) Write down the modal number of laptops sold.

6. The results for examinations in Science and French for a class of students are shown in the back-to-back stem and leaf diagram below:

	Science		French	
	7 5	2		
	8 0	3	6	
	5 5	4	0 5 7 8	
9 5 4 3 2	5	1 5 8	
	9 7 5	6	2 4 4 5 7	
	3 1	7	2 4 5 6	
	6 3	8	3 5	
	1	9		

Key: 1|7 = 71 marks

Key: 3|6 = 36 marks

(i) How many students took the examinations?
(ii) What is the range of marks in (a) Science (b) French?
(iii) What is the median mark in Science?
(iv) What is the interquartile range of the French marks?

7. The back-to-back stem and leaf diagram below shows the rested pulse rates of a group of college students. They are split into those who smoked and those who didn't.

	Smoke		Do not smoke	
		5	0 8 9	
	9 8 5	6	0 4 4 5 6 6 6 8 8	
6 6 5 0 0	7	0 1 1 8 9	
8 8 6 3 0	8	0 1 6 8 8	
	2 0	9		

Key: 5|6 = 65 bpm

Key: 5|8 = 58 bpm

(i) Find the median and range of the pulse rates of the group who smoked.
(ii) Find the median and range of the pulse rates of the group who did not smoke.
(iii) If a lower pulse rate indicates a higher level of fitness, which of the two groups is the fitter? Explain your answer.

8. The table below gives the examination marks in French and English for a class of 20 pupils.

French	75	69	58	58	46	44	32	50	53	78
	81	61	61	45	31	44	53	66	47	57
English	52	58	68	77	38	85	43	44	56	65
	65	79	44	71	84	72	63	69	72	79

   (i)   Construct a back-to-back stem and leaf diagram to represent these results.
   (ii)   What is the median mark in French?
   (iii)   What is the median mark in English?
   (iv)   In which subject did the pupils perform better? Explain your answer.

9. The lengths of time (in minutes) that twenty people had to wait to buy tickets at two cinema complexes were recorded.
The back-to-back stem and leaf diagram below shows the results.

Cinema

Movie Matrix 1		Movie Matrix 2
6 5 3 2 2	0	2 4 5 6
8 7 6 5 3 1	1	0 2 4 ☐ 6 7 8 8 9
8 6 4 3 3 2 1	2	1 2 4 5 5
2 0	3	3 3

Key: 1|2 = 21 mins   Key: 2|4 = 24 mins

   (i)   What is the range of waiting times at Movie Matrix 2?
   (ii)   What is the median waiting time at Movie Matrix 1?
   (iii)   One time is missing from Movie Matrix 2.
          Give a possible value for this missing time.
   (iv)   A patron is selected at random from Movie matrix 1.
          What is the probability that this person waited longer than 10 minutes for tickets?
   (v)   At which cinema would you have the shorter wait?
          Justify your answer.

10. Ten men and ten women were asked how much television they watched the previous weekend. Their times, in minutes, were as follows:

| Men | 40 | 41 | 42 | 52 | 52 | 52 | 64 | 65 | 65 | 71 |
| Women | 40 | 41 | 51 | 62 | 63 | 75 | 87 | 88 | 93 | 95 |

Copy and complete the back-to-back stem and leaf diagram opposite.

Men		Women
	4	0
	5	
4	6	
	7	
	8	
	9	

Key: 4|6 = 64 mins   Key: 4|0 = 40 mins

   (i)   What is the modal time for men?
   (ii)   What is the median time for
          (a) men   (b) women?
   (iii)   What is the range of times for
          (a) men   (b) women?
   (iv)   Use the results in (ii) and (iii) to show that women spend more time watching television than men do.

Section 2.7 Histograms

One of the most common ways of representing a frequency distribution is by means of a **histogram**.

Histograms are very similar to bar charts but there are some important differences:

> there are no gaps between the bars in a histogram
> histograms are used to show **continuous data**
> the data is always **grouped**; the groups are called classes
> the **area** of each bar or rectangle represents the frequency.

Histograms may have equal or unequal class intervals.

For our course, we will confine our study to histograms with **equal class intervals**.

When the class intervals are equal, drawing a histogram is very similar to drawing a bar chart.

Example 1

The frequency table below shows the times taken by 32 students to solve a problem.

Time (in secs)	0–10	10–20	20–30	30–40	40–50	50–60
No. of students	1	2	8	12	6	3

(i) Draw a histogram to represent this data.
(ii) Write down the modal class.
(iii) In which interval does the median lie?

We first draw two axes at right angles to each other.

We plot the variables (time in this case) on the horizontal axis and plot the frequencies (number of students) on the vertical axis.

(i) The histogram is shown below.

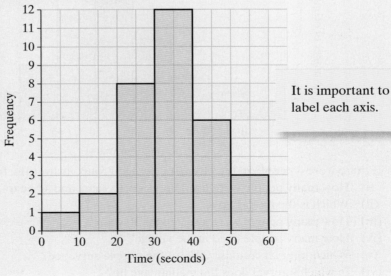

It is important to label each axis.

(ii) The modal class is the class with the highest frequency.
This is the (30–40) second class.

∴ the modal class is (30–40) seconds.

(iii) The median is the value halfway through the distribution.

There are 32 students altogether; so the middle students are the 16th and 17th students.

The sum of the numbers of students in the first three intervals is

1 + 2 + 8 i.e. 11

The 16th and 17th students will lie in the next interval, i.e., (30–40) seconds.

Thus the median lies in the (30–40) second interval.

Exercise 2.7

1. At the end of their journeys, 30 motorists were asked how many kilometres they had travelled. Their responses are shown in the table opposite.
   (i) Draw a histogram to illustrate this data.
   (ii) How many motorists had travelled 40 km or more?
   (iii) What is the modal class?
   (iv) What percentage of the motorists travelled between 20 km and 40 km?

Distance (in km)	Frequency
0–20	6
20–40	12
40–60	7
60–80	4
80–100	1

[0–20 means ⩾0 and <20]

2. The histogram below shows the ages of people living in a village.

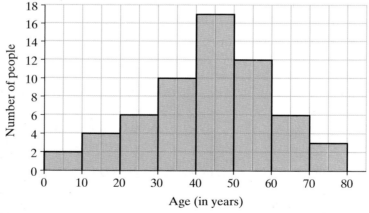

If there were 4 people in the (10–20) year age-group, answer the following questions:
   (i) How many people were aged between 30 years and 40 years?
   (ii) Which is the modal class?
   (iii) How many people were aged under 30 years?
   (iv) How many people lived in the village?
   (v) Which interval contains 20% of the people surveyed?
   (vi) In which interval does the median age lie?

3. The frequency table below gives the waiting times of a group of patients at a doctor's surgery.

Waiting time (in mins)	0–4	4–8	8–12	12–16	16–20
No. of patients	2	6	10	12	8

   (i)   Draw a histogram to illustrate this data.
   (ii) How many patients were included in the survey?
   (iii) Which is the modal class?
   (iv) In which interval does the median lie?
   (v)   What is the greatest number of patients who could have waited longer than 10 minutes?
   (vi) What is the least number of patients who could have waited longer than 14 minutes?

4. The histogram below shows the times taken, in seconds, for a group of pupils to solve a puzzle.

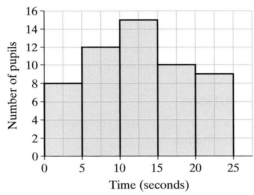

   (i)   How many pupils took 15 seconds or longer to solve the puzzle?
   (ii) How many pupils took part?
   (iii) Which is the modal class?
   (iv) In which interval does the median lie?
   (v)   What is the greatest number of pupils who could have solved the puzzle in less than 8 seconds?
   (vi) What is the least number of pupils who could have solved the puzzle in less than 12 seconds?

5. The grouped frequency table opposite shows the minutes spent in a shopping complex by a number of people:

Minutes	Number of people
5–15	8
15–25	14
25–35	28
35–45	20

   (i)   Draw a histogram to illustrate the data.
   (ii) Write down the modal class.
   (iii) In which interval does the median lie?
   (iv) Which interval contains exactly 20% of the people?
   (v)   What is the greatest number of people who could have spent more than 30 minutes in the shopping complex?
   (vi) Use the mid-interval values to calculate the mean time spent in the shopping complex, correct to the nearest minute.

Section 2.8 The shape of a distribution

In the previous section, we encountered histograms of various shapes.

The diagrams below show four histograms, all with different shapes.

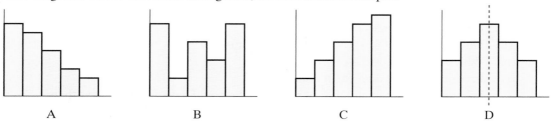

| A | B | C | D |

Only histogram D appears balanced or symmetrical as it has an axis of symmetry. The other three histograms are less balanced or **skewed** in some way.

Histograms are very useful when you want to see where the data lies and so get a clear picture of the shape of the distribution. For example, in histogram A above, we can see that most of the data is concentrated at the lower values. In histogram C, the data is concentrated at the higher values.

There are some shapes that occur frequently in distributions and you should be able to recognize and name them. The most common and frequently occurring shapes follow.

1. Symmetrical distributions

> This distribution has an axis of symmetry down the middle.
  It is called a **symmetrical distribution**.

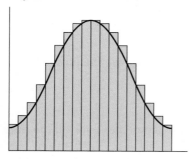
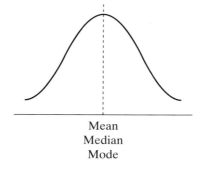

Mean
Median
Mode

Mean = Median = Mode

> It is one of the most common and most important distributions in statistics. It is generally referred to as the **normal distribution**.

> Real-life examples of a symmetrical (or normal) distribution are
>   (i)   the heights of a random sample of people
>   (ii) the intelligence quotients (IQ) of a population.

2. Positive skew

> When a distribution has most of the data at the lower values, we say it has a **positive skew**. The following histogram shows a positive skew as most of the data, represented by the higher bars, is mainly to the left.

If there is a positive skew, most of the data is to the left.

Notice that there is a long tail to the right of the distribution.

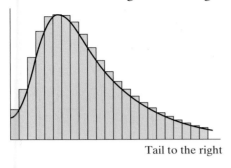

Tail to the right

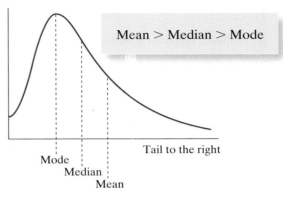

Mean > Median > Mode

Tail to the right

Mode
Median
Mean

> Real-life examples of a distribution with a
positive skew are
  (i)   the number of children in a family
  (ii) the age at which people first learn to ride a bicycle
  (iii) the age at which people marry.

3. Negative skew

> When a distribution has most of the data at the higher values, we say that the distribution
has a **negative skew**.

When a distribution has a negative skew, the tail will be to the left.

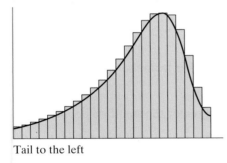

Tail to the left

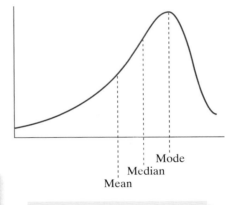

Mode
Median
Mean

In a distribution with a **positive**
skew, the tail is to the **right**; with a
negative skew, the tail is to the **left**.

Mean < Median < Mode

> Real-life examples of a distribution with a negative skew are
  (i) the ages at which people have to get their first pair of reading glasses
  (ii) the heights of players playing in a professional basketball league.

4. Uniform distributions

In a uniform distribution, the data is evenly
spread throughout.

It does not have a modal class.

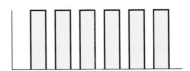

5. Bimodal distributions

This distribution has two modes.

It is called a **bimodal distribution**.

The modes are 6 and 16.

A distribution that has three or more modes is said to be **multimodal**.

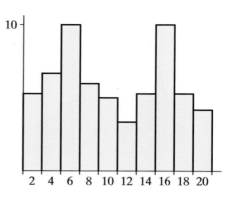

6. Distributions and standard deviation

Consider the two distributions, (A) and (B), shown below:

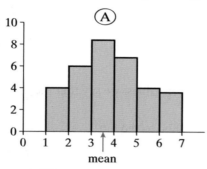

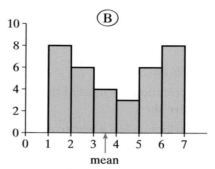

In distribution (A), most of the data lies between 2 and 5.

In distribution (B), the data is more spread out and further from the mean than the data in distribution (A).

The more spread out the data is in a distribution, the greater the standard deviation will be.

In the distributions above, we can conclude that (B) has a higher standard deviation than (A).

In the two distributions (C) and (D) below, the mean μ is given in each.

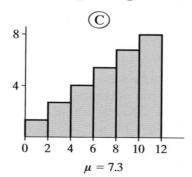

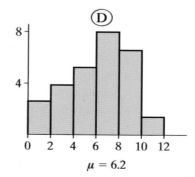

From the diagrams, we can see that more of the data is further from the mean in (C) than in (D).

Thus distribution (C) has the greater standard deviation.

Exercise 2.8

1. Describe the distribution shown.
   (i) What is this distribution commonly known as?
   (ii) Give one real-life example of this distribution.

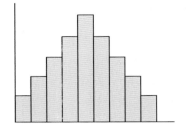

2. Is this distribution positively or negatively skewed?
   You will notice that most of the values are
   at the lower end of the distribution.
   Give one real-life situation that is an example
   of this type of distribution.

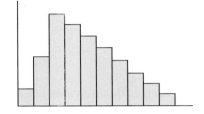

3. Here are three distributions:

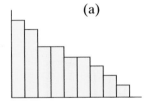
(a)
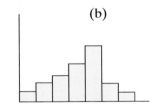
(b)
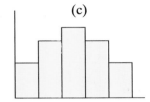
(c)

   (i) Which of these distributions is symmetrical?
   (ii) Which distribution is positively skewed?
   (iii) Which distribution is negatively skewed?
   (iv) Which distribution is the most likely to represent this data?
        'The weights of international rugby players'.
   (v) Which distribution best represents this data?
        'The intelligence quotients (IQ) of a large number of second-level students.'

4. Describe the distribution illustrated below.

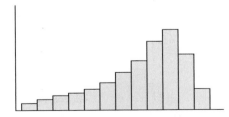

   For the mode, mean and median of this distribution,
   (i) state which of the three is the smallest
   (ii) state which of the three is the largest.

5. Consider the two distributions (A) and (B) shown below.

Explain why the standard deviation of the data in (B) is greater than the standard deviation of the data in (A).

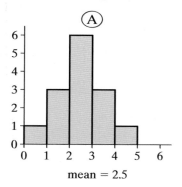

mean = 2.5

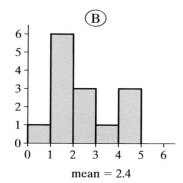

mean = 2.4

For each of the following pairs of distributions, state whether (A) or (B) has the larger standard deviation.

If they are the same, state so.

6. (i)

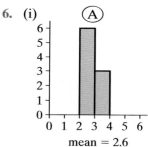

mean = 2.6

mean = 3.5

(ii)

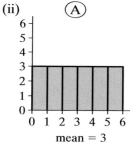

mean = 3

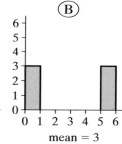

mean = 3

7. (i)

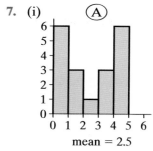

mean = 2.5

mean = 2.5

(ii)

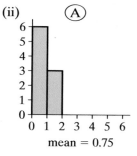

mean = 0.75

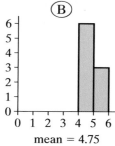

mean = 4.75

8. (i)

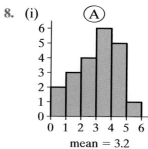

mean = 3.2

mean = 3.5

(ii)

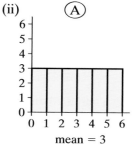

mean = 3

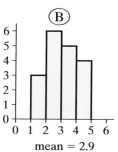

mean = 2.9

9. (i)

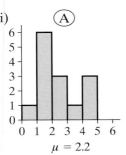

$\mu = 2.2$

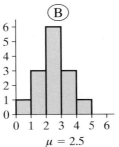

$\mu = 2.5$

(ii)

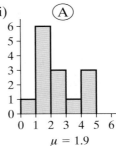

$\mu = 1.9$

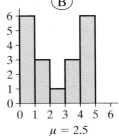

$\mu = 2.5$

10. The shapes of the histograms of four different sets of data are shown below.

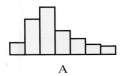

A

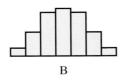

B

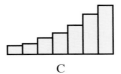

C

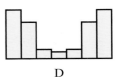

D

(i) Complete the table below, indicating whether the statement is correct (✓) or incorrect (✗) with respect to each data set.

	A	B	C	D
The data is skewed to the left.				
The data is skewed to the right.				
The mean is equal to the median.				
The mean is greater than the median.				
There is a single mode.				

(ii) Assume that the four histograms are drawn on the same scale.
State which of them has the largest standard deviation, and justify your answer.

Test yourself 2

A – questions

1. State whether each of the following is primary data or secondary data:
   (i) Counting the number of hatchback cars passing the school gate.
   (ii) Looking at records to see how many people passed through Shannon Airport each day in June one year.
   (iii) Phoning local supermarkets and stores to find the hourly pay rates for part-time work.
   (iv) Going online to see how many medals each country won at the Vancouver Winter Olympics.
   (v) Examining tourist brochures to find the average midday temperatures of selected cities for the month of June.

2. Here are the times, in minutes, for a bus journey:

   15, 7, 9, 12, 9, 19, 6, 11, 9, 16, 8

   (i) Find the range of these times.
   (ii) Find the lower quartile.
   (iii) Find the upper quartile.
   (iv) Write down the interquartile range.

3. The mean of the numbers 3, 6, 7, x and 14 is 8.
   Find x and the standard deviation of the set of numbers.

4. (i) What is the main difference between obtaining information by census and by sampling?
   (ii) A student discovered that his mark in a recent test was at the 72nd percentile. If 90 students took the test, how many students received a higher mark than he did?

5. The following stem and leaf diagram shows the amounts of money spent on a Friday night by a group of college students.

Males			Females
8	0	6	
7 6 5	1	0 5 5 5 8 8
9 9 9 8 6 6	2	5 5 8 8 9
8 8 5 5 5	3	5 5
8 5	4	0

   Key: 5|4 = €45   Key: 3|5 = €35

   (i) How many students were in the group?
   (ii) Write down the largest amount of money spent by the males.
   (iii) What is the median amount of money spent by the females?
   (iv) What is the median amount of money spent by the males?
   (v) Comment on whether males or females spent the most money.

6. (i) Without doing any calculations, state which of the following arrays of numbers has the greater standard deviation:
   (a) 2, 7, 10, 11, 12, 14, 15
   (b) 1, 5, 9, 10, 15, 18, 21
   Give a reason for your answer.

(ii)   The data below gives the number of books read in the last month by a class of 20 students.

Number of books, x	0	1	2	3	4
Number of students, f	2	5	6	5	2

Find the mean and standard deviation of the number of books.

7.   The principal of an 800-pupil school wishes to carry out a survey to determine how the pupils feel about the introduction of e-books instead of hard-copy textbooks. There are roughly the same number of pupils in each of the five year-groups. The principal decides to take a random sample of 100 students, with equal numbers from each year-group.
   (i)   The principal is using two sampling methods in this survey. Name these two methods.
   (ii)   How many students should she select from the first-year group?
   (iii)   Describe one method of selecting a random sample of 10 students from 100 students.

8.   A pollster working for RTE wants to know how many people are watching a new series which is being shown. She questions 200 people as they are leaving a supermarket between 10:00 and 12:00 one Thursday.
   (i)   Do you think that this sample might be biased? Explain your answer.
   (ii)   Suggest a more suitable way of selecting a sample.

9.   Explain what is meant by **stratified sampling** and **cluster sampling**.
   Your explanation should include
   (i)   a clear indication of the difference between the two methods
   (ii)   one reason why each method might be chosen instead of simple random sampling.

10.   Alexandrine enjoys listening to popular music.
   On one CD she noted that the lengths of the tracks varied greatly.
   These are the times, in minutes, of the tracks.

   4.6   3.8   4.0   3.1   4.2   3.2   3.5   4.7
   4.7   3.3   4.7   4.1   3.6   3.4   4.6   5.9

   (i)   Construct a stem and leaf diagram to show these times.
   (ii)   Write down the mode of the distribution.
   (iii)   Find the median and interquartile range.

B – questions

1.   The table below lists some statistics for the performances of Nicola and David in their mathematics tests over a term.

Student	Mean	Standard deviation	Range
Nicola	70	3.8	11
David	64	2.5	11

Which student, Nicola or David, had the more consistent test results?
Give a reason for your answer.

2. Here are the marks, out of 100, of 24 students in a national test:

46	73	68	65	37	48	74	68	76	55	42	38
57	63	68	71	46	54	82	78	66	46	64	59

   (i) Find P_{40}, the 40th percentile.
   (ii) Gillian scored 71 marks in the test.
       At what percentile was her mark?

3. The size, mean, and standard deviation of four different data sets are given in the table below.

	A	B	C	D
size (N)	1000	100	100	10
mean (μ)	10	100	1000	100
standard deviation (σ)	20	30	20	10

   Complete the sentences below by inserting the relevant letter in each space:
   (i) The biggest data set is _____ and the smallest is _____.
   (ii) In general, the data in set _____ is the biggest and the data in set _____ is the smallest.
   (iii) The data in set _____ is more spread out than the data in the other sets.
   (iv) Set _____ must contain some negative numbers.
   (v) If the four sets are combined, the median is most likely to be a value in set _____.

4. Using the mid-interval values, find the standard deviation of the given grouped frequency distribution. Give your answer correct to 1 decimal place.

Class interval	1–3	3–5	5–7	7–9
Frequency	4	3	0	2

5. The histogram below represents a certain distribution.

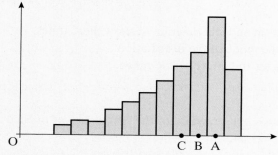

   (i) Is the distribution positively or negatively skewed?
       Explain your answer.
   (ii) The mean, mode and median of the distribution are represented by the points A, B and C.
       State what each point represents.
   (iii) Give a real-life example of a distribution that is likely to have this shape.

6. A meat-canning factory supplies a supermarket with cans of meat in three sizes: large, medium and small.

The regular consignment is of 300 large cans, 500 medium cans and 400 small cans.

If the supermarket applies the method of *stratified random sampling* to select a sample of 60 cans to test the quality of the goods, how many of each size should be selected?

7. The number of road accidents recorded per day at a busy junction were recorded over a 400-day period as follows:

Accidents per day	0	1	2	3	4	5	6
Number of days	26	90	57	19	5	3	200

(i) Calculate the mean number of accidents per day.
(ii) Calculate the standard deviation of the number of accidents per day.

An earlier study at the same road junction produced the results shown below.

Daily road accidents	
Mean	3.2
Standard deviation	1.15

(iii) Compare the results of the two studies.

8. State which is the explanatory variable and which is the response variable in each of the following.
(i) The wheat yield per hectare and the quantity of fertilizer applied.
(ii) The number of suitable habitats and the number of species.
(iii) The length of time it takes for a container of hot water to cool and the amount of water in the container.
(iv) The petrol consumption of a car and the size of its engine.

9. Name the sampling method employed in each of the following surveys:
A: Taking every 20th name from a school list arranged in alphabetical order.
B: Surveying the first 50 people you meet in the street.
C: Putting all the names into a box and picking out 20 names without looking.
D: Selecting a random sample of boys and girls from each year-group in proportion to their numbers.
E: Selecting 40 interviewers and asking each interviewer to question fifty people in any way they wish.

10. The runs scored by a cricketer in 11 innings during a season were as follows:

47   63   0   28   40   51   *a*   77   0   13   35

The exact value of *a* was unknown but it was greater than 100.

(i) Calculate the median and interquartile range of these 11 values.
(ii) Give a reason why, for these 11 values,
(a) the mode is **not** an appropriate measure of average
(b) the range is **not** an appropriate measure of spread.

C – questions

1. For each of the football seasons 2008/09 and 2009/10 of a major European league, a count is made of the number of goals scored in each of the 380 matches. The results are shown in the table on the right:

Number of goals scored in a match	Number of matches	
	2008/09	2009/10
0	30	32
1	79	82
2	99	95
3	68	78
4	60	48
5	24	30
6	11	9
7	6	6
8	2	0
9	1	0
Total	380	380

   (i) For the number of goals scored in a match during the 2008/09 season,

      (a) determine the median and the interquartile range

      (b) calculate the mean and standard deviation, correct to 2 decimal places.

   (ii) Two statistics students, Jole and Katie, independently analyse the data on the number of goals scored in a match during the 2009/10 season.

     ❯ Jole determines correctly that the median is 2 and that the interquartile range is also 2.

     ❯ Katie calculates correctly, to two decimal places, that the mean is 2.48 and that the standard deviation is 1.59.

   Use your answers from part (i), together with Jole's and Katie's results, to compare briefly the two seasons with regard to the average and the spread of the number of goals scored in a match.

2. Sophie and Jack do a survey every day for three weeks. Sophie counts the number of pedal cycles using Market Street. Jack counts the number of pedal cycles using Strand Road. The data they collected is summarised in the back-to-back stem and leaf diagram.

Sophie	Stem	Jack
9 9 7 5	0	6 6
7 6 5 3 3 2 2 2 1 1	1	1 1 5
5 3 3 2 2	2	1 2 2 2 3 7 7 8 9
2 1	3	2 3 4 7 7 8
	4	2

Key: 1|3 = 31   Key: 2|1 = 21

   (i) Write down the modal number of pedal cycles using Strand Road.
   The quartiles for these data are summarised in the table opposite.

	Sophie	Jack
Lower quartile	X	21
Median	13	Y
Upper quartile	Z	33

   (ii) Find the values for X, Y and Z.

   (iii) Write down the road you think has the most pedal cycles travelling along it overall. Give a reason for your answer.

3. The diagrams show the age distribution of road-user casualties.

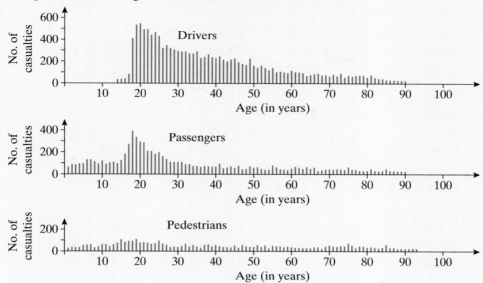

(i) Comment on the shape of the distributions of driver and passenger casualties mentioning skewness and clustering.

(ii) At what age are you most likely to be injured in a road accident if your are
(a) the driver   (b) a passenger?

(iii) Comment on the shape of the distribution of pedestrian casualties.

(iv) If you were running a road safety campaign to help lower the number of casualties on our roads, whom would you target and why?

4. Some research was carried out into the participation of girls and boys in sport. The researchers selected a simple random sample of fifty male and fifty female teenagers enrolled in GAA clubs in the greater Cork area. They asked the teenagers the question: *How many sports do you play?*

The data collected was as follows:

Boys	Girls
0, 4, 5, 1, 4, 1, 3, 3, 3, 1,	3, 3, 3, 1, 1, 3, 3, 1, 3, 3,
1, 2, 2, 2, 5, 3, 3, 4, 1, 2,	2, 2, 4, 4, 4, 5, 5, 2, 2, 3,
2, 2, 2, 3, 3, 3, 4, 5, 1, 1,	3, 3, 4, 1, 6, 2, 3, 3, 3, 4,
1, 1, 1, 2, 2, 2, 2, 2, 3, 3,	4, 5, 3, 4, 3, 3, 3, 4, 4, 3,
3, 3, 3, 3, 3, 3, 3, 3, 3, 3	1, 1, 3, 2, 1, 3, 1, 3, 1, 3

(i) Display the data in a way that gives a picture of each distribution.

(ii) State **one difference** and **one similarity** between the distributions of the two samples.

(iii) Do you think that there is evidence that there are differences between the two populations?

(iv) The researchers are planning to repeat this research on a larger scale.
List **two** improvements they could make to the design of the research to reduce the possibility of bias in the samples. Explain why each improvement you suggest will reduce the likelihood of bias.

5. 224 athletes completed a triathlon which consisted of a 750 metre swim, followed by a 20 kilometre cycle, followed by a 5 kilometre run.

Some of the summary statistics are given in the table below:
Three of the entries in the table have been removed and replaced with question marks (?).

	Swim	Cycle	Run
Mean	18.329	41.927	?
Median	17.900	41.306	?
Mode			
Standard Deviation	?	4.553	3.409
Sample Variance	10.017	20.729	11.622
Skewness	1.094	0.717	0.463
Range	19.226	27.282	20.870
Minimum	11.350	31.566	16.466
Maximum	30.576	58.847	37.336
Count	224	224	224

Histograms of the times for the three events were produced.
Here are the three histograms without their titles.

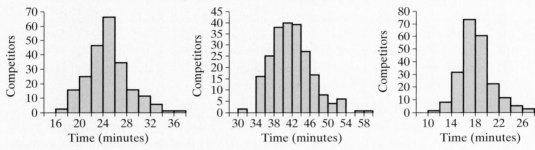

(i) Use the summary statistics in the table to decide which histogram corresponds to each event.

(ii) The mean and median time for the run are approximately equal. Estimate this value from the corresponding histogram.

(iii) Estimate, from the relevant histogram, the standard deviation of the times for the swim.

(iv) When calculating the summary statistics, the software failed to find a *mode* for the data sets. Why do you think this is?

6. Some students are using a database of earthquakes to investigate the times between the occurrences of serious earthquakes around the world. They extract information about all of the earthquakes in the 20th century that caused at least 1000 deaths. There are 115 of these.

The students wonder whether there are patterns in the timing of these earthquakes, so they look at the number of days between each successive pair of earthquakes.

They make the following table, showing the number of earthquakes for which the time interval from the previous earthquake is as shown.

Time in days from previous earthquake	0–100	100–200	200–300	300–400	400–500	500–600	600–700	700–800	800–1000	1000–1300
Number of earthquakes	31	24	12	14	8	7	5	6	5	3

[Source: National geophysical data center, significant earthquake database: www.ngdc.noaa.go]

(i) Create a suitable graphical representation of the distribution.

(ii) Describe the distribution. Your description should refer to the shape of the distribution and should include an estimate of the median.

(iii) The mean time between these earthquakes is 309 days and the standard deviation is 277 days. Suppose that such an earthquake has just occurred and that we want to find the probability that the time to the next one will be between 100 and 200 days. Explain why it would **not** be correct to use standard normal distribution tables (z-tables) to do this.

(iv) Based on the information presented in this question so far, what is the best estimate for the probability described in part (iii) above? Explain your reasoning.

(v) As stated at the beginning, the students chose to analyse earthquake timings by looking at the time intervals between the occurrences of a particular type of earthquake. Suggest a different way that they could have looked at the data in the database in order to try to find patterns in the timing of earthquakes.

3 Probability 2

Key words

tree diagram   probability distribution   expected value   random variable
fair game   binomial distribution   Bernoulli trials   multiplication rule
independent events   normal distribution   normal curve
Empirical rule   standard score   Probability simulations

In Chapter 1 of this book, we dealt with permutations, combinations and the fundamentals of probability. In this chapter, we continue the study of probability and that will include more difficult concepts such as expected value and independent events as well as an introduction to the normal distribution.

Section 3.1 Tree diagrams

The possible outcomes of two or more events can be shown in a particular type of diagram called a **tree diagram**. Each branch represents a possible outcome of one event. The probability of each outcome is written on the branch.

Consider this problem:

A fair coin is tossed three times.
Determine the probability that exactly 2 heads are obtained.

Here is the sample space of possible outcomes:

HHH, HHT, HTH, HTT, THH, THT, TTH and TTT

Since 2 heads appear on 3 occasions,

$$P(2\text{heads}) = \tfrac{3}{8}$$

The same possibilities can be represented in a more structured way on a tree diagram.

The branches that contain 2 heads are highlighted.

Again $P(\text{ 2 heads}) = \tfrac{3}{8}$.

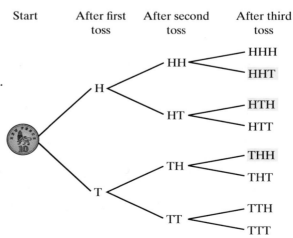

Start	After first toss	After second toss	After third toss
		HH	HHH
			HHT
	H		
		HT	HTH
			HTT
		TH	THH
			THT
	T		
		TT	TTH
			TTT

Example 1

Box A contains 3 red beads and 4 blue beads
Box B contains 2 red beads and 3 blue beads
One bead is taken at random from each box.
(i) Draw a tree diagram to show all the outcomes.
(ii) Work out the probability that they both will
have the same colour.

(i) The tree diagram below shows all the possible outcomes.
Taking a red bead from box A and taking a red bead from box B are
independent events.
So P(red, red) = P(red) × P(red)

$$\frac{3}{7} \times \frac{2}{5} = \frac{6}{35}$$

Box A	Box B	Outcome	Probability
$\frac{3}{7}$ R	$\frac{2}{5}$ R	R R	$\frac{3}{7} \times \frac{2}{5} = \frac{6}{35}$
	$\frac{3}{5}$ B	R B	$\frac{3}{7} \times \frac{3}{5} = \frac{9}{35}$
$\frac{4}{7}$ B	$\frac{2}{5}$ R	B R	$\frac{4}{7} \times \frac{2}{5} = \frac{8}{35}$
	$\frac{3}{5}$ B	B B	$\frac{4}{7} \times \frac{3}{5} = \frac{12}{35}$

(ii) P(same colour) = P(both red or both blue)

= P(R, R) + P(B, B)   OR implies addition

$= \frac{6}{35} + \frac{12}{35} = \frac{18}{35}$

Note: Notice that the probabilities at the end of the branches sum to 1, i.e.,

$$\frac{6}{35} + \frac{9}{35} + \frac{8}{35} + \frac{12}{35} = \frac{35}{35} = 1$$

Tree diagrams for events without replacement

The tree diagram in the following example illustrates events that are not independent. The
outcome of the first event affects subsequent events.

Example 2

A box contains 12 beads. Five are yellow and the rest are green. A bead is removed
from the box and its colour is noted. It is not returned to the box. A second
selection is then made and the process is repeated, followed by a third selection.
(i) Draw a tree diagram outlining this situation
(ii) Find the probability of selecting exactly two green beads.

(i)

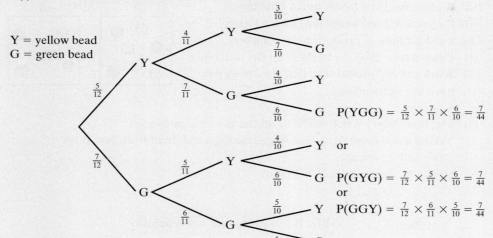

First selection   Second selection   Third selection

Y = yellow bead
G = green bead

$P(YGG) = \frac{5}{12} \times \frac{7}{11} \times \frac{6}{10} = \frac{7}{44}$

or

$P(GYG) = \frac{7}{12} \times \frac{5}{11} \times \frac{6}{10} = \frac{7}{44}$

or

$P(GGY) = \frac{7}{12} \times \frac{6}{11} \times \frac{5}{10} = \frac{7}{44}$

(ii) So P (exactly two green beads) $= \frac{7}{44} + \frac{7}{44} + \frac{7}{44}$

$= \frac{21}{44}$

Note: 1. In the example above, the calculations of probabilities were confined to the relevant branches.

2. The problems in the two worked examples above may be done more quickly by using the general multiplication rule.

Exercise 3.1

1. (i) Draw a tree diagram for these two spinners.

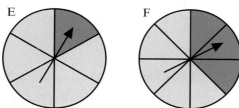

E   F

(ii) Find the probability that the two spinners show the same colour.

2. Paula has a dice with 5 red faces and 1 green face. She rolls the dice twice.
   (i) Copy and complete the tree diagram.
   (ii) Find the probability that the dice shows the same colour each time.
   (iii) Find the probability that the dice shows green and red in that order.

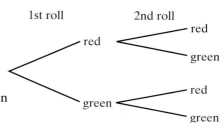

1st roll   2nd roll

red
red
green

red
green
green

3. Bag A contains 2 blue counters and 3 white counters.
   Bag B contains 3 blue counters and 4 white counters.
   A counter is taken at random from each bag.
   Copy and complete the tree diagram to show all the
   possible outcomes.
   Work out the probability that the counters
   will both be:
   (i)   white
   (ii) blue
   (iii) the same colour.

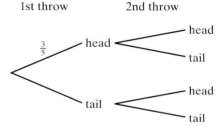

4. Kevin has a coin which is weighted so that the
   probability that it lands 'head' is $\frac{3}{5}$ and 'tail' $\frac{2}{5}$.
   (i)   Copy and complete the tree diagram for two
         throws of the weighted coin.
   (ii) What is the probability of two heads?
   (iii) Find the probability of getting one 'head' and
         one 'tail' (in either order).

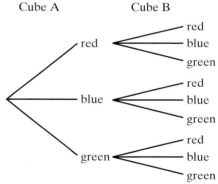

5. Patrick has two cubes, A and B.
   The faces of cube A are coloured red, red, blue,
   blue, green, green.
   The faces of cube B are coloured red, blue, blue,
   blue, green, green.
   Patrick rolls the two cubes to see which colours
   come on top.
   (i)   Copy and complete the tree diagram,
         writing the probabilities on the branches.
   (ii) Find the probability that both cubes land
         with the same colour on top.
   (iii) Find the probability that one of the cubes lands blue and the other green.

6. Harry throws an ordinary dice
   three times.
   (i)   Copy and complete this tree
         diagram.
   (ii) Find the probability that Harry
         gets two or more sixes in his
         three throws.

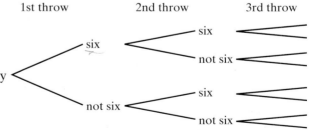

7. A bag contains 2 black counters and 4 white counters.
   A counter is taken from the bag and not replaced.
   A second counter is then taken.
   Find the probability that the two counters are
   (i)   the same colour   (ii) different colours.

8. A bag contains 3 red cubes and 2 blue cubes.
   A cube is taken at random from the bag and not replaced.
   Then a second cube is taken at random.
   (i) Draw a tree diagram for this situation.
   (ii) Find the probability that both of the cubes taken out are the same colour.
   (iii) Find the probability that the two cubes are of different colours.

9. The probability that it will be raining tomorrow morning is $\frac{1}{3}$.
   If it is raining, the probability that Simon will be late for school is $\frac{1}{4}$.
   If it is not raining, the probability that he will be late is $\frac{1}{5}$.
   (i) Copy and complete this tree diagram.

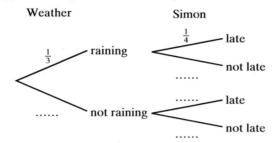

   (ii) Find the probability that Simon will be late for school tomorrow.

10. On his way to work, Nick goes through a set of traffic lights and then passes over a level crossing.
    Over a period of time, Nick has estimated the probability of stopping at each of these.
    The probability that he has to stop at the traffic lights is $\frac{2}{3}$.
    The probability that he has to stop at the level crossing is $\frac{1}{5}$.
    The probabilities are independent.
    (i) Construct a tree diagram to show this information.
    (ii) Calculate the probability that Nick will not have to stop at either the lights or the level crossing on his way to work.

11. Karen is looking at a job advert in the paper.
    On past experience, she estimates that she has a 70% chance of getting the job if she can get an interview.
    Karen thinks that she has a two in five chance of getting an interview.
    Draw a tree diagram to illustrate these events.
    Use the tree diagram to find each of these:
    (i) Given that she gets an interview, what then is the probability that she does not get the job?
    (ii) What is the probability that Karen does not get the job?

12. The probability that Aidan passes his driving test at the first attempt is $\frac{1}{3}$.
    If the test is failed, the probability that Aidan passes his driving test at the next attempt is $\frac{7}{12}$.
    Draw a tree diagram to illustrate the probabilities of these events.
    Hence calculate the probability that Aidan passes his driving test at his third attempt.

Section 3.2 Probability distributions – Expected value ——

Probability distributions

Consider the following experiments
  (i)   4 coins are tossed: x is the number of heads obtained
  (ii) Three dice are thrown: x is the number of sixes obtained
  (iii) A hand of 7 cards is dealt: x is the number of kings
  (iv) 100 people are selected: x is the number of people of weight $\geqslant 150\,\text{kg}$
  (v)   One person is selected at random: x cm is the height of that person
  (vi) One person is selected at random: x is the I.Q. of that person.

In each of the above experiments, x is called a **random variable** whose value depends, to some extent, on chance. In experiments (i) to (iv), x can take discrete values such as 0, 1, 2, 3… and for that reason x is said to be a *discrete random variable*. In experiments (v) and (vi), x can take any value within a certain range and is said to be a **continuous random variable**. In this section, we will consider only discrete random variables.

If a coin is tossed 3 times, the sample space of all possible outcomes is

   TTT, TTH, THT, THH, HTT, HTH, HHT, HHH

If x is the number of heads obtained, a table of the results can be formulated as follows:

x	0	1	2	3
$P(x)$	$\frac{1}{8}$	$\frac{3}{8}$	$\frac{3}{8}$	$\frac{1}{8}$

This is called a **probability distribution**, where $P(x)$ is the probability that x occurs.

Probability distributions are particularly useful when dealing with expected values, as shown below.

Expected value

This circle is divided into 3 sectors.
When the spinner is spun, it will land on 4, 8 or 12.
If the spinner is spun twice and we get 4 and 12,
then the average of the two results is $\dfrac{4+12}{2}=8$.

If the spinner is spun 100 times, is there a quick way of finding the 'average' of these spins?

Yes and it is found by multiplying each outcome (4, 8 or 12) by the probability of that outcome occurring and then adding the results.
This average is called the **expected value**.

This is set out in the table below:

Outcome (x)	Probability (P)	$x \times P$
12	$\frac{1}{2}$	6
8	$\frac{1}{4}$	2
4	$\frac{1}{4}$	1

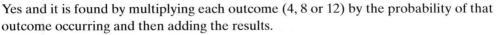

When each outcome is multiplied by its corresponding probability, we get 6, 2 and 1.
The sum of these results is 9.
The number 9 is the **expected value**.

If the spinner above is spun a large number of times, the mean value of outcomes approaches the expected value, 9. Statisticians call this the *Law of large numbers*.

Notice that the expected value 9 is not one of the possible outcomes, i.e., 4, 8 and 12.

> In general, the expected value need not be one of the possible outcomes.

The expected value of the outcome of an experiment is denoted by E(X).

When all the outcomes are multiplied by their corresponding probabilities and the results added, the operation can be expressed in a concise way as follows

$$E(X) = \sum(x).P(x), \text{ where } \sum \text{ represents 'the sum of'.}$$

The expected value is widely used in the insurance industry and in the operation of casino games. If you would like to know whether or not a casino game is fair, you would need to know what the payout is and the probability of getting that payout. In simple terms, you need to know the expected value of the payouts.

You also have to take into account the money you pay to play the game.

Let us consider this fun-park spinning-wheel on the right.
It costs €8 to spin the wheel and you win the amount to which the arrow is pointing.

Is this a fair game?

First we calculate the expected value of the payout.

Payout (x)	Probability (P)	$x \times P$
€10	$\frac{1}{2}$	€5
€5	$\frac{1}{4}$	€1.25
€4	$\frac{1}{4}$	€1

$$\sum x.P(x) = €5 + €1.25 + €1 = €7.25$$

The expected value of the payout is €7.25.
But it costs €8 to spin the wheel.
The expected payout now is €7.25 − €8, i.e. −€0.75.
Thus if the wheel is spun a large number of times, you could expect to lose €0.75 on average on each spin.

When is a game fair?

To determine whether or not a game is **mathematically fair**, we need to take into account
  (i)   the expected value of the payout
  (ii) the cost of playing the game.

Then (a) if the expected payout is zero, the game is fair

(b) if the expected payout is greater than zero, you will win in the long-run

(c) if the expected payout is less than zero, you will lose in the long-run.

A game is **equitable** or **fair** if the player's mathematical expectation is zero.

Example 1

This circle is divided into 6 equal sectors.

You pay €10 to spin the arrow and you win the amount in the sector where the arrow stops.

What is the expected amount you win or lose in this game?

We find the expected value of the payout by constructing the table below which shows the probability of each outcome.

Payout (x)	Probability (P)	Payout × Probability ($x \times P$)
€0	$\frac{2}{6}$	€0
€5	$\frac{1}{6}$	€$\frac{5}{6}$
€10	$\frac{2}{6}$	€$\frac{20}{6}$
€30	$\frac{1}{6}$	€5

Expected payout $= \sum x.P(x) = $ €$0 + $ €$\frac{5}{6} + $ €$\frac{20}{6} + $ €5

$$= \text{€}5 + \text{€}\frac{25}{6}$$

$$= \text{€}5 + \text{€}4\frac{1}{6} = \text{€}9\frac{1}{6} = \text{€}9.17$$

The expected payout is €9.17.

When you include the €10 you pay to play, the expected payout is

€9.17 − €10 = −€0.83

So you can expect to lose €0.83 if you play this game.

Example 2

Luke rolls a pair of dice in a game of chance that costs €2 to play.

The table on the right gives the financial outcome for each event.

(i) Calculate the financial expectation for this game.

(ii) Is this game fair? Explain your answer.

Event	Financial outcome
Any double	Win €4
Total of 7	Win €3
Odd sum (except 7)	Money back (€2)
Even sum (except doubles)	Lose €3

There are 36 possible outcomes, as shown on the right.

(i) $P(\text{double}) = \frac{6}{36} = \frac{1}{6}$

6	7	8	9	10	11	12
5	6	7	8	9	10	11
4	5	6	7	8	9	10
3	4	5	6	7	8	9
2	3	4	5	6	7	8
1	2	3	4	5	6	7
	1	2	3	4	5	6

$P(\text{total of } 7) = \frac{6}{36} = \frac{1}{6}$

$P(\text{odd sum} - \text{except } 7) = \frac{12}{36} = \frac{1}{3}$

$P(\text{even sum} - \text{except doubles}) = \frac{18-6}{36} = \frac{12}{36} = \frac{1}{3}$

We now multiply each financial outcome by its probability.

$$\sum x.P(x) = €4 \times \tfrac{1}{6} + €3 \times \tfrac{1}{6} + €2 \times \tfrac{1}{3} - €3 \times \tfrac{1}{3}$$
$$= €\tfrac{4}{6} + €\tfrac{1}{2} + €\tfrac{2}{3} - €1$$
$$= €\tfrac{11}{6} - €1 = €1.83 - €1 = €0.83$$

We now deduct the cost to play the game which is €2.

$$€0.83 - €2 = -€1.17$$

The financial expectation is $-€1.17$ per game.

(ii) This game is not fair as you expect to lose €1.17 each time you play this game.

Exercise 3.2

1. Find the expected value when this spinner is spun.

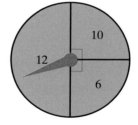

2. A card is selected at random from the cards shown and then replaced.
   The process is repeated several times.
   Find the expected value of the number selected.

   2   6   8
   12   9   2

3. When this spinner is spun, the amount in the sector in which the arrow stops is paid out.
   What is the expected value of the payout?

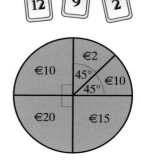

4. The probability of throwing each of the numbers 1 to 6 with a biased dice are given below.

Outcome (x)	1	2	3	4	5	6
Probability (P)	0.1	0.05	0.25	0.15	0.25	0.2
$x \times P(x)$						

Find the expected value when this dice is thrown.

5. The probability distribution of a set of numbers is shown in this table:
Find the expected value of x.

x	-2	-1	0	1	2
$P(x)$	0.3	0.1	0.15	0.4	0.05

6. The Garda chief of a city knows that the probabilities for 0, 1, 2, 3, 4 or 5 car thefts on any given day are, respectively, 0.21, 0.37, 0.25, 0.13, 0.03 and 0.01. How many car thefts can he expect per day?

7. List the eight different outcomes when three fair coins are tossed.
Now find the expected number of heads when the three coins are tossed.

8. In the given wheel, you win the amount in the sector in which the arrow stops.
It costs €10 to play the game.
How much would you expect to win or lose if you play this game?
Explain why the game is not fair.

9. When a fair dice is thrown, you win €10 when 1 or 2 shows and lose €5 when 3, 4, 5 or 6 shows.
Find the expected gain or loss when the dice is thrown.
Is the game fair? Explain your answer.

10. Grandad bet €5 on each of these 5 horses in a horserace.

Horse	Probability of win	Payout from €5
Likely lad	0.32	€11
Just a Minute	0.07	€68
Everyone's a Critic	0.11	€42
Sauerkraut	0.01	€480
Solar Eclipse	0.05	€96

   (i) Calculate his financial expectation from this bet.
   (ii) On average, will Grandad make a gain or a loss?

11. For a particular age group, statistics show that the probability of dying is 1 in 1000 people and the probability of suffering some sort of disability is 3 in 1000 people. The *Hope Life Insurance Company* offers to pay out €50 000 if you die and €20 000 if you are disabled.
What profit is the insurance company making per customer, based on the expected value, if it charges a premium of €300 to its customers for the above policy?

12. The probability distribution of a random variable x is shown in this table:

x	1	2	3	4	5
$P(x)$	0.1	0.3	y	0.2	0.1

   (i) Find the value of y.
   (ii) Find the expected value of x.

13. In a casino, it costs €5 to throw a fair dice.
    If you throw a 2 or a 6, you win €20.
    If you throw a 1, you lose €15.
    For all other scores, you neither win nor lose.
    If you played this game 20 times, how much would you expect to lose?

14. The probability distribution of a random variable x is given below:

x	1	2	3	4	5
$P(x)$	0.1	p	0.3	q	0.2

   (i) Given $E(x) = 3$, write down two equations in p and q.
   (ii) Find the value of p and the value of q.

15. The table below gives details of claims made by households against the *Coverall Insurance Company* for a particular year.

	No. of households	No. of claims	Average cost per claim
Urban area	6250	480	€2840
Rural area	4600	210	€1705

   Use the table above to answer the following questions, giving your answer correct to two decimal places:
   (i) What is the probability that a rural household, selected at random, made a claim during the year?
   (ii) What is the expected value of the cost of a claim from a rural household?
   (iii) The urban households paid an average annual premium of €580. Calculate the average profit the insurance company made on each urban household premium.
   (iv) A rural household in County Galway has a probability of 0.05 of making a claim during the year. The average cost of such a claim is €1550. What premium should the insurance company charge this household to make a profit of €350 on the transaction?

16. A test consists of three sections:

   Section 1 has 20 multiple-choice questions in which students select 1 correct answer from 4 options (A, B, C, D).

   Section 2 has 10 true-or-false questions in which students choose either true or false.

   Section 3 has 10 multiple-choice questions in which students select 1 correct answer from 3 options (A, B, C).

   If every question in the test is randomly answered, what is the expected number of correct answers?

17. On one table in a casino there is a deck of normal playing cards.
On another table there are two fair dice.
It costs €10 to play at each table.
At the card table, you select one card from the deck.
You win €30 if you draw a heart but lose €5 if you draw any other suit.
At the other table, you throw the two dice and add the numbers showing.
If you get a total of 10, 11 or 12 you win €50.
For any other total you lose €2.
Which game should you play to get the better expected return?
What is the difference between the two expected returns?

Section 3.3 Binomial distribution – Bernoulli trials

A coin is biased in such a way that the probability of a head is always $\frac{2}{5}$.

Robbie tosses the coin four times. He wants to know the probability that there will be three heads and one tail.

The 3 heads and 1 tail can be arranged in **four** different ways.

$$P(\text{H, H, H, T}) = \tfrac{2}{5} \times \tfrac{2}{5} \times \tfrac{2}{5} \times \tfrac{3}{5} = \left(\tfrac{2}{5}\right)^3 \times \tfrac{3}{5}$$

$$P(\text{H, H, T, H}) = \tfrac{2}{5} \times \tfrac{2}{5} \times \tfrac{3}{5} \times \tfrac{2}{5} = \left(\tfrac{2}{5}\right)^3 \times \tfrac{3}{5}$$

$$P(\text{H, T, H, H}) = \tfrac{2}{5} \times \tfrac{3}{5} \times \tfrac{2}{5} \times \tfrac{2}{5} = \left(\tfrac{2}{5}\right)^3 \times \tfrac{3}{5}$$

$$P(\text{T, H, H, H}) = \tfrac{3}{5} \times \tfrac{2}{5} \times \tfrac{2}{5} \times \tfrac{2}{5} = \left(\tfrac{2}{5}\right)^3 \times \tfrac{3}{5}$$

The total probability for 3 heads and 1 tail $= 4 \times \left(\tfrac{2}{5}\right)^3 \times \tfrac{3}{5} = \tfrac{96}{625}$

Notice that the 4 in the answer is the value of $\binom{4}{3}$ and is the number of selections of 3 heads from 4 coins.

Thus the probability of 3 heads and 1 tail $= \binom{4}{3}\left(\tfrac{2}{5}\right)^3 \times \tfrac{3}{5}$

The example above is a special type of probability model called the **binomial distribution**.

A binomial distribution can be used in any experiment that has these 4 characteristics:

❯ A fixed number, n, of trials are carried out
❯ Each trial has two possible outcomes: success or failure
❯ The trials are independent
❯ The probability of success in each trial is constant.
   The probability of a success is generally called p.
   The probability of a failure is q, where $p + q = 1$.

In general, the probability of r successes in n trials is given by the formula on the right, where p is the probability of success and q is the probability of failure.

$$P(r \text{ successes}) = \binom{n}{r} p^r q^{n-r}$$

Experiments which satisfy the four conditions listed above are also called **Bernoulli Trials** after the Swiss mathematician James Bernoulli (1654–1705).

Consider the event of obtaining a 6 from a single throw of an unbiased die.

$$P(\text{success}) = \frac{1}{6} \quad \text{and} \quad P(\text{failure}) = \frac{5}{6}$$

If there are 8 such trials, then the probability of 0, 1, 2, 3, ... successes from 8 attempts is given by the terms of the expansion of

$$\left(\frac{5}{6} + \frac{1}{6}\right)^8$$

Since the probability of r successes is given by $\binom{n}{r} p^r q^{n-r}$

(i) $P(\text{no six}) = \binom{8}{0}\left(\frac{1}{6}\right)^0 \left(\frac{5}{6}\right)^8 = \binom{8}{0}\left(\frac{5}{6}\right)^8$

(ii) $P(1 \text{ six}) = \binom{8}{1}\left(\frac{1}{6}\right)^1 \left(\frac{5}{6}\right)^7$

(iii) $P(2 \text{ sixes}) = \binom{8}{2}\left(\frac{1}{6}\right)^2 \left(\frac{5}{6}\right)^6$

....

$P(8 \text{ sixes}) = \binom{8}{8}\left(\frac{1}{6}\right)^8 \left(\frac{5}{6}\right)^0 = \binom{8}{8}\left(\frac{1}{6}\right)^8$

Example 1

An unbiased die is thrown 5 times. Find the probability of obtaining

    (i)   1 six   (ii)   3 sixes   (iii)   at least 1 six.

Let $p = P(\text{success, i.e. getting a six})$ and $q = P(\text{failure})$.

$$\Rightarrow \quad p = \frac{1}{6} \quad \text{and} \quad q = \frac{5}{6} \quad \text{and} \quad n = 5$$

(i)   To find $P(1 \text{ six})$, we substitute 1 for r and 4 for $(n-r)$ in the formula $\binom{n}{r} p^r q^{n-r}$.

$$\Rightarrow \quad P(1 \text{ six}) = \binom{5}{1} p^1 q^4 = \binom{5}{1}\left(\frac{1}{6}\right)\left(\frac{5}{6}\right)^4$$

$$= 5 \cdot \frac{1}{6} \cdot \frac{5^4}{6^4} = \frac{5^5}{6^5} = \frac{3125}{7776}$$

(ii) $P(3 \text{ sixes}) = \binom{5}{3}\left(\frac{1}{6}\right)^3 \left(\frac{5}{6}\right)^2$

$$= 10 \cdot \frac{1}{6^3} \cdot \frac{25}{36} = \frac{250}{7776} = \frac{125}{3888}$$

(iii) $P(\text{at least 1 six}) = 1 - P(\text{no six})$

$$P(\text{no six}) = \binom{5}{0}\left(\frac{1}{6}\right)^0 \left(\frac{5}{6}\right)^5 = \left(\frac{5}{6}\right)^5$$

$$\Rightarrow \quad P(\text{at least 1 six}) = 1 - \left(\frac{5}{6}\right)^5 = \frac{4651}{7776}$$

Example 2

Given that 10% of apples are bad, find the probability that in a box containing 6 apples, there is
  (i) no bad apple
 (ii) just one bad apple
(iii) at least one bad apple.

$P(\text{bad apple}) = \dfrac{1}{10} \;\Rightarrow\; P(\text{good apple}) = \dfrac{9}{10}$

$\Rightarrow\;\; p = \dfrac{1}{10} \quad \text{and} \quad q = \dfrac{9}{10} \quad \text{and} \quad n = 6$

(i) $P(\text{no bad apple})$ is the term where the power of p is zero.

$$= \binom{6}{0}\left(\frac{1}{10}\right)^0 \left(\frac{9}{10}\right)^6 = \left(\frac{9}{10}\right)^6 = \frac{9^6}{10^6}$$

(ii) $P(1 \text{ bad apple}) = \binom{6}{1}\left(\dfrac{1}{10}\right)^1 \left(\dfrac{9}{10}\right)^5$ .... the power of $p = 1$

$$= 6 \cdot \frac{1}{10} \cdot \left(\frac{9}{10}\right)^5 = \frac{6.9^5}{10^6}$$

(iii) $P(\text{at least 1 bad apple}) = 1 - P(\text{no bad apple})$

$$= 1 - \frac{9^6}{10^6}$$ .... from (i) above

Probability of kth success on n^{th} Bernoulli trial

In example 1 on the previous page, we worked out the probability of getting 3 sixes when a dice is thrown 5 times. If the same dice is thrown continuously until a six appears for the fourth time, how do we find the probability that the 4th six appears on the tenth throw?

For a 4th six to appear on the 10th throw,
  (i) we need to get 3 sixes on the first nine throws, and then
 (ii) get a six on the 10th throw.

Three sixes on the first nine throws is given by

$\binom{9}{3} p^3 q^{9-3}$ i.e. $\binom{9}{3}\left(\dfrac{1}{6}\right)^3 \left(\dfrac{5}{6}\right)^6$

$$84 \times \frac{5^6}{6^9} = 0.13$$

$P(\text{six on the 10th throw}) = \dfrac{1}{6}$

Thus $P(\text{4th six on the 10th throw}) = 0.13 \times \dfrac{1}{6} = 0.0217.$

Example 3

A card is drawn at random from a normal deck of playing cards and then replaced. The process is repeated until the third diamond appears. Find the probability that this happens when the tenth card is drawn.

$$P(\text{drawing a diamond}) = \frac{1}{4}$$

The probability of drawing the third diamond on the 10th draw is

$$P(\text{drawing 2 diamonds in the first nine draws}) \times$$
$$P(\text{drawing a diamond on the 10th draw})$$

$$P(\text{2 diamonds on 1st nine draws}) = \binom{9}{2}\left(\frac{1}{4}\right)^2\left(\frac{3}{4}\right)^7$$

$$= 0.3$$

$$P(\text{diamond on 10th draw}) \qquad = \frac{1}{4} = 0.25$$

Thus $P(\text{third diamond on the 10th draw}) = 0.3 \times 0.25$

$$= 0.075$$

Exercise 3.3

1. A fair coin is tossed 8 times.
   We require the probability of getting 3 heads on these 8 tosses.
   (i) Explain why the binomial distribution is a suitable method of solving this problem.
   (ii) If p = probability of getting a head
   q = probability of not getting a head
   and n = number of trials,
   write down the values of p, q and n.

2. A coin is tossed 5 times. What is the probability of getting
   (i) exactly 1 head
   (ii) exactly 3 heads?

3. Find the probability that, in five throws of a fair dice, a 3 will occur
   (i) on no occasion
   (ii) once only
   (iii) twice.

4. The probability that a marksman hits the target is $\frac{1}{3}$.
   What is the probability that, in 7 attempts, he hits the target three times?

5. Assuming that a couple are equally likely to produce a boy or a girl, find the probability that in a family of 5 children there are 3 boys and 2 girls.

6. Jean either walks to school or goes by bus. The probability that she walks to school on a summer morning is 0.7. For a school week of five days during the summer, find the probability that
   (i) she walks to school only once
   (ii) she walks to school exactly three times.

7. The probability that a person votes for Party X is $\frac{3}{5}$.
   Find the probability that, in a randomly selected sample of 8 voters, there are exactly 3 who vote for Party X.

8. The probability that a first-year university student will complete four years of study is $\frac{1}{3}$. What is the probability that, of four first-year students, at least three will complete four years of study?

9. If 20% of the bolts produced by a machine are defective, determine the probability that, out of 4 bolts selected at random,
   (i) 2 bolts are defective
   (ii) not more than 2 bolts are defective.

10. The probability that any child in a certain class travels to school by bus is $\frac{2}{5}$. If four children from the class are selected at random, what is the probability that
    (i) none of them travels to school by bus
    (ii) three of them travel to school by bus
    (iii) at least one of them travels to school by bus?

11. A certain golfer estimates that the probability that he will sink any one putt is $\frac{7}{10}$. Find the probability that
    (i) he will sink two putts in three attempts
    (ii) he will miss three putts in four attempts.

12. The probability that horse A will win any given race is $\frac{2}{5}$.
    What is the probability that in five races
    (i) A will win exactly 3 races
    (ii) A will win the first, third and fifth races and lose the others?

13. Out of 2000 families with 4 children each, how many would you expect to have
    (i) 2 boys   (ii) no girls   (iii) at least one boy?

14. In a multiple-choice test, each question has three alternative answers with only one answer correct.
    Part A of the test consists of four of these questions.
    (i) Explain why the binomial distribution is appropriate in this situation.
    (ii) If Ray guesses each answer, calculate the probability that he gets all answers correct.
    (iii) Calculate the probability that he gets the first answer correct.
        Hence calculate the probability that he gets exactly one answer correct.

15. A fair coin is tossed repeatedly until the third head appears.
    Explain how you would use the binomial distribution to work out the probability of this happening.

16. A fair dice is thrown repeatedly.
    (i) Find the probability of getting two fives in the first ten throws.
    (ii) Hence find the probability of getting the third five on the eleventh throw.

17. A card is drawn at random from a normal deck of playing cards and then replaced.
    (i) What is the probability that the card drawn is a picture card?
    (ii) A card is drawn repeatedly and then replaced until the third picture card is drawn.
        Find the probability that the third picture card is drawn on the thirteenth attempt.

18. When a spinner is spun, the probability that it lands on red is 0.3. The spinner is spun until four reds are got.
    Find the probability that the fourth red is got on the tenth spin.

19. A bag contains counters of which 40% are red and the rest yellow. A counter is taken from the bag, its colour is noted and then replaced. This is performed eight times.
    (i)   Find the probability that exactly three counters will be red.
    (ii) If the process is repeated until a fourth red counter is drawn, find the probability that this happens on the ninth draw.

20. In a multiple-choice test, there are ten questions and for each question there is a choice of four answers, only one of which is correct. If a student guesses at each of the answers, find the probability that he gets
    (i)   none correct   (ii) 7 correct.
    Now find the probability that he gets his third correct answer on the tenth question.

Section 3.4 How to show events are independent

In Section 1.6 of this book, it was stated that two events are **independent** when the outcome of one event does not affect the outcome of the other event.

We also used the **multiplication rule** for independent events A and B which stated that

$$P(A \text{ and } B) = P(A \cap B)$$

$$P(A \text{ and } B) = P(A) \times P(B).$$

Using set notation, this rule may be written as:

$$P(A \cap B) = P(A).P(B)$$

Multiplication rule for independent events

In this section, we will use the multiplication rule to determine whether or not two events are independent.

The following examples will illustrate this procedure.

┌─ **Example 1** ───

In a group of 60 students, 20 study History, 24 study French, 8 study both History and French and 24 study neither.

Illustrate this information on a Venn diagram.

Now investigate if the events 'a student studies History' and 'a student studies French' are independent.

$P(\text{History}) = \frac{20}{60} = \frac{1}{3}$

$P(\text{French}) = \frac{24}{60} = \frac{2}{5}$

$P(\text{History and French}) = \frac{8}{60} = \frac{2}{15}$

Now $P(\text{History}) \times P(\text{French}) = \frac{1}{3} \times \frac{2}{5} = \frac{2}{15}$

Thus $P(\text{History and French}) = P(\text{History}) \times P(\text{French}) = \frac{2}{15}$

The two events are independent.

Two rules that we have already dealt with are highlighted in the box opposite. They are used frequently when we are investigating whether or not two events are independent. These two rules should be memorised.

1. The addition rule:
$$P(A \cup B) = P(A) + P(B) - P(A \cap B)$$

2. Conditional probability: $P(A|B) = \dfrac{P(A \cap B)}{P(B)}$

Example 2

Two events A and B are such that $P(A) = 0.5$, $P(B) = 0.4$ and $P(A|B) = 0.3$.
(i) Find $P(A \cap B)$.
(ii) Investigate whether or not the events A and B are independent.

(i) Using the conditional probability rule, we have:
$$P(A|B) = \frac{P(A \cap B)}{P(B)}$$
$$\therefore \qquad 0.3 = \frac{P(A \cap B)}{0.4}$$
$$\therefore \qquad P(A \cap B) = (0.3)(0.4) = 0.12$$
$$\therefore \qquad P(A \cap B) = 0.12$$

(ii) $P(A \cap B) = 0.12 \qquad P(A) = 0.5 \qquad P(B) = 0.4$
$$P(A) \times P(B) = 0.5 \times 0.4 = 0.2$$
Since $P(A \cap B) = 0.12 \Rightarrow P(A \cap B) \neq P(A) \times P(B)$
Thus the events A and B are not independent.

Example 3

Two ordinary fair dice, one red and one blue, are to be rolled once.
(i) Find the probability of the following events:

Event A: the number showing on the red dice will be a 5 or a 6.
Event B: the total of the numbers showing on the two dice will be 7.
Event C: the total of the numbers showing on the two dice will be 8.

(ii) Show that events A and B are independent.
(iii) Investigate if events A and C are independent.

(i) The events A, B and C are shown on the right.

$\#A = 12 \qquad \therefore \quad P(A) = \frac{12}{36} = \frac{1}{3}$

$\#B = 6 \qquad \therefore \quad P(B) = \frac{6}{36} = \frac{1}{6}$

$\#C = 5 \qquad \therefore \quad P(C) = \frac{5}{36}$

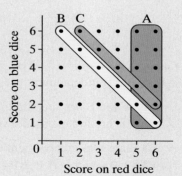

(ii) There are two ways to score 7 with the red dice showing 5 or 6.

These are $(5, 2)$ and $(6, 1)$

So $\#(A \cap B) = 2 \Rightarrow P(A \cap B) = \frac{2}{36} = \frac{1}{18}$

Now $P(A) \times P(B) = \frac{1}{3} \times \frac{1}{6} = \frac{1}{18}$

Since $P(A \cap B) = P(A) \times P(B) = \frac{1}{18}$, events A and B are independent.

(iii) From the diagram $\#(A \cap C) = 2$.

These are $(5, 3)$ and $(6, 2)$.

Thus $\#(A \cap C) = 2 \Rightarrow P(A \cap C) = \frac{2}{36} = \frac{1}{18}$

Now $P(A) \times P(C) = \frac{1}{3} \times \frac{5}{36} = \frac{5}{108}$

Since $\frac{5}{108} \neq \frac{1}{18}$, then $P(A \cap C) \neq P(A) \times P(C)$.

Thus events A and C are not independent.

Note: To show that two events A and B are mutually exclusive, we must show that
$$P(A \text{ or } B) = P(A) + P(B).$$

Exercise 3.4

1. The given Venn diagram shows the number of elements in the different regions.

   Find (i) $P(A)$ (ii) $P(B)$ (iii) $P(A \cap B)$.

   Hence show that A and B are independent events.

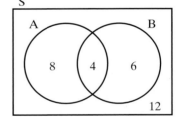

2. From the given Venn diagram, write down
   (i) $P(A)$ (ii) $P(B)$.

   Now show that A and B are independent.

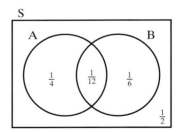

3. Given that $P(A) = 0.8$, $P(B) = 0.6$ and $P(A \cap B) = 0.48$. Are A and B independent events? Explain your answer.

4. Events A and B are such that $P(A) = 0.4$ and $P(B) = 0.25$. If A and B are independent events, find $P(A \cap B)$.

5. A and B are two independent events. If $P(A) = 0.4$ and $P(A \cup B) = 0.7$, use the formula $P(A \cup B) = P(A) + P(B) - P(A \cap B)$ to find $P(B)$.

6. The events A and B are such that

$$P(A) = 0.45, P(B) = 0.35 \text{ and } P(A \cup B) = 0.7.$$

Remember:

$$P(A|B) = \frac{P(A \cap B)}{P(B)}.$$

   (i)   Find the value of $P(A \cap B)$.
   (ii) Explain why the events A and B are not independent.
   (iii) Find the value of $P(A|B)$.

7. Given that $P(A) = 0.8$, $P(B) = 0.7$ and $P(A|B) = 0.8$.
   (i)   Find $P(A \cap B)$
   (ii) Show that A and B are independent.

8. The events A and B are such that $P(A) = \frac{2}{5}$, $P(B) = \frac{1}{6}$ and $P(A \cup B) = \frac{13}{30}$.
   (i)   Find $P(A \cap B)$.
   (ii) Explain why A and B are not independent.

9. Given that events C and D are independent and that $P(C|D) = \frac{2}{3}$ and $P(C \cap D) = \frac{1}{3}$, find
   (i) $P(C)$ (ii) $P(D)$.

10. Given $P(B) = 0.7$, $P(C) = 0.6$ and $P(C|B) = 0.7$, find $P(B \cap C)$.
    Now investigate if B and C are independent.

11. A and B are two independent events such that

$$P(A) = 0.2 \text{ and } P(B) = 0.15$$

    Evaluate the following probabilities:
    (i) $P(A \cap B)$ (ii) $P(A|B)$ (iii) $P(A \cup B)$

12. Two events A and B are such that

$$P(A) = 0.2, P(A \cap B) = 0.15 \text{ and } P(A' \cap B) = 0.6.$$

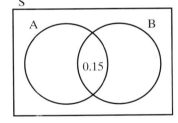

    (i)   Copy and complete the given Venn diagram.
    (ii) Find the probability that neither A nor B happens.
    (iii) Find the conditional probability, $P(A|B)$.
    (iv) State whether A and B are independent and justify your answer.

13. Two events A and B are such that $P(A) = \frac{8}{15}$, $P(B) = \frac{1}{3}$, $P(A|B) = \frac{1}{5}$.
    Calculate the probability that
    (i)   both events occur
    (ii) only one of the two events occurs
    (iii) neither event occurs.

14. (i) Given that two events, A and B, are such that $P(A \text{ and } B) = P(A) \times P(B)$, state what you can say about the events A and B.
        If event A is 'obtaining a 6 on a single throw of a dice', suggest a possible description for event B.
    (ii) Given that two events, C and D, are such that $P(C \text{ or } D) = P(C) + P(D)$, state what you can say about the events C and D.
        Write down the value of $P(C \text{ and } D)$.

15. Two events, A and B, are such that $P(A|B) = 0.4$, $P(B|A) = 0.25$ and $P(A \cap B) = 0.12$.
    (i) Calculate the value of $P(A)$ and $P(B)$.
    (ii) Give a reason why A and B are not independent.
    (iii) Find $P(A \cap B')$

16. Two events, E and F, are such that $P(E) = \frac{2}{5}$, $P(F) = \frac{1}{6}$ and $P(E \cup F) = \frac{13}{30}$.
    Show that E and F are neither mutually exclusive nor independent.

Section 3.5 Probability involving permutations and combinations

Many of the more difficult problems in probability involve the use of permutations or combinations to identify the number of possible outcomes or the number of favourable outcomes. While many problems can be solved in more than one way, the following worked examples will illustrate how combinations, in particular, can be used to solve certain types of problem.

Example 1

In Class 6A, two boys and four girls study music.
In Class 6B, four boys and six girls study music.
Two pupils are chosen at random from each of the two classes to perform at a concert.
(i) In how many ways can the 4 pupils be selected?
(ii) Calculate the probability that the four chosen consist of 2 boys from 6A and 2 girls from 6B.
(iii) Calculate the probability that the four pupils are of the same gender.

For convenience, we will set out the information in the form of a table.

6A	2 Boys	4 Girls
6B	4 Boys	6 Girls

(i) The number of ways 2 pupils can be selected from 6A and 2 pupils from 6B is,
$$\binom{6}{2} \times \binom{10}{2} = 675 \text{ ways.}$$

(ii) Two boys from 6A and two girls from 6B can be chosen in
$$\binom{2}{2} \times \binom{6}{2} = 1 \times 15 = 15 \text{ ways}$$
$$P(\text{2 boys from 6A and 2 girls from 6B}) = \frac{15}{675} = \frac{1}{45}$$

(iii) If the four pupils are of the same gender, they will consist of
    (a) 2 girls from 6A and 2 girls from 6B
or (b) 2 boys from 6A and 2 boys from 6B.
$$P(a) = \frac{\binom{4}{2} \times \binom{6}{2}}{675} = \frac{6 \times 15}{675} = \frac{90}{675}$$
$$P(b) = \frac{\binom{2}{2} \times \binom{4}{2}}{675} = \frac{1 \times 6}{675} = \frac{6}{675}$$
$$\therefore \quad P(a \text{ or } b) = P(a) + P(b) = \frac{90}{675} + \frac{6}{675} = \frac{96}{675} = \frac{32}{225}$$

Example 2

Three cards are drawn at random, and without replacement, from a pack of 52 playing cards. Find the probability that
  (i)   the three cards drawn are the Jack of spades, the Queen of clubs and the King of clubs
  (ii) the three cards are aces
  (iii) two cards are red and the third one is a club
  (iv) the three cards are of the same colour.

  (i)   Three cards can be selected from 52 cards in $\binom{52}{3}$ ways.

$$\binom{52}{3} = \frac{52 \times 51 \times 50}{3 \times 2 \times 1} = 22100$$

The three cards mentioned can be selected in $\binom{3}{3}$ i.e. 1 way

$$\therefore \quad P(J..Q..K) = \frac{1}{22100}$$

  (ii) Three aces can be selected from four aces in $\binom{4}{3}$ ways

$$\therefore \quad P(3 \text{ aces}) = \frac{\binom{4}{3}}{\binom{52}{3}} = \frac{4}{22100} = \frac{1}{5525}$$

  (iii) Two red cards and one club can be selected in

$$\binom{26}{2} \times \binom{13}{1} = \frac{26 \times 25}{2 \times 1} \times 13 = 4225 \text{ ways}$$

$$\therefore \quad P(2 \text{ red and 1 club}) = \frac{4225}{22100} = \frac{169}{884} = \frac{13}{68}$$

  (iv) $P(3 \text{ cards of the same colour}) = P(3 \text{ black or 3 red})$

$$= P(3 \text{ black}) + P(3 \text{ red})$$

$$= \frac{\binom{26}{3}}{\binom{52}{3}} + \frac{\binom{26}{3}}{\binom{52}{3}} = \frac{5200}{22100} = \frac{4}{17}$$

Note: Most of the problems involving combinations can be done more quickly using the multiplication rule. Where a choice of methods exist, it is better to use the multiplication rule.

Events occurring at least once

Many questions in probability contain phrases such as "at least once", "at least one red disc", etc. Take, for example, the probability of getting at least one 4 when a pair of dice are thrown.

First get the probability that no 4 is thrown.

$$P(\text{no 4}) = P(\text{no 4 on 1st throw}) \times P(\text{no 4 on 2nd throw}) = \tfrac{5}{6} \times \tfrac{5}{6} = \tfrac{25}{36}$$

$$P(\text{at least one 4}) = 1 - P(\text{no 4}) = 1 - \tfrac{25}{36} = \tfrac{11}{36}$$

Similarly, if a coin is tossed four times, the probability of getting at least two heads is

$$P(\text{at least 2 heads}) = 1 - P(\text{no head}) - P(\text{1 head})$$

In general, if E is any event, then

$$P(E \text{ occurring at least once}) = 1 - P(E \text{ not occurring at all})$$

Exercise 3.5

1. A hand of four cards is dealt at random from a normal pack of 52 cards.
   Find the probability that the hand contains
   (i)   exactly two queens   (ii) four spades
   (iii) four red cards   (iv) four cards of the same suit.

2. A team of four people is chosen at random from six men and five women.
   In how many ways can the team be chosen?
   Now find the probability that the team will consist of
   (i) 2 men and 2 women   (ii) 1 man and 3 women   (iii) all women.

3. There are sixteen discs in a board-game: five blue, three green, six red and two yellow.
   Four discs are chosen at random.
   What is the probability that
   (i)   the four discs are blue
   (ii) the four discs are the same colour
   (iii) all four discs are different in colour
   (iv) two of the discs are blue and two are not blue?

4. Nine discs were each given a natural number from two to ten inclusive, each number different from the others. All nine were placed in a box.
   (i) A disc was picked at random and replaced. A second disc was then picked.
        Find the probability that both discs showed prime numbers.
   (ii) Three discs were picked at random. What is the probability that three odd-numbered discs or three even-numbered discs were picked?

5. Nine cards are numbered from 1 to 9, with each number different from the others.
   Three cards are drawn at random from the nine cards.
   (i) Find the probability that the card numbered 8 is not drawn.
   (ii) Find the probability that all three cards drawn have odd numbers.

6. In a class of 24 students, there are 14 boys and 10 girls.
   In a particular week three students celebrate their birthdays.
   What is the probability that these three students
   (i) are three boys or three girls
   (ii) have their birthdays falling on different days of the week?

7. In an examination a candidate is required to select any seven questions from ten.
   (i) In how many ways can this be done?
   (ii) How many of the selections contain the first and second questions?
   Now calculate the probability that the candidate selects
   (iii) both the first and second questions
   (iv) at least one of the first two questions.

8. A class of 16 pupils consists of 10 girls, 3 of whom are left-handed, and 6 boys, only one of whom is left-handed. Two pupils are to be chosen at random from the class to act as prefects. Calculate the probability that the chosen pupils will consist of
   (i) one girl and one boy
   (ii) one girl who is left-handed and one boy who is left-handed
   (iii) two left-handed pupils
   (iv) at least one pupil who is left-handed.

9. Three dice, each numbered 1 to 6 are rolled. One dice is fair and the others are biased so that, for each of them, a six is twice as likely as any other score.
   Find the probability of rolling exactly two sixes.

10. A box contains letters used in a word-game. At a certain stage in the game, the 8 letters in the box are A, A, C, E, L, P, P, P. One player draws, at random, 3 letters in succession without replacing them. Calculate the probability that
    (i) the letters P, E, A are drawn in that order
    (ii) the letters P, E, A are drawn in any order
    (iii) the 3 letters drawn do not include E or P
    (iv) the 3 letters drawn are either all consonants or all vowels.

Section 3.6 The normal distribution

When the physical characteristics, such as height or weight, of a large number of individuals are arranged in order, from lowest to highest, in a frequency distribution, the same pattern shows up repeatedly. This pattern shows that large numbers cluster near the middle of the distribution, as illustrated by the symmetrical histogram shown below.

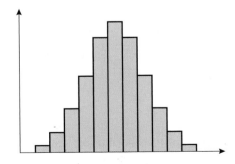

If the distribution is very large and continuous, and the class intervals become sufficiently small, the distribution forms a symmetrical bell-shaped smooth curve called **the curve of normal distribution** or simply the **normal curve** as shown on the following page:

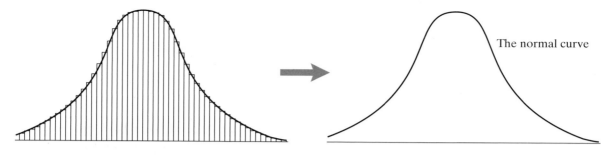

The normal curve

The normal distribution is the most important continuous distribution in statistics.

The curve on the right shows a normal distribution with mean μ.
The red line is the axis of symmetry.

The mode, median and mean are all equal.
They lie on the axis of symmetry.

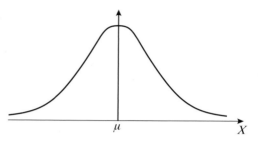

Standard deviation and the normal curve

Here are two normal curves, both with the same mean of 15.
The green curve is narrower and has the smaller spread.
It has the smaller standard deviation.

The red curve is wider and has the larger spread.
It has the larger standard deviation.

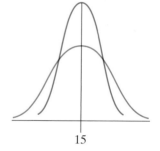

The diagram below shows three normal curves with different means but the same standard deviation.

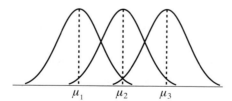

For any normal distribution:

- approximately 68% of the distribution lies within one standard deviation of the mean, i.e., 68% lies between $\bar{x} - \sigma$ and $\bar{x} + \sigma$.
- 95% lies between $\mu - 2\sigma$ and $\mu + 2\sigma$.
- 99.7% lies between $\mu - 3\sigma$ and $\mu + 3\sigma$.

This is known as the **Empirical Rule**.

The normal curve opposite illustrates the Empirical Rule.

Based on the Empirical Rule, the probability that a score, selected at random, will be within one standard deviation of the mean is 68% or 0.68.

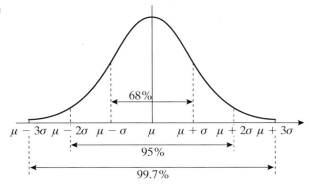

The normal curve is discussed in a more comprehensive way in Chapter 4 of this book.

The standard normal distribution

There are many different normal distributions, all of the same bell-shape, but with different means and standard deviations. To avoid the necessity of having separate tables for each normal curve, we convert the units in a given curve to **standard units** to get the **standard normal distribution**. The standard units are often referred to as z units.

The change of scale from x-units to z-units is shown in the diagram below.

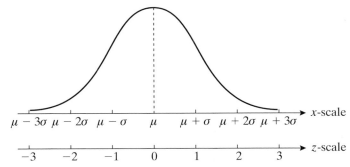

A **z-score** or **standard score** is the number of standard deviations that a value lies above or below the mean.

> a z-score of 1 represents a score that is 1 standard deviation **above** the mean
> a z-score of -2 represents a score that is 2 standard deviations **below** the mean

The standard normal distribution has mean 0 and standard deviation 1.

The formula which changes the given units (x-units) into z-units is given below:

Standard scores
$$z = \frac{x - \mu}{\sigma}$$

> x is the given score or variable
> μ is the given mean
> σ is the given standard deviation

Example 1

Milk cartons are designed to hold 600 ml of milk.
Their capacities are normally distributed with mean 600 ml and standard deviation 10 ml.

  (i)   Calculate the standard scores for these capacities
        (a) 610 ml   (b) 595 ml   (c) 625 ml.
 (ii) Mark these z-scores on the diagram of a standard normal curve.
(iii) What can you conclude about a carton containing 625 ml?

  (i) $z = \dfrac{x - \mu}{\sigma}$, where $\mu = 600$ and $\sigma = 10$

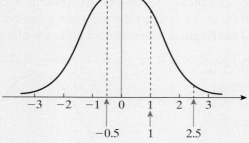

       (a) 610 ml: $z = \dfrac{610 - 600}{10} = \dfrac{10}{10} = 1$ $z = 1$ means 1 standard deviation above the mean.

       (b) 595 ml: $z = \dfrac{595 - 600}{10} = \dfrac{-5}{10} = -0.5$ $z = -0.5$ means 0.5 standard deviations below the mean.

       (c) 625 ml: $z = \dfrac{625 - 600}{10} = 2.5$ $z = 2.5$ means 2.5 standard deviations above the mean.

 (ii) The z-scores -0.5, 1 and 2.5 are shown on the right.

(iii) A carton containing 625 ml is most unlikely as the capacity is over 2σ above the mean, that is, outside the 95% limit.

Probability and the normal distribution

The area between the standard normal curve and the z-axis is 1.

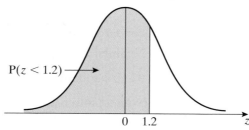

Pages (36–37) of *formulae and tables* gives the area under the curve as far as a particular value of z.

The shaded area in the diagram above represents the probability that $z \leqslant 1.2$.

However, since the curve is symmetrical about the line $z = 0$, the tables allow us to find the area under the curve for any value of z.

The method of finding various areas under the curve are shown below:

$P(z \leqslant 1.68)$ can be read directly from the tables.

$$P(z \leqslant 1.68) = 0.9535$$

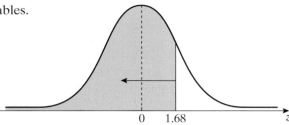

$P(z \geqslant 0.85)$
To find the area to the right of 0.85 use the equation,

$$P(z \geqslant 0.85) = 1 - P(z \leqslant 0.85)$$
$$= 1 - 0.8023$$
$$= 0.1977$$

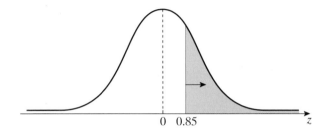

$P(z \leqslant -1.23)$
To find the area left of -1.23, we use the fact that the curve is symmetrical and find the area to the left of 1.23

i.e. $P(z \leqslant -1.23) = 1 - P(z \leqslant 1.23)$
$$= 1 - 0.8907$$
$$= 0.1093$$

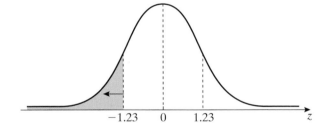

$P(-1.21 \leqslant z \leqslant 0.93)$
To find this area
  (i) find area to the left of 0.93
  (ii) find area to the right of -1.21.

Then subtract (ii) from (i)

For example,
Area to the left of 0.93 = 0.8238
Area to the right of $-1.21 = 1 - P(z \leqslant 1.21)$
$$= 1 - 0.8869 = 0.1131$$
$\Rightarrow$ area of shaded portion $= 0.8238 - 0.1131$
$$= 0.7107$$

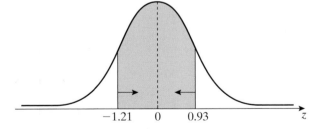

If we are given the probability that $z \leqslant k$, we can still use the tables to find the value of z that corresponds to k.

The following example illustrates this.

Example 2

Find a in each of the following:
  (i) $P(z \leqslant a) = 0.7324$ (ii) $P(z \leqslant a) = 0.1724$

  (i) The area to the left of $z = 0$ is 0.5.
      Thus $P(z \leqslant a) = 0.7324 \Rightarrow a$ is positive
      From the tables, $0.7324 \Rightarrow a = 0.62$

 (ii) $P(z \leqslant a) = 0.1724 \Rightarrow a$ is negative
      Thus $P(z \leqslant -a) = 1 - P(z \leqslant a)$

                          $= 1 - 0.1724$

                          $= 0.8276$

                $\Rightarrow a = 0.94$

    $\Rightarrow -a = 0.94$

    $\Rightarrow \quad a = -0.94$

Example 3

The mean height of all the students in a certain school is 175 cm and the standard deviation is 15 cm. If a student is selected at random, find the probability that he is less than, or equal to, 190 cm tall.

If 90% of the students are less than or equal to x cm, find the value of x, assuming that the distribution is normal.

In the given distribution, $\mu = 175$ and $\sigma = 15$

Using the formula $\qquad z = \dfrac{x - \mu}{\sigma}$

$\quad x = 190 \qquad \Rightarrow \qquad z = \dfrac{190 - 175}{15} = 1$

$\quad \Rightarrow P(x \leqslant 190) = P(z \leqslant 1)$

$\qquad\qquad\qquad = 0.8413$

$\quad \Rightarrow P(\text{student} \leqslant 190\,\text{cm}) = 0.8413$

If 90% of the students are less than or equal to x cm, we need to find the value of z_1 in the diagram on the right.

From the tables on page 36,

$\qquad P(z \leqslant z_1) = 0.9$

$\qquad\quad \Rightarrow z_1 = 1.28$

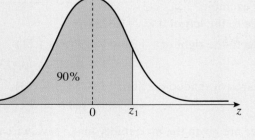

To find the value for x, we must "transform back" by expressing x in terms of z.

$$z = \frac{x - \mu}{\sigma} \Rightarrow x = z\sigma + \mu$$
$$= 1.28(15) + 175 = 194.2$$

Therefore 90% of the students are less than or equal to 194.2 cm.

Exercise 3.6

1. Using your *Formulae and Tables* book, find the area of the shaded region under each of the following standard normal curves:

(i)

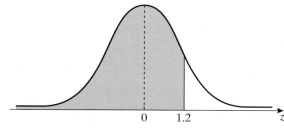

(ii)

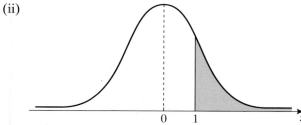

(iii)

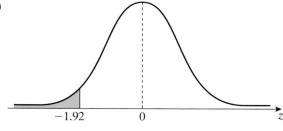

(iv)

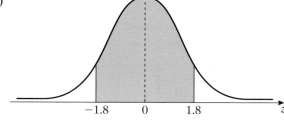

If z is a random variable with standard normal distribution, find

2. $P(z \leqslant 1.42)$ 3. $P(z \leqslant 0.89)$ 4. $P(z \leqslant 2.04)$

5. $P(z \geqslant 2)$ 6. $P(z \geqslant 1.25)$ 7. $P(z \geqslant 0.75)$

8. $P(z \leqslant -2.3)$ 9. $P(z \leqslant -1.3)$ 10. $P(z \leqslant -2.13)$

11. $P(z \leqslant 0.56)$ 12. $P(-1 \leqslant z \leqslant 1)$ 13. $P(-1.5 \leqslant z \leqslant 1.5)$

14. $P(0.8 \leqslant z \leqslant 2.2)$ 15. $P(-1.8 \leqslant z \leqslant 2.3)$ 16. $P(-0.83 \leqslant z \leqslant 1.4)$

Find the value of z_1 in each of the following if z is a random variable with normal distribution.

17. $P(z \leqslant z_1) = 0.8686$ 18. $P(z \leqslant z_1) = 0.6331$

19. $P(-z_1 \leqslant z \leqslant z_1) = 0.6368$ 20. $P(-z_1 \leqslant z \leqslant z_1) = 0.8438$

21. If x is a random variable with normal distribution and has mean $\mu = 50$ and standard deviation $\sigma = 10$, find
(i) $P(x \leqslant 60)$ (ii) $P(x \leqslant 55)$ (iii) $P(x \geqslant 45)$

In each of the following, x is a random variable with normal distribution with a given mean (μ) and standard deviation (σ). Find the required probability in each case.

22. $\mu = 300$, $\sigma = 25$, find   (i) $P(x \geqslant 294)$ (ii) $P(x \leqslant 312)$.

23. $\mu = 250$, $\sigma = 40$, find   (i) $P(x \geqslant 300)$ (ii) $P(x \leqslant 175)$.

24. $\mu = 50$, $\sigma = 8$, find   (i) $P(52 \leqslant x \leqslant 55)$ (ii) $P(48 \leqslant x \leqslant 54)$.

25. $\mu = 100$, $\sigma = 80$, find   (i) $P(85 \leqslant x \leqslant 112)$ (ii) $P(105 \leqslant x \leqslant 115)$.

26. $\mu = 200$, $\sigma = 20$, find   (i) $P(190 \leqslant x \leqslant 210)$ (ii) $P(185 \leqslant x \leqslant 205)$.

27. The life of a particular light bulb is normally distributed with a mean life of 210 hours and a standard deviation of 20 hours. Find
(i) the probability that a bulb, selected at random, will last more than 240 hours
(ii) the probability that a bulb will last less than or equal to 200 hours.

28. The chest measurements of teenage male customers for T-shirts may be modelled by a normal distribution with mean 101 cm and standard deviation 5 cm. Find the probability that a randomly-selected customer will have a chest measurement which is
(i) less than 103 cm
(ii) 98 cm or more
(iii) between 95 and 100 cm.

29. The time taken by a postman to deliver letters to a certain apartment block is normally distributed with mean 12 minutes and standard deviation 2 minutes. Estimate the probability that he takes
(i) longer than 17 minutes
(ii) less than 10 minutes
(iii) between 9 and 13 minutes.

30. A mobile phone company finds that its phone bills are normally distributed with a mean of €53 and a standard deviation of €15.
   Find the probability that, if a mobile phone bill is chosen at random, the amount due will be between €47 and €74.

31. The heights of a large group of female students are normally distributed with a mean of 165cm and a standard deviation of 3.5 cm. A student is selected at random from this group.
   (i) Find the probability that she is less than 160 cm in height.

   The Drama teacher is looking for a student with a height between 168 cm and 174 cm for a part in a school play.
   (ii) Find the proportion of students from this group that would satisfy these conditions.

32. The mean length of 500 laurel leaves from a certain bush is 151 mm and the standard deviation is 15 mm. Assuming that the lengths are normally distributed, find how many leaves measure
   (i) greater than 185 mm
   (ii) between 120 mm and 155 mm.

33. A biscuit company knows that the weights of the packets of one of their brands are normally distributed with a mean of 300 grams and a standard deviation of 6 grams. How many of 1000 packets, selected at random, can be expected to weigh
   (i) less than 295 grams
   (ii) between 306 and 310 grams?

34. The mean percentage mark achieved by students in Geography in a state examination was 60% and the standard deviation was 10%.
   (i) What is the probability that a randomly selected student scored
      (a) below 45%
      (b) between 50% and 75%?
   (ii) Students got a special award if they obtained a mark greater than 90% of all the other students in the examination.
      What percentage mark would the student need to get a prize?

Section 3.7 Probability simulations ———————

The word **simulate** means to imitate or model. The use of simulation is becoming an increasingly-powerful tool in the modern world of business. In the past, when an engineer was designing a new car or aeroplane, he would build a physical model first and test its performance in wind tunnels. Now, initial tests are done on computers through the use of simulation programmes.

A **probability simulation** is the use of some method to model or represent a real experiment or situation.

Simulations can involve

> dice, spinners, discs and counters
> calculators and computers to generate random numbers
> random number tables

You may also use experiments in simulation.

Example 1

With every breakfast cereal pack there is a free coloured toy. There are 6 different colours of toys.

How many packs of breakfast cereal do you need to buy to collect the 6 different-coloured toys?

A simulation can give you some indication of how many packets you need to buy.

  (i) Match each colour to a number on a dice.

 (ii) Roll the dice until each colour has appeared once.

$$2, 2, 6, 4, 2, 2, 5, 1, 4, 5, 4, 3$$

All six numbers have occurred in the first 12 rolls.
Based on this simulation, you would need to buy 12 packets.

(iii) Repeat the simulation.

$$3, 1, 3, 1, 4, 6, 6, 5, 3, 5, 6, 3, 5, 2$$

This time you would need to buy 14 packets.

(iv) Repeat this as many times as you like.

> The more times you repeat the experiment, the more confidence you have in the results.

Think!

Can you propose an alternative way to find how many packets you need to buy?
Perhaps your method might include the following:

> generate a random number table
> use a spreadsheet
> use a spinner
> get your friends to buy some boxes to see how many you need to buy to get a full set.

The **advantages** of simulation are:

> It is quick and inexpensive
> When using a spreadsheet, you can get several hundred pieces of data
> You can adjust the probability to cater for events that are not equally likely.

Example 2

In families that have 5 children, we wish to investigate the probability that boys outnumber girls.

Devise a simulation of this situation and use it to determine whether the probability is more than, less than, or equal to $\frac{1}{2}$.

Assume that each child has an equal chance of being a boy or a girl.

Suppose you choose to toss 5 coins at a time to simulate the genders of the 5 children in the family, where head stands for boy and tail stands for girl.

In 4 tosses we get the following results:

TTTTT	5 girls	Girls outnumber boys
THHHH	1 girl, 4 boys	Boys outnumber girls
THTHH	2 girls, 3 boys	Boys outnumber girls
HHTTT	3 girls, 2 boys	Girls outnumber boys

After 100 tosses, we get the following results:

Outcome	Frequency
Boys outnumbering	53
Girls outnumbering	47

It appears that the outcomes are fairly even and that the probability that boys outnumber girls is about $\frac{1}{2}$.

Using a spreadsheet, this experiment was simulated and the result is shown in the table below:

Outcome	Frequency
Boys outnumbering	48
Girls outnumbering	52

This outcome shows a similar result.

This example could also be modelled by

 (i)   Rolling a dice with 1 − 3 indicates boy and 4 − 6 indicates girl

 (ii) Random numbers using a calculator or a table of random numbers:

       0 − 4 indicates boy   and   5 − 9 indicates girl

 (iii) selecting from a deck of playing cards:

       red indicates girl   and   black indicates boy

Example 3

Four people are selected at random from a large crowd.

What is the probability that two or more of them have birthdays in the same month?

  (i) Devise a simulation that could determine the probability of this happening.

 (ii) Run the simulation 100 times and approximate the probability.

  (i) Possible simulations:

  ❯ Write down the 12 months of the year on separate cards and draw them out of a box.

  ❯ Remove all the kings from a deck of cards, then select a card from the remaining 48:

  Ace = January, 2 = February, ... etc.

  ❯ Use a calculator or spreadsheet to generate random numbers from 1 to 12.

  ❯ Toss a dice and coin together (there are 12 possible outcomes).

  H1 = January, H2 = February, ... etc.

 (ii)

Simulation result				Shared birthday
6	8	1	2	No
1	8	1	11	Yes
5	11	6	10	No
8	8	10	12	Yes
10	8	2	4	No
5	6	12	10	No

  ❯ The above 6 results were found using the random number function on a calculator.

  ❯ When this experiment was conducted 100 times, the following results were recorded.

Shared birthday	Frequency
Yes	45
No	55

From these results, we can conclude that the probability of two, three or more people, from a random group of four sharing the same birthday, is about 45%.

Note: This answer seems surprisingly high but the true (calculated) probability is 42.7%.

Exercise 3.7

1. One of twenty different vouchers are given away in packets of crisps.
   You need a full set of vouchers to get a model car.
   Carry out a simulation to estimate the number of packets of crisps you would need to buy to get a car.

2. A menu has three options – meat, fish and vegetarian.
   $\frac{2}{8}$ of diners choose fish; $\frac{1}{8}$ choose vegetarian; $\frac{5}{8}$ choose meat.
   Explain how you would simulate the choices of the next ten customers.

3. Carry out a simulated experiment to determine the probability, correct to two decimal places, that in a family with four children
   (i) the girls outnumber the boys
   (ii) all the children are girls.

4. At a road junction, it is known that 80% of cars turn left and 20% of cars turn right.
   Suggest how you might allocate numbers to simulate the probability of cars turning right or left when approaching this junction.

5. The *Ringdogs* have a 0.7 chance of winning their home games and a 0.4 chance of winning their away games.
   (i) If they play 12 home games and 13 away games, how many games should they win?
   (ii) Make a simulation of this situation and find out how many of the 25 games they should win.
   Does your result agree with part (i)?

6. Every packet of *Chocopops* breakfast cereal contains a superhero figure for children to collect. David wants to collect the entire set of eight different superhero figures.
   Devise a simulation to determine the approximate number of packets of *Chocopops* he will need to purchase to collect the full set.

7. What is the probability of rolling at least one 6 in four rolls of a fair dice?
   Give your answer correct to 2 decimal places.
   Simulate an experiment over a number of trials to determine an approximate probability of rolling a 6.
   Compare your result to the answer already found.

8. What is the likely size of a family that contains one child of each gender?
   Explain how you could simulate this experiment.

Test yourself 3

A – questions

1. If z is a random variable with standard normal distribution, use *Tables and Formulae* to find $P(z \geqslant 0.93)$.

2. Which of these events can be illustrated by this tree diagram?

   (i) tossing a coin three times
   (ii) selecting two counters from a bag of red, blue and yellow counters.

   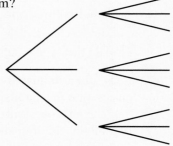

3. A golfer estimates that the probability she will sink a 1-metre putt is 0.7.
   Find the probability that she will sink three 1-metre putts in four attempts.

4. Five children are selected at random from a class containing 10 boys and 20 girls.
   (i) In how many ways can this be done?
   (ii) How many of the selections have 2 boys and 3 girls?
   (iii) What is the probability that exactly two boys are selected?

5. If z is a random variable having a standard normal distribution, use your *Tables and Formulae* to find $P(-1 \leqslant z \leqslant 1.24)$.

6. 20% of the items produced by a machine are defective. Four items are chosen at random.
   Find the probability that none of the chosen items is defective.

7. The school team has two tennis matches to play.
   The probability that they win the first match is $\frac{2}{5}$.
   If they win the first match, the probability that they win the second is $\frac{3}{4}$.
   If they lose the first match, the probability that they win the second is $\frac{1}{3}$.
   Copy this tree diagram. Fill it in.

   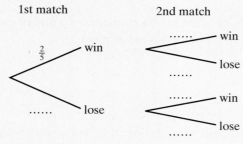

   Find the probability that the team:
   (i) loses both matches   (ii) wins only one match.

8. From the given Venn diagram, write down
   (i) $P(E)$
   (ii) $P(F)$
   (iii) $P(E \cup F)$

   Now show that E and F are independent.
   Find also $P(E|F)$.

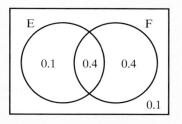

9. At a bazaar held to raise money for a charity, it costs €1 to try one's luck in drawing an ace from an ordinary deck of 52 playing cards.
   What is the expected profit per customer if the prize is €10 if, and only if, the person draws an ace?

10. Jack takes a card at random from this pack.

   He keeps the card and then takes a second card at random.
   What is the probability that the second number he takes is higher than the first?

B – questions

1. A tennis player A has a probability of $\frac{2}{3}$ of winning a set against a player B. The match is won by the player who first wins two sets.
   Find the probability that A wins the match.

2. The probability that my football club has all their first-team players fit is 70%. When they do have a fully-fit team, they win 90% of their home games. When their first team is not fully-fit, they win 40% of their home games.
   Calculate the probability that they win their next home game.

3. Two events E and F are independent.
   If $P(E) = \frac{1}{5}$ and $P(F) = \frac{1}{7}$, find
   (i) $P(E \cap F)$ (ii) $P(E \cup F)$.

4. In a class of 56 students, each studies at least one of the subjects Biology, Chemistry, Physics. The Venn diagram shows the numbers of students studying the various combinations of subjects.

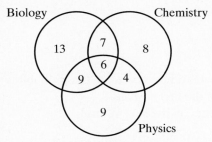

   (i) A student is picked at random from the whole class.
       Find the probability that the student does not study Biology.
   (ii) A student is picked at random from those who study at least two of the subjects.
        Find the probability that the student does not study Biology.

(iii) Two students are picked at random from the whole class.
Find the probability that they both study Physics.
(iv) Two students are picked at random from those who study Chemistry.
Find the probability that exactly one of them studies Biology.

5. (i) Find P$(1 < z < 2)$, where z is a random variable having a normal distribution.
   (ii) If z is a random variable with normal distribution, and $P(z \leqslant k) = 0.8686$, find k.

6. Two athletes, A and B, are attempting to qualify for an international competition in both the 5000 m and 10 000 m races.
The probabilities of each qualifying are shown in the following table:

Athlete	5000 m	10 000 m
A	$\frac{3}{5}$	$\frac{1}{4}$
B	$\frac{2}{3}$	$\frac{2}{5}$

Assuming that the probabilities are independent, calculate the probability that
   (i) athlete A will qualify for both races
   (ii) exactly one of the athletes qualifies for the 5000 m race
   (iii) both athletes qualify for the 10 000 m race.

7. (i) Amy throws a biased dice three times.
   For each throw, the probability of Amy not scoring a 6 is $\frac{2}{3}$.
   Using a tree diagram, or otherwise, find the probability that she gets at least one 6 in the three throws.
   (ii) For events A and B, it is known that $P(A) = \frac{2}{3}$, $P(A \cup B) = \frac{3}{4}$ and $P(A \cap B) = \frac{5}{12}$.
   Find $P(B)$.

8. The given diagram shows a roulette wheel in a casino.
It costs €25 to spin the spinner once and you win the money in the sector in which it stops.
How much do you expect to win or lose if you play this game?
Explain why the game is not fair.

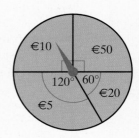

9. A fair dice is rolled several times. Calculate the probability that
   (i) two sixes occur on the first six rolls
   (ii) the second six occurs on the seventh roll.

10. Events E and F are such that $P(E) = \frac{2}{3}$, $P(E|F) = \frac{2}{3}$ and $P(F) = \frac{1}{4}$.
Find (i) P$(E \cap F)$ (ii) $P(F|E)$
Investigate if E and F are independent events.
Explain your answer.

C – questions

1. A marble falls down from A and must follow one of the paths indicated on the diagram. All paths from A to the bottom row are equally likely to be followed.

   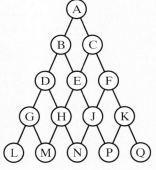

   (i) One of the paths from A to H is A-B-D-H. List the other two possible paths from A to H.
   (ii) Find the probability that the marble passes through H or J.
   (iii) Find the probability that the marble lands at N.
   (iv) Two marbles fall from A, one after the other, without affecting each other. Find the probability that they both land at P.

2. A soccer player knows that he has a 70% success rate when taking penalties. He takes ten penalty shots against the same goalkeeper. Calculate, correct to three decimal places, the probability that
   (i) he scores his first goal on his third attempt
   (ii) he scores exactly three goals in five attempts
   (iii) he scores his third goal on his seventh attempt.

3. (a) A and B are two events such that $P(A) = \frac{13}{25}$, $P(B) = \frac{9}{25}$ and $P(A|B) = \frac{5}{9}$. Determine each of these probabilities:
       (i) $P(A \text{ and } B)$ (ii) $P(B|A)$ (iii) $P(A \cup B)$.
   (b) A dice is biased in such a way that the probability of rolling a six is p. The other five numbers are all equally likely. This biased dice and a fair dice are rolled simultaneously. Show that the probability of rolling a total of 7 is independent of p.

4. The time a mobile phone battery lasts before needing to be recharged is assumed to be normally distributed with a mean of 48 hours and a standard deviation of 8 hours.
   (i) Find the probability that a battery will last for more than 60 hours.
   (ii) Find the probability that a battery lasts less than 35 hours.

5. A bag contains 4 red counters and 6 green counters. Four counters are drawn at random from the bag. Calculate the probability that
   (i) all counters drawn are green
   (ii) at least one counter of each colour is drawn
   (iii) at least two green counters are drawn
   (iv) at least two green counters are drawn, given that at least one of each colour is drawn. State, giving a reason, whether or not the events "at least two green counters are drawn" and "at least one counter of each colour is drawn" are independent.

6. (i) If z is a random variable with normal distribution, find the value of k if $P(-k \leqslant z \leqslant k) = 0.8438$.
   (ii) Events X and Y are such that $P(X) = \frac{2}{3}$, $P(X|Y) = \frac{2}{3}$ and $P(Y) = \frac{1}{4}$. Find   (a) $P(X \cap Y)$ (b) $P(Y|X)$.

7. (a) The random variable X has the following probability distribution.

x	1	2	3	4	5
$P(x)$	0.1	a	b	0.2	0.1

   (i) Write down the value of $a + b$.
   (ii) Given that E(x), the expected value of x, is 2.9, find the value of a and the value of b.

   (b) There are 16 girls and 8 boys in a class. Half of these 24 students study French. The probability that a randomly-selected girl studies French is 1.5 times the probability that a randomly-selected boy studies French. How many of the boys in the class study French?

8. In a game, Ann uses a dice and Jane uses two equilateral triangle spinners, adding the scores together. Ann rolls the dice and Jane spins the spinners. After each turn they compare the scores.
   (i) If the winner gets 1 point, who do you think is the more likely to reach 20 points first?
   (ii) To test if your judgement is correct, now construct a probability distribution for each event and, by finding the expected values, state which of the two has the better chance of reaching 20 points first.

9. Five unbiased coins are tossed.
   (i) Find the probability of getting three heads and two tails.
   (ii) The five coins are tossed eight times. Find the probability of getting three heads and two tails exactly four times.
   Give your answer correct to three decimal places.

10. (i) What relationship exists between the mean, mode and median of a normal distribution?
    (ii) List the other properties of a normal distribution.
    (iii) A long-life bulb has a mean life of 12 000 hours and a standard deviation of 300 hours. Work out the probability that a light bulb, chosen at random, will last
    (a) less than 11 400 hours   (b) between 11 400 hours and 12 600 hours.
    If 5000 light bulbs are tested, estimate the number of bulbs that could last longer than 12 600 hours.

11. A bag contains the following cardboard shapes:
    10 red squares, 15 green squares, 8 red triangles and 12 green triangles.
    One of the shapes is drawn at random from the bag.
    E is the event that a square is drawn.
    F is the event that a green shape is drawn.
    (i) Find $P(E \cap F)$.
    (ii) Find $P(E \cup F)$.
    (iii) State whether E and F are independent events, giving a reason for your answer.
    (iv) State whether E and F are mutually exclusive events, giving a reason for your answer.

Statistics 2

Key words

scatter diagram   correlation   causal relationship   causality
correlation coefficient   line of best fit   normal distribution   normal curve
Empirical Rule   standard scores (z-scores)   margin of error
confidence interval   hypothesis testing   null hypothesis

Section 4.1 Scatter diagrams

A **scatter graph** or **scatter diagram** is a graph consisting of points plotted on an x–y plane. Each point represents the values of two different variables such as the heights and weights of different individuals. Such data connecting two variables is called **bivariate data**.

After plotting the points on a scatter graph, we look for a pattern, particularly a **linear** pattern. If the points on a scatter graph lie approximately on a straight line, we say that there is a linear relationship between the two sets of data. The closer the points are to a straight line, the stronger the relationship will be.

The table below shows the number of ice-creams sold by a shop over a 12-day period.

Average temperature (°C)	10	12	16	20	13	16	14	17	19	20	21	16
No. of ice-creams sold	1	5	20	50	15	25	14	30	32	42	50	30

Using the horizontal axis for the temperature and the vertical axis for the numbers of ice-creams sold, we get the following scatter graph.

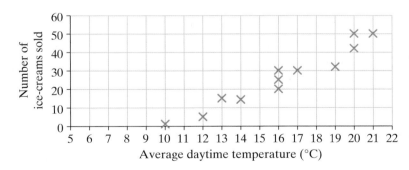

The scatter graph shows that the number of ice-creams sold increases as the temperature increases. Since the points lie close to a straight line, we say that there is a linear relationship between the two sets of data.

Correlation

Correlation is a measure of the strength of a relationship between two variables, say x and y. We say x and y are correlated if a scatter graph shows a linear pattern to the plotted points (x, y). If no pattern exists, the variables are not correlated.

The three diagrams below illustrate **positive correlation**, **negative correlation** and **no correlation**.

The variables x and y have a **positive correlation** if y increases as x increases.

The variables x and y have a **negative correlation** if y decreases as x increases.

The variables x and y show no linear pattern.

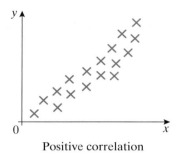

Positive correlation

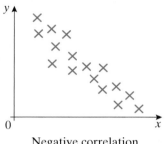

Negative correlation

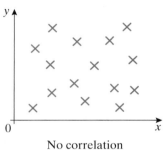

No correlation

The correlation is **high** if the points are close to a straight line.
The correlation is **low** if the points are more spread out.

It is possible to have strong and weak positive correlations as well as strong and weak negative correlations.
The scatter diagrams below illustrate these possibilities:

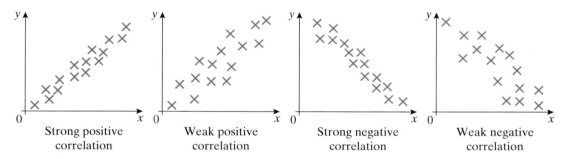

Strong positive correlation

Weak positive correlation

Strong negative correlation

Weak negative correlation

Example 1

The table shows the weights and heights of 12 people.

Height (cm)	150	152	155	158	158	160	163	165	170	175	178	180
Weight (kg)	57	62	63	64	58	62	65	66	65	70	66	67

(i) Draw a scatter graph to show this data.
(ii) Describe the strength and type of correlation between these heights and weights.

(i) We draw two axes at right angles.
We put the heights on the horizontal axis.
We start with 140 cm and go up to 180 cm.
We put the weights on the vertical axis, starting at 55 kg and going up to 70 kg.
We then plot the points (150, 57), (152, 62), ... etc.
The scatter graph is shown below.

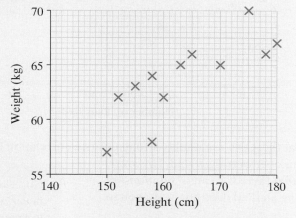

(ii) The correlation is weak positive as the points do not lie very close to a straight line. The correlation is positive because the weight generally increases as the height increases.

Causal relationships and correlation

The price of a used car depends, among other things, on the age of the car. The age of the car **causes** the price of the car to decrease. We say that there is a **causal relationship** between the price of the car and the age of the car.

Definition When a change in one variable causes a change in another variable, we say that there is a causal relationship between them.

The scatter graph shows the relationship between the sales of iced drinks and temperature. The correlation is strong and positive. You would expect this as a rise in temperature would tend to result in an increase in the sales of iced drinks.

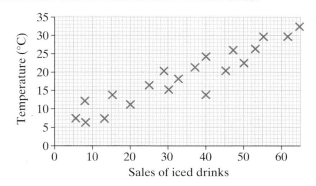

It would therefore be reasonable to conclude that there is a **causal relationship** between the sales of iced drinks and an increase in temperature.

The scatter diagram below shows the number of iPads and the number of fridges sold by an electrical shop over a ten-month period.

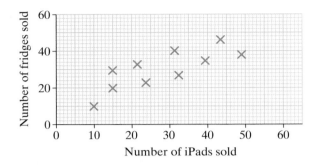

The graph shows that there is a reasonably strong positive correlation between the number of iPads sold and the number of fridges sold. However, this does not mean that there is a causal relationship between them; buying an iPad does not cause you to buy a fridge.

> Correlation does not necessarily mean that there is a causal relationship.

Exercise 4.1

1. Here are sketches of six scatter graphs:

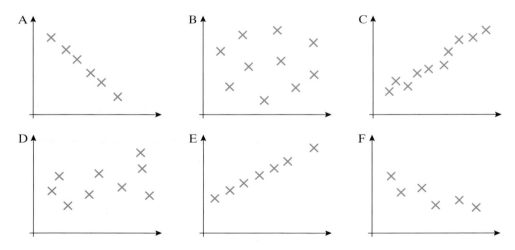

   Which diagram(s) show
   (i) positive correlation
   (ii) negative correlation
   (iii) no correlation
   (iv) strong negative correlation?
   Describe the correlation in graph F.

2. Four scatter graphs are shown below.

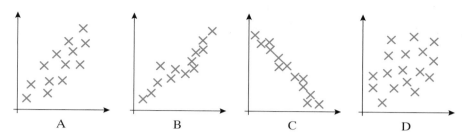

         A   B   C   D

   (i) Which of these graphs shows the strongest positive correlation?
   (ii) Which of these graphs shows negative correlation?
   (iii) Which of these graphs shows the weakest correlation?

3. The examination marks of a sample number of
   students in both their mock and final examinations
   are shown in the given scatter graph.

   (i) Describe the correlation shown in the graph.
   (ii) What can you say about the relationship
        between the mock and final marks of the
        students?

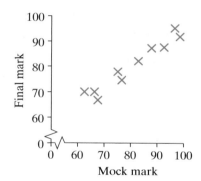

4. Brian recorded the percentages achieved in Statistics and Mathematics exams by
   ten students.

Statistics %	78	82	74	75	93	70	66	62	77	89
Mathematics %	70	76	61	70	89	65	59	58	73	82

   (i) Draw a scatter diagram of this data.
   (ii) Describe the correlation shown.
   (iii) Describe the relationship between the percentages achieved in Statistics and
         Mathematics for these students.

5. Describe the type of correlation – positive, negative or no correlation – that you would
   expect between these variables:
   (i) the age of a boat and its second-hand selling price
   (ii) the heights of children and their ages
   (iii) the shoe sizes of children and the distances they travel to school
   (iv) time spent watching television and time spent studying
   (v) the number of cars on the road and the number of accidents.

6.

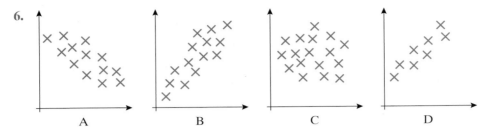

A   B   C   D

Four scatter graphs are shown above. For each of the following situations, choose the most appropriate of the scatter graphs. Explain your choice in each case.
  (i) Boys' heights and their shoe sizes.
 (ii) Men's weights and the times taken by them to complete a crossword puzzle.
(iii) Ages of cars and their selling prices.
(iv) Marks achieved in Maths Paper 1 and Maths Paper 2.

7. The scatter graph below shows the relationship between the ages and prices of used motorcycles.

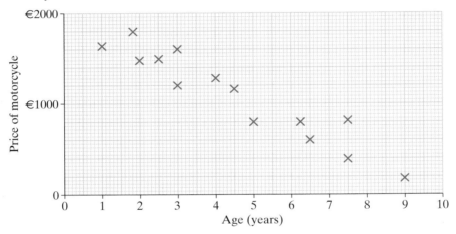

  (i) Describe the correlation shown in this scatter graph.
 (ii) Is there a causal relationship between the variables?
      Explain your answer.

8. A small electrical shop recorded the yearly sales of radio sets and television sets over a period of ten years. The results are shown in the table below.

Year	1	2	3	4	5	6	7	8	9	10
No. of televisions sold	60	68	73	80	85	88	90	96	105	110
No. of radios sold	80	60	72	65	60	55	52	44	42	36

  (i) Using scales going from 50 to 120 for the sales of televisions and 30 to 90 for the sales of radios, draw a scatter graph.
 (ii) What sort of correlation does the scatter graph suggest?
(iii) Is there a causal relationship between the television sales and radio sales?
      Explain your answer.

Section 4.2 Measuring correlation – Line of best fit ———

1. Calculating the correlation coefficient

Correlation is a measure of the strength of the relationship between two sets of data.
We use the letter *r* to denote the **correlation coefficient**.
The value of *r* will always lie between -1 and 1.

- $r = 0$ indicates no correlation.
- $r = 1$ indicates **perfect positive** linear correlation.
- $r = -1$ indicates **perfect negative** linear correlation.

Here are some examples of the value of *r*:

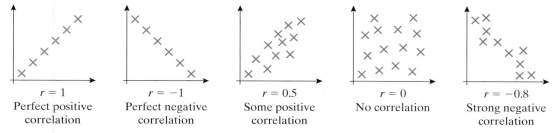

$r = 1$	$r = -1$	$r = 0.5$	$r = 0$	$r = -0.8$
Perfect positive correlation	Perfect negative correlation	Some positive correlation	No correlation	Strong negative correlation

The nearer the value of *r* is to 1 or -1, the closer the points on the scatter diagram are to a straight line.

There are several methods of calculating a correlation coefficient.
The method selected for our course is called the **product–moment correlation coefficient, *r*.**
The formula that is used to find this coefficient involves a lot of tedious calculations.

For our course, it is recommended that we use the electronic calculator to find the value of *r*.

The steps involved in the input of data and finding the value of *r* are given in *Appendix 1* at the end of the book.

2. The line of best fit

We have already stated that when points on a scatter diagram lie on, or close to, a straight line a strong correlation exists.
When a line is drawn through the points on a scatter diagram, it is called a **line of best fit**. Try to draw the line that fits best through the points. You should aim to have roughly the same number of points on either side of your line. This method is generally referred to as drawing the line of best fit **by eye**.

This scatter diagram shows the average daytime temperature plotted against the number of ice-creams sold.

> A line that is drawn to pass as close as possible to all the plotted points on a scatter diagram is called the **line of best fit**.

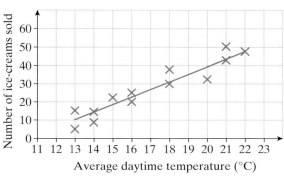

The line drawn is called the line of best fit.
It can go through some, all or none of the points.
This line shows the general trend of the relationship between the two sets of data. The line can be used to estimate other values. However, estimating values where the line has been extended beyond the existing points is less reliable.

Example 1

The table below shows the number of hours of sunshine and the maximum temperature in ten Irish towns on a particular day.

Maximum temperature (°C)	12	13	14	15	16	17	18	19	20	21
Hours of sunshine	9.6	11.6	10.2	13.25	11.8	13.6		15.4	15.2	15

   (i) Plot a scatter diagram and draw a line of best fit for the data.
  (ii) Use your line of best fit to estimate the number of hours of sunshine when the maximum temperature was 18°C.
 (iii) Describe the correlation shown in your diagram.
  (iv) Use your calculator to find the correlation coefficient.

   (i) The scatter diagram and line of best fit are shown below:

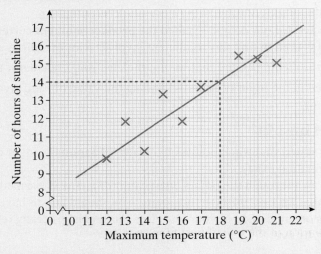

  (ii) The dotted lines on the diagram show that there are 14 hours of sunshine when the temperature is 18°C.
 (iii) The diagram shows that there is strong positive correlation between the two sets of data.
  (iv) The correlation coefficient, by calculator, is 0.9176.

3. Finding the equation of the line of best fit

From our knowledge of coordinate geometry, we should be familiar with the equation of a line in the form $y = mx + c$.
In statistics, it is more usual to use it in the form $y = ax + b$.

The equation $y = ax + b$ has a gradient a and its intercept on the y-axis is $(0, b)$.

Thus to find the equation of a line of best fit drawn by eye,
  (i) find two points on the line and use these points to find the slope of the line.
  (ii) Use the slope found and one of the points to find the equation of the line using
$$y - y_1 = m(x - x_1).$$
  (iii) Express the equation in the form $y = ax + b$.

Example 2

This scatter diagram shows the results of a scientific experiment involving two variables x and y.
  (i) Find the equation of the line of best fit.
  (ii) Assuming that this line is valid for larger values of x, find the value of y when $x = 52$.

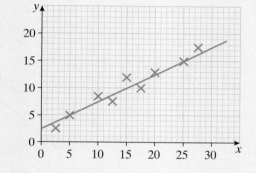

(i) (15, 10) and (25, 15) are two points on the line.

Slope $m = \dfrac{15 - 10}{25 - 15} = \dfrac{5}{10} = \dfrac{1}{2}$

Equation of line: $\quad y - y_1 = m(x - x_1)$
$\qquad\qquad\qquad y - 10 = \frac{1}{2}(x - 15)$ ... (15, 10) is a point on the line
$\qquad\qquad \Rightarrow 2y - 20 = x - 15$
$\qquad\qquad \Rightarrow \qquad y = \frac{1}{2}x + \frac{5}{2}$

The equation of the line of best fit is $y = \frac{1}{2}x + \frac{5}{2}$.

(ii) We use the equation $y = \frac{1}{2}x + \frac{5}{2}$ to find the value of y when $x = 52$.

$x = 52 \Rightarrow y = \frac{1}{2}(52) + \frac{5}{2}$, i.e., $y = 28\frac{1}{2}$

Thus $y = 28\frac{1}{2}$ when $x = 52$.

Example 3

The table below shows the weights and heights of 12 pupils.

Height (cm)	150	152	155	158	158	160	163	165	170	175	178	180
Weight (kg)	57	62	63	64	58	62	65	66	66.5	70	66	67

  (i) Draw a scatter diagram to show this data.
  (ii) Describe the strength and type of correlation between these heights and weights.
 (iii) Draw a line of best fit on your scatter diagram.
 (iv) Tony is 162 cm tall.
      Use your line of best fit to estimate his height.
  (v) Use your calculator to find the correlation coefficient, correct to two decimal places.
 (vi) Find the equation of the line of best fit in the form $y = ax + b$.

  (i) The scatter diagram and line of best fit are shown below:

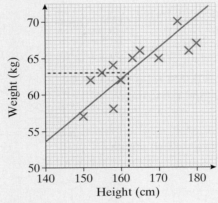

 (ii) Weak positive correlation.
 (iv) Draw a line from 162 cm on the height axis to meet your line of best fit.
      Now draw a horizontal line and read off the value where it meets the weight axis.
      Tony's probable weight is about 63 kg.
  (v) By calculator, the correlation coefficient is 0.8.
 (vi) Two points on the line are: (162, 63) and (155, 60).

$$\text{Slope of line} = \frac{60 - 63}{155 - 162} = \frac{-3}{-7} = \frac{3}{7}$$

Equation of line: $y - y_1 = m(x - x_1)$

$$y - 63 = \tfrac{3}{7}(x - 162)$$

$$y = \frac{3x}{7} - \frac{486}{7} + 63$$

$$\Rightarrow \qquad y = \frac{3x}{7} - \frac{45}{7}$$

Exercise 4.2

1. Four scatter graphs A, B, C and D are shown below.

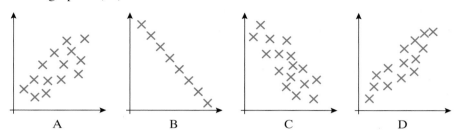

    Match one of the following numbers with each of the graphs above so that it best represents the correlation:

    0.1,   −0.4,   1,   −1,   0.6,   −0.8,   0.8

2. Match one of these correlation coefficients to each of the descriptions below:

    0.9,   −0.1,   −1,   −0.8,   0,   0.2

    (i)   Strong positive correlation   (ii) Strong negative correlation
    (iii) No correlation   (iv) Perfect negative correlation
    (v)   Very weak negative correlation   (vi) Very weak positive correlation

3. The scatter diagram below shows the heights and weights of a group of children. A line is drawn through some of these points.

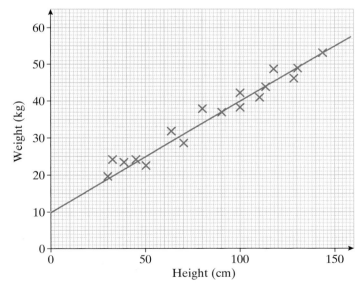

    (i)   What is the name given to this line?
    (ii) Explain why this is a suitable line of best fit.
    (iii) Use the line to find the likely weight of a child who is 150 cm in height.
    (iv) Describe the correlation between the two sets of data.

4. Use your calculator to show that the correlation coefficient of the following set of data is 0.86.

x	1	1	1	2	2	2	3	3	3	9
y	1	2	3	1	2	3	1	2	3	8

5. The following table shows the marks of ten candidates in Physics and Mathematics. Use your calculator to find the correlation coefficient, correct to two decimal places.

Mark in Physics (x)	18	20	30	40	46	54	60	80	88	92
Mark in Mathematics (y)	42	54	60	54	62	68	80	66	80	100

6. The number of forest fires and the annual rainfall (in cm) were recorded over an 8-year period.
   The results are given in the table below:

Rainfall (cm)	19	23	24	7	22	27	20	16
No. of fires	24	9	12	32	18	10	21	20

   (i) Plot the data on a scatter diagram.
   (ii) Construct a line of best fit by eye.
   (iii) Calculate the value of r, the correlation coefficient.
   (iv) Find the equation of the line of best fit.
   (v) Use your equation to predict the number of fires in a year with a rainfall of 25 cm.

7. The table below shows the pairs of scores obtained by eight pupils on two types of tests.

Test A	21	6	43	48	8	31	29	14
Test B	58	94	28	18	84	41	54	71

   (i) Draw a scatter diagram for these results.
   (ii) Describe the correlation between the two sets of scores.
   (iii) Draw a line of best fit on your scatter diagram.
   (iv) Find the equation of this line.
   (v) Another pupil sat Test A and was given a score of 18, but was absent for Test B. Use your line of best fit to estimate the score on Test B for this pupil.

8. The table below shows the heights of five fathers and their sons.

Height of father (cm)	163	185	185	193	197
Height of son (cm)	167	180	187	188	182

   Use your calculator to find the correlation coefficient, r, correct to two decimal places.

9. Ten students were selected at random from those visiting the tuck shop at mid-morning break. The students were asked their age and for how many hours they watched television each week.

The results are shown in the table.

Student	1	2	3	4	5	6	7	8	9	10
Age, x (years)	17	16	18	13	10	$11\frac{1}{2}$	14	11	15	12
Hours of TV watching, y	12	15	20	10	2	2.25	10.5	2.5	11	13

(i) Draw a scatter diagram of this data.
(ii) Add a line of best fit by eye.
(iii) Find the equation of the line of best fit.
(iv) Use the equation of the line to find how many hours a child of $16\frac{1}{2}$ years watches television.

10. This data shows the engine size and the fuel economy of a range of petrol cars.

Engine size (litres)	1.6	1.4	3.0	1.2	1.1	1.0	2.0	1.7	1.3	4.0	3.5
Fuel economy	12	14	11	14	15	18	11	12	15	6	8

(i) Show this information on a scatter diagram.
(ii) Describe the correlation between the engine size and the fuel economy of these cars.
(iii) Calculate the correlation coefficient, r.
(iv) Draw the line of best fit and find its equation.
(v) A Lamborghini has a 5.7 litre engine.
What fuel economy would you expect from this car, using the equation of the line of best fit?
Explain why this result may not be reliable.

11. The manager of a factory decided to give the workers an incentive by introducing a bonus scheme. After the scheme was introduced, the manager thought that the workers might be making more faulty products because they were rushing to make articles quickly. A study of the number of articles rejected, y, and the amount of bonus earned, €x, gave the figures shown in the table.

Employee	A	B	C	D	E	F	G	H
Bonus, x (€)	14	23	17	32	16	19	18	22
Number of rejects, y	6	14	5	16	7	12	10	14

(i) Draw a scatter diagram for this data and add a line of best fit by eye.
(ii) What sort of correlation is there between the two variables?
(iii) Calculate the correlation coefficient, r.
(iv) Calculate the equation of the line of best fit.
(v) If the maximum number of rejects acceptable is 9, what level should the maximum bonus be set at?

Section 4.3 The normal distribution

In Section 3.6 of this book, we were introduced to the **normal distribution** which is the cornerstone of modern statistics.

The **normal curve** is a smooth bell-shaped and symmetrical curve.
The red line is the axis of symmetry.

The mean, the mode and the median are all equal and they lie on the axis of symmetry.

Normal distributions occur frequently in nature. For example the heights and weights of all adult males in Ireland will be **normally distributed**.
If all the heights of these adult males were plotted on a graph, the result would be a smooth bell-shaped curve, as shown above.

All normal distributions will have a mean (μ) and standard deviation (σ).
Different values for μ and σ will give different normal distributions.

The diagram on the right shows two normal distributions with the same mean but different standard deviations.

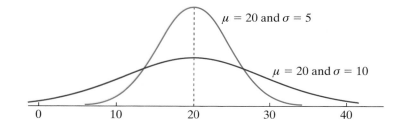

This diagram shows two normal distributions with the same standard deviation but different means.

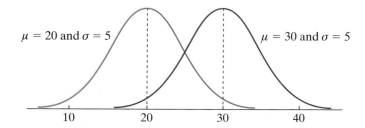

All normal distributions share some very important characteristics.

1. About 68% of all the values of any normal distribution lie within one standard deviation of the mean, i.e., in the range $[\mu - \sigma$ and $\mu + \sigma]$.

   34% lie to the right of the mean.
   34% lie to the left of the mean.

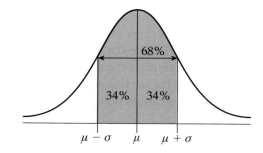

2. About 95% of all values lie within two standard deviations of the mean, i.e., in the range $[\mu - 2\sigma$ and $\mu + 2\sigma]$.

$47\frac{1}{2}\%$ lie to the right of the mean.

$47\frac{1}{2}\%$ lie to the left of the mean.

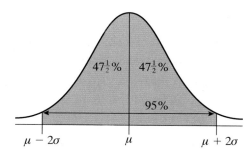

3. Almost all (99.7%) of the values lie within three standard deviations of the mean.

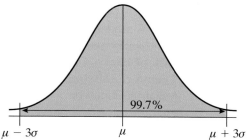

The three characteristics of the normal distribution listed above are generally known as **The Empirical Rule**.
This rule is highlighted below.

The Empirical Rule
- Approximately 68% of a normal distribution lie within one standard deviation of the mean
- 95% lie within two standard deviations of the mean
- 99.7% lie within three standard deviations of the mean.

Example 1

The marks, out of 100, in an examination are normally distributed.
The mean mark is 60 and the standard deviation is 6 marks.
  (i) Work out the mark that is two standard deviations above the mean.
 (ii) What percentage of the marks lie between 48 and 72 marks?
(iii) What percentage of the marks lie between 60 and 72 marks?
 (iv) If 1000 students took the examination, how many students scored less than 54 marks?

  (i) The mark that is two standard deviations above the mean is:

   mean + twice standard deviation = $60 + 2(6) = 72$ marks.

 (ii) $48 = 60 - 12 = \mu - 2\sigma$ and $72 = 60 + 12 = \mu + 2\sigma$
    There are 95% of all values in the range $[\mu - 2\sigma$ and $\mu + 2\sigma]$.
    $\therefore$ 95% of the marks lie between 48 and 72.

(iii) $60 = \mu$ and $72 = 60 + 12 = \mu + 2\sigma$

Since 95% of the marks lie between $\mu - 2\sigma$ and $\mu + 2\sigma$,

$\frac{1}{2}(95\%)$, i.e. $47\frac{1}{2}\%$, lie between μ and $\mu + 2\sigma$.

Thus, $47\frac{1}{2}\%$ lie between 60 and 72 marks.

(iv) $54 = 60 - 6 = \mu - \sigma$

From the curve, 34% of the marks lie between μ and $\mu - \sigma$.

∴ $50\% - 34\% = 16\%$

∴ 16% are less than $\mu - \sigma$, i.e.,
less than 54 marks.

16% of 1000 = 160

Therefore 160 students scored less than 54 marks.

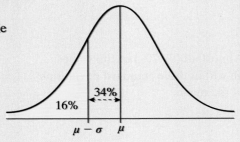

Example 2

Bottles of 300 ml shampoo are filled with the amounts in the bottles normally distributed with a mean of 300 ml and a standard deviation of 3 ml.
If 10 000 bottles are filled, how many bottles contain amounts that are
  (i) within one standard deviation of the mean?
  (ii) more than two standard deviations above the mean?
  (iii) If the manufacturer rejects bottles that contain amounts more than 3 standard deviations from the mean, what is the largest amount of shampoo in a bottle you would find for sale?

  (i) 68% of the bottles lie within one standard deviation of the mean.
     68% of 10 000 = 6800.
     ∴ 6800 bottles lie within one standard deviation of the mean.
  (ii) 95% of the bottles lie within 2 standard deviations of the mean.
     $\frac{1}{2}$ of 95%, i.e. $47\frac{1}{2}\%$, lie within 2 standard deviations **above** the mean.
     ∴ $50\% - 47\frac{1}{2}\%$, i.e. $2\frac{1}{2}\%$, lie more than two standard deviations above the mean.
     $2\frac{1}{2}\%$ of 10 000 = 250.
     250 bottles are more than 2 standard deviations above the mean.
  (iii) 3 standard deviations above the mean is $300 + 3(3) = 309$.
     Therefore, 309 ml is the largest amount you would find in a bottle.

Example 3

The weights of a group of 1000 school children were normally distributed with a mean of 42 kg and a standard deviation of σ.
If 950 of the children were in the range 30 kg to 54 kg,
  (i) find the value of σ
 (ii) find the probability that a child selected at random was in the range 36 kg to 48 kg.

  (i) 950 is 95% of 1000
      $\therefore$ 95% are in the range 30 kg to 54 kg
      But 95% are within 2 standard deviations of the mean.
      Thus $\mu - 2\sigma, \mu + 2\sigma$ is equivalent to 30 kg, 54 kg.
      $\therefore 42 - 2\sigma = 30$
      $\qquad 2\sigma = 12$
      $\qquad\ \sigma = 6$
 (ii) The range 36 kg to 48 kg is $42 - \sigma, 42 + \sigma$.
      $\therefore$ 68% of the weights lie in the range 36 kg to 48 kg
      $\therefore$ the probability = 68% or 0.68

Standard scores (z-scores)

In a state examination, Karen got 72% in her English examination and 68% in her Maths examination. In which examination did she achieve the better result? To determine this, we would need to know the average mark and standard deviation for each subject. We would then need to find the number of standard deviations Karen's mark was above or below the mean in each subject. If her mark was 1 standard deviation above the mean in English and 0.75 standard deviations above the mean in Maths, then Karen would have done relatively better in her English examination.

The number of standard deviations that a value lies above or below the mean is called a **standard score** or **z-score**.

In general, if x is a measurement belonging to a set of data with mean μ and standard deviation σ, then its value in z-units is given below:

$$z = \frac{x - \mu}{\sigma}, \text{ where } \begin{array}{l} x \text{ is the score or value} \\ \mu \text{ is the mean} \\ \sigma \text{ is the standard deviation} \end{array}$$

Standard scores are very useful when comparing values from different normal distributions.

Example 4

Simon and Susan did a test in French and a test in Science.
Both tests had a maximum mark of 100. The results are given in the table below:

	Susan's mark	Simon's mark	Mean mark	Standard deviation
French	75	50	60	10
Science	65	40	50	5

Work out the z-scores for each subject and comment on the performance of
Simon and Susan.

Susan: z-score in French $= \dfrac{x - \mu}{\sigma} = \dfrac{75 - 60}{10} = \dfrac{15}{10} = 1.5$

z-score in Science $= \dfrac{x - \mu}{\sigma} = \dfrac{65 - 50}{5} = \dfrac{15}{5} = 3$

Simon: z-score in French $= \dfrac{50 - 60}{10} = \dfrac{-10}{10} = -1$

z-score in Science $= \dfrac{40 - 50}{5} = \dfrac{-10}{5} = -2$

Overall, Susan did better as her standard scores were 1.5 and 3 above the mean.
Each of Simon's scores was below the mean.
The 'best' mark was Susan's Science mark because it had the highest standard score.
The 'worst' mark was Simon's Science mark because it had the lowest standard score.

Exercise 4.3

1. For each of the following normal curves, find the percentage of all the values that are in
   the shaded area:

(i)

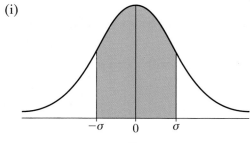

(ii)

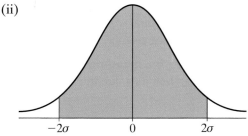

(iii)

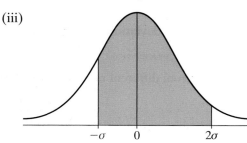

(iv)

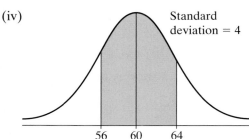

Standard
deviation = 4

2. The normal distribution shown on the right represents the heights, in cm, of a group of teenagers.

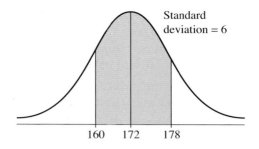

   (i) What percentage of the teenagers are between 172 cm and 178 cm in height?
   (ii) What percentage of the teenagers are taller than 178 cm?
   (iii) What percentage of the teenagers are between 160 cm and 178 cm in height?

3. The mean speed of vehicles on a road can be modelled by a normal distribution with mean 55 km/h and standard deviation 9 km/h.
   What would be the speed of a vehicle that was travelling at
   (i) one standard deviation below the mean
   (ii) two standard deviations above the mean
   (iii) three standard deviations above the mean?

4. A normal distribution has a mean $\mu = 60$ and standard deviation $\sigma = 5$.
   (i) Find the range within which 68% of the distribution lie.
   (ii) Find the range within which 95% of the distribution lie.

5. The heights of a large sample of adults are normally distributed with a mean of 170 cm and a standard deviation of 8 cm.
   Within what limits do
   (i) 68% of the heights lie
   (ii) 99.7% of the heights lie?

6. The mean time it takes factory workers to get to a factory is 35 minutes.
   The times can be modelled by a normal distribution with a standard deviation of 6 minutes.
   (i) What percentage of workers will take between 23 and 47 minutes to get to work?
   (ii) What percentage of the workers will take longer than 47 minutes?
   (iii) If there are 600 factory workers, how many will take between 23 and 47 minutes to get to work?

7. The lifetime of light bulbs were tested and found to be normally distributed with a mean of 620 hours and a standard deviation of 12 hours.
   (i) If 12 000 bulbs were manufactured, how many lifetimes would fall within one standard deviation of the mean?
   (ii) How many of the 12 000 bulbs would last between 620 and 644 hours?
   (iii) How many of the 12 000 bulbs would last longer than 644 hours?

8. To test tennis balls, they are dropped from a given height and the height they rebound is measured. Balls that rebound less than 128 cm are discarded. Assuming that the rebound height can be modelled by a normal distribution with a mean of 134 cm and a standard deviation of 3 cm, work out how many tennis balls in a batch of 1000 will be rejected.

9. Chicken portions produced for a fast-food restaurant have weights that are normally distributed with a mean of 160 g and a standard deviation of 10 g.
   (i) What percentage of the portions have weights between:
       (a) 140 and 180 g?   (b) 130 and 190 g?

   Portions are packed in boxes of 100 portions.
   (ii) How many portions in a box would you expect to weigh between 140 and 190 g?

10. In a normal distribution the mean μ is 80 and the standard deviation σ is 4.
    Use the formula $z = \dfrac{x - \mu}{\sigma}$ to convert each of these values to z-scores:

    (i) 84   (ii) 72   (iii) 86   (iv) 70

11. Explain what is meant by
    (i) a z-score of 2   (ii) a z-score of -1.5.

12. In a class test, the average mark was 70 and the standard deviation was 15. Karl received a z-score of 1.8 and Tanya received a z-score of -0.6.
    (i) Explain the meaning of each z-score in terms of the average mark and standard deviation.
    (ii) What were Karl's and Tanya's marks in the test?

13. The table shows Carmel's height and weight, alongside the mean and standard deviation for her class.

	Carmel's values	Class mean	Class standard deviation
Weight (kg)	48	44	8
Height (cm)	160	175	10

   Calculate the z-scores for Carmel's height and weight.

14. Anna's marks for Maths and History, as well as the mean and standard deviations of the marks for each subject, are given in the table below:

Subject	Anna's mark	Mean mark	Standard deviation
Maths	80	75	12
History	70	78	10

   (i) Find Anna's z-score for each subject.
   (ii) In which subject did she perform better?
        Justify your answer.
   (iii) Anna's friend Ciara got a z-score of 0.5 in History.
         What raw score did Ciara get in History?

15. Sarah-Jane received a z-score of 1.8 in a mathematics test.
    (i) What does this mean?
    (ii) If her raw score is 80 and the standard deviation of scores in the test is 12, what is the mean score?
    (iii) If Senan's score is 50 in the same test, what is his z-score?

16. The mean and standard deviation of two French papers are shown.
The marks for both papers are normally distributed.

	Mean	Standard deviation
Paper 1	45	8
Paper 2	56	12

Sarah was present for Paper 1 but absent for Paper 2.
In Paper 1, she scored 59 marks.

(i) What was Sarah's z-score on Paper 1?

(ii) Sarah expected to do equally well on Paper 2.
What would be the best estimate for her mark in this paper?

17. A class of students is given a History test and Physics test.
Both the History and Physics marks are approximately normally distributed.
The mean and the standard deviation of each distribution are shown in the table.

	Mean	Standard deviation
History	52	6
Physics	60	8

The graph shows a sketch of the distribution for the History marks.

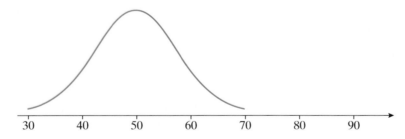

(i) Show, on a copy of the same graph, a sketch of the distribution of the
Physics marks.

Kelly scores 64 in the History test and 72 in the Physics test, but she claims that she is
better at History than at Physics.

(ii) By standardizing her marks, find out whether her test results support
her claim.

18. As part of her geography fieldwork, Alison is measuring and comparing the lengths of
pebbles on two beaches. On the first beach, the mean length is 8 mm and the standard
deviation is 1.4 mm. On the second beach, the mean length is 9 mm and the standard
deviation is 0.8 mm. She finds a pebble of length 10 mm on each beach. She claims that
this is less likely to happen on the first beach.
Use the standardised scores to test her claim.

Section 4.4 Margin of error – Confidence intervals – Hypothesis testing

When dealing with sampling in *Statistics 1*, it was stated that the purpose of sampling is to gain information about the whole population by surveying a small part of the population. If data from a sample is collected in a proper way, then the sample survey can give an accurate indication of the population characteristic that is being studied.

Before a general election, a national newspaper generally requests a market research company to survey a sample of the electorate regarding their voting intentions in the election. The number surveyed is generally about 1000.

The result of the survey might appear in the daily newspaper as follows:

> *40% support for* **The Democratic Right**.

The **40%** support is called the **sample proportion**, that is, the part or portion of the sample who indicated that they would vote for **The Democratic Right**.
A sample proportion is used to give an estimate of the **population proportion** who intend to vote for **The Democratic Right**.

The notation $\hat{p}$ is used to denote **sample proportion**.
The notation p is used to represent **population proportion**.
Since p is generally not known, $\hat{p}$ is used as an **estimator** for the true population proportion, p.

Of course everybody knows that sample surveys are not always 100% accurate. There is generally some 'element of chance' or **error** involved.

The newspaper might add to their headline the following sentence:

> *The margin of error is 3%.*

The **margin of error** of 3% is a way of saying that the result of the survey is 40% $\pm$ **3%**. That means that the research company is quite 'confident' that the proportion of the whole electorate who intend to vote for **The Democratic Right** could be anywhere between 37% and 43%.

How does the research company calculate 'the margin of error'?

The margin of error in opinion polls is generally calculated using the formula,

$$E = \frac{1}{\sqrt{n}},$$ where n is the sample size.

> **Margin of error**
> $$E = \frac{1}{\sqrt{n}}$$

If the sample size is 1000, then $E = \frac{1}{\sqrt{1000}} \approx 3\%$.

If the sample size is increased, the margin of error will be reduced.

Confidence interval

The result of the opinion poll above was given as 40% $\pm$ 3%.

That could be written as 37% $< p <$ 43%, where p is the population proportion.

37% $< p <$ 43% is called the **confidence interval**.

The 'confidence' level is pitched at 95%.

The 95% confidence implies that the interval was obtained by a method which 'works 95% of the time'.

The confidence interval, 37% $< p <$ 43%, is a way of stating that if you surveyed many samples of 1000 people on the same day, the results would be in the interval 37% to 43% in 95% of the samples.

In our course, the confidence level is always at 95%.

At the 95% confidence level, the confidence interval for a population proportion is given on the right.

Confidence interval is
$$\hat{p} - \frac{1}{\sqrt{n}} < p < \hat{p} + \frac{1}{\sqrt{n}}$$

The confidence interval above may be also expressed as $\hat{p} \pm \frac{1}{\sqrt{n}}$.

Example 1

What sample size would be required to have a margin of error of
(i) 0.05   (ii) $2\frac{1}{2}$%?

(i) $\frac{1}{\sqrt{n}} = 0.05$

$\therefore \frac{1}{n} = (0.05)^2$

$\therefore n = \frac{1}{(0.05)^2}$

$n = 400$

(ii) $\frac{1}{\sqrt{n}} = 2\frac{1}{2}\% = 0.025$

$\frac{1}{n} = (0.025)^2$

$n = \frac{1}{(0.025)^2}$

$n = 1600$

Example 2

A random sample of 400 persons are given a flu vaccine and 136 of them experienced some discomfort.
Construct a 95% confidence interval for p, the population proportion who might experience discomfort.

The sample proportion $\hat{p} = \frac{136}{400} = 0.34$

The margin of error $= \frac{1}{\sqrt{n}} = \frac{1}{\sqrt{400}} = \frac{1}{20} = 0.05$

The confidence interval is $0.34 - 0.05 < p < 0.34 + 0.05$
$$= 0.29 < p < 0.39$$

Example 3

A survey of 100 residents of a Dublin suburb were asked if they remembered seeing an advertisement for McCain's chips on television. 60 respondents said that they had.
   (i)   Calculate the sample proportion, $\hat{p}$.
   (ii) Find the margin of error, E.
   (iii) Construct a 95% confidence interval for p.

   (i) $\hat{p} = \dfrac{60}{100} = 0.6$

   (ii) $E = \dfrac{1}{\sqrt{n}} = \dfrac{1}{\sqrt{100}} = \dfrac{1}{10} = 0.1$

   (iii) Confidence interval: $\hat{p} - \dfrac{1}{\sqrt{n}} \qquad < p < \hat{p} + \dfrac{1}{\sqrt{n}}$

$$0.6 - 0.1 < p < 0.6 + 0.1$$
$$0.5 < p < 0.7$$
$$\text{or } 50\% < p < 70\%$$

Note: The confidence interval is very high here because the sample was small.
A sample of 100 has a margin of error of 10%.
A sample of 1000 has a margin of error of 3%.

Hypothesis testing

A **hypothesis** is a statement or conjecture made about some statistic or characteristic of a population.
Here is an example of a hypothesis:

'A football team is most likely to concede a goal just after it has scored a goal'.

A **hypothesis test** is a statistical method of proving the truth or otherwise of the statement or claim.

A local council reduced the speed limit on a dangerous 8 km stretch of country road from 80 km/hr to 60 km/hr. The number of accidents on the stretch was reduced from 5 per month to 3 per month. The council claimed that the speed reduction was effective. Is the council correct in its claim?

In cases like this, a hypothesis test is set up to prove or disprove the claim.

Procedure for carrying out a hypothesis test
The procedure for carrying out a hypothesis test will involve the following steps:

1. Write down $\mathbf{H_0}$, the **null hypothesis**, and $\mathbf{H_1}$, the **alternative hypothesis**
    For example, to test if a coin is biased if we get 7 heads in 10 tosses, we could formulate the following hypothesis:
        H_0 : The coin is not biased.
        H_1 : The coin is biased.

2. Write down or calculate the sample proportion, $\hat{p}$.

3. Find the margin of error.

4. Write down the confidence interval for p, using

$$\hat{p} - \frac{1}{\sqrt{n}} < p < \hat{p} + \frac{1}{\sqrt{n}}$$

5. (i) If the value of the population proportion stated is within the confidence interval, accept the null hypothesis H_0 and reject H_1.
   (ii) If the value of the population proportion is outside the confidence interval, reject the null hypothesis H_0 and accept H_1.

Example 4

A drugs company produced a new pain-relieving drug for migraine sufferers and claimed that the drug had a 90% success rate. A group of doctors doubted the company's claim. They prescribed the drug for a group of 150 patients. After six months, 120 of these patients said that their migraine symptoms had been relieved by the drug.
At the 95% level of confidence, can the company's claim be upheld?

1. State H_0 and H_1.
   H_0: The success rate of the drug is 90%.
   H_1: The success rate of the drug is not 90%.

2. Sample proportion $\hat{p} = \dfrac{120}{150} = 0.8$

3. Margin of error $= \dfrac{1}{\sqrt{n}} = \dfrac{1}{\sqrt{150}} = 0.08$

4. Confidence interval $= \hat{p} - \dfrac{1}{\sqrt{n}} < p < \hat{p} + \dfrac{1}{\sqrt{n}}$

   $= 0.8 - 0.08 < p < 0.8 + 0.08$

   $= 0.72 < p < 0.88$

5. The population proportion, 0.9 (90%), is not within the confidence interval. So we reject the null hypothesis and accept H_1.
   We conclude that the success rate of the drug is not 90%.

Example 5

A coin is tossed 1000 times and heads occur 550 times.
At the 95% confidence level, does the result indicate that the coin is biased?

1. H_0: The coin is not biased
   H_1: The coin is biased

2. Sample proportion, $\hat{p} = \dfrac{550}{1000} = 0.55$

3. Margin of error $= \dfrac{1}{\sqrt{n}} = \dfrac{1}{\sqrt{1000}} = 0.03$

4. Confidence interval $= \hat{p} - \dfrac{1}{\sqrt{n}} < p < \hat{p} + \dfrac{1}{\sqrt{n}}$

$$0.55 - 0.03 < p < 0.55 + 0.03$$
$$0.52 < p < 0.58$$

5. Since $P(\text{head}) = 0.5$, the population proportion $= 0.5$.
   The population proportion 0.5 is not within the confidence interval found.
   We reject the null hypothesis and conclude that the coin is biased.

Exercise 4.4

1. In a random sample of 500 cars, it was found that 150 of them were coloured silver.
   (i) Calculate the sample proportion, $\hat{p}$.
   (ii) At the 95% confidence level, calculate the margin of error, correct to two decimal places.
   (iii) Construct a 95% confidence interval for the proportion of all cars that are coloured silver.

2. In a random sample of 400 computer shops, it was discovered that 136 of them sold computers at below the list price recommended by the manufacturer.
   (i) Estimate the percentage of all computer shops selling below the list price.
   (ii) Construct an approximate 95% confidence interval for the proportion of shops selling below the list price.
   Briefly explain what this means.

3. The results of a survey showed that 3600 out of 10 000 families regularly purchased a specific weekly magazine.
   Construct a 95% confidence interval for the proportion of families buying the magazine.

4. A survey was undertaken to find the level of use of the internet by residents of a city.
   In a random sample of 150 residents, 45 said that they log on to the internet at least once a day.
   Construct a 95% confidence interval for p, the population proportion that log on to the internet once a day.

5. A college principal decides to consult the students about a proposed change in the times of lectures. She finds that, out of a random sample of 80 students, 57 of them are in favour of the change.
   Construct a 95% confidence interval for the proportion of students who are **not** in favour of the change.

6. At the 95% level of confidence, what sample size is required to have a margin of error of
    (i) 5%   (ii) 3%   (iii) 1.5%?

7. A survey was carried out in order to gauge the response to a new school "healthy eating"
   menu. A random sample of 200 schoolchildren was selected from different schools.
   It was found that 84 children approved of the new menu.
   Construct an approximate 95% confidence interval for the population proportion, p,
   who approve of the new menu.

8. In a public opinion poll, 1000 randomly-chosen electors were asked whether they would
   vote for the *Purple Party* at the next election and 357 replied "Yes".
   The leader of the *Purple Party* believes that the true proportion is 0.4.
   At the 95% confidence level, is the leader's belief justified?

9. A large college claims that it admits equal numbers of men and women. A random
   sample of 500 students gave 267 men. At the 95% confidence level, is there evidence to
   suggest that the college is not evenly divided between men and women?

10. A dice was rolled 240 times and 52 sixes were recorded.
    (i)   Write down the sample proportion, $\hat{p}$.
    (ii) What is the margin of error?
    (iii) If the dice is fair, write down the probability of throwing a 6.
    (iv) At the 95% confidence level, test the hypothesis that the dice is fair.

11. A survey in a university library revealed that 12% of returned books were overdue.
    After an increase in fines, a random sample of 200 returned books revealed that only 15
    were overdue. The university claimed that the proportion of overdue books had decreased.
    At the 95% level of confidence, is the university's claim justified?

12. A seed company sells pansy seeds in mixed packets and claims that 20% of the resulting
    plants will have red flowers. A packet of seeds is sown by a gardener who finds that only
    11 out of 82 plants have red flowers.
    Test the company's claim at the 95% confidence level.

13. The 'Daily Mensa' claims that at least 60% of its readers have third level degrees.
    In a random sample of 312 readers, there were 208 with third level degrees.
    At the 95% confidence level, is the paper's claim justified?

14. A manufacturer wants to assess the proportion of defective items in a large batch
    produced by a particular machine. He tests a random sample of 300 items and finds that
    45 items are defective.
    (i)   Construct an approximate 95% confidence interval for the proportion of defective
          items in the batch.
    (ii) Explain what the 95% confidence interval means in the context of the question.
    (iii) If 200 such tests are performed and a 95% confidence interval constructed for each,
          how many would you expect to include the proportion of defective items in the batch?

Test yourself 4

A – questions

1. For the given normal curve, find the percentage of the data that is in the shaded region.

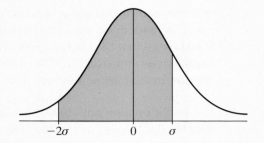

2. Four scatter diagrams are shown below:

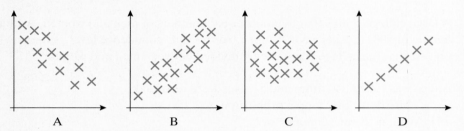

| A | B | C | D |

For each of the following, choose the most appropriate of the scatter diagrams above:
(i) Number of caps of an international rugby player and number of points scored.
(ii) Distance (north) from equator and winter daylight hours.
(iii) Men's percentage body fat and the time taken for them to solve a Rubik's Cube.
(iv) An example of negative correlation.
(v) A scatter diagram showing a correlation coefficient of 0.7.

3. The heights of students in a certain university are normally distributed with a mean of 180 cm and a standard deviation of 10 cm.
(i) Make a copy of the given normal curve and write down the values of a, b, c, d and e, where each interval represents one standard deviation.
(ii) Find the z-score that corresponds to 190 cm.
(iii) What percentage of students have a height greater than 190 cm?

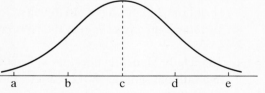

4. The table shows the marks of 15 students taking Paper 1 and Paper 2 of a maths exam. Both papers were marked out of 40.

Paper 1	36	34	23	24	30	40	25	35	20	15	35	34	23	35	27
Paper 2	39	36	27	20	33	35	27	32	28	20	37	35	25	33	30

(i) Draw a scatter diagram to show this information.
(ii) Describe the correlation shown in the scatter diagram.

(iii) Draw a line of best fit on your scatter diagram.

(iv) Find the equation of the line of best fit.

(v) Joe scored 32 on Paper 1 but was absent for Paper 2.
Use your line of best fit to estimate his score on Paper 2.

5. The heights of a large number of students can be modelled by a normal distribution
with mean 175 cm.
95% of students have heights between 160 and 190 cm.
Work out the standard deviation of the students' heights.

6. In a survey of 250 households in a large city, 170 households owned at least one pet.

(i) At the 95% confidence level, calculate the margin of error, correct to two decimal
places.

(ii) Find an approximate 95% confidence interval for the proportion of households in
the city that own at least one pet.

7. (i) Explain briefly what you understand by the term 'correlation'.

(ii) The table below gives the marks, out of 20, obtained by five students in two tests:

Test 1	8	9	7	2	13
Test 2	7	10	5	4	14

(a) Use your calculator to calculate r, the correlation coefficient.

(b) What does this value tell us about the performance of the students in
the tests?

8. The length, X, of bamboo canes sold in a garden centre can be modelled by the normal
distribution shown in the diagrams below. Work out the probability of a cane chosen at
random falling in the shaded area of each diagram.

(i)
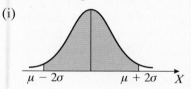

(ii)
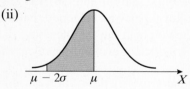

9. Simon takes French and German tests.
The marks for both tests are normally distributed.
In French he scores 76 and in German he scores 78.
The French marks have a mean of 68 and a standard deviation of 10.
The German marks have a mean of 70 and a standard deviation of 12.

(i) Calculate Simon's z-score in French.

(ii) Calculate Simon's z-score in German.

(iii) Use the z-scores to compare Simon's results.

10. Explain, with the aid of an example, what is meant by the statement:

"Correlation does not necessarily imply causality".

B – questions

1. In an opinion poll, 2000 people were interviewed and 527 said they preferred white chocolate to milk chocolate.
   (i) Calculate the margin of error at the 95% confidence level.
   (ii) Calculate the 95% confidence interval for the proportion of the population who prefer white chocolate.

2. Television tubes have a mean life of 4000 hours and a standard deviation of 500 hours. Assuming that their life can be modelled by a normal distribution, estimate:
   (i) the percentage of tubes lasting less than 3000 hours
   (ii) the **probability** that a tube will last for between 3000 and 5000 hours.
   (iii) In a batch of 10 000 tubes, after how many hours would you expect only $2\frac{1}{2}$% of the tubes to be still working?

3. The following table gives the number of employees and the units produced for a certain company over a 4-month period.

Month	Number of employees	Units produced
January	100	80
February	85	75
March	76	64
April	60	60

   (i) Use your calculator to find r, the correlation coefficient.
   (ii) Comment briefly on the value of r that you found.

4. A survey is conducted of voters' opinions on several different issues.
   (i) What is the overall margin of error of the survey, at 95% confidence, if it is based on a simple random sample of 1111 voters?
   (ii) A political party had claimed that it has the support of 23% of the electorate.
   Of the voters in the sample above, 234 stated that they support the party.
   Is this sufficient evidence to reject the party's claim, at the 95% confidence level?

5. Mr Cross has two very different trees in his garden. He knows that the lengths of the leaves on both trees are approximately normally distributed. For the first tree, the mean length is 5 cm and the standard deviation is 1 cm. For the second tree, the mean length is 8 cm and the standard deviation is 1.5 cm. He picks leaves which measure exactly 7 cm from both trees. He claims that this is more likely to happen on the second tree. Use the standardised scores to test his claim.

6. The table below shows the temperature of water as it cools in a freezer:

Time (minutes)	5	10	15	20	25	30
Temperature (°C)	36	29	25	20	15	8

   (i) Use this information to draw a scatter diagram.
   (ii) What type of correlation is shown?

    (iii) Draw a line of best fit and find its equation.

    (iv) Use the equation of the line to estimate the time when the temperature of the water reaches 0°C.

    (v) Use your calculator to calculate r, the correlation coefficient, correct to 2 decimal places.

7. A company states that 20% of the visitors to its website purchase at least one of its products. A sample of 400 people who visited the site is checked and the number who purchased a product is found to be 64.

    (i) Calculate the margin of error in this case.

    (ii) Based on this sample, should the company's claim be accepted? Explain your reasoning.

8. The table shows the mean and the standard deviation of the heights of a sample of adult males and a sample of boys aged nine.

The heights of both the adult males and the boys are normally distributed.

	Adult males	Boys aged nine
Mean	180 cm	135 cm
Standard deviation	18 cm	10 cm

David is a boy aged nine whose height is 120 cm.

    (i) How many standard deviations below the mean is David's height?

It is believed that the height of a boy aged nine is a good indicator of his adult height.

    (ii) Estimate the height that David will be when he is an adult.

The diagram below shows the distribution of the heights of the boys aged nine.

    (iii) Copy the diagram and sketch the distribution of the heights of the adult males.

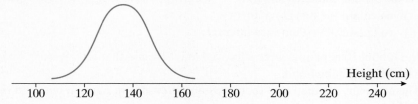

9. The NCCB believed that 70% of maths teachers were in favour of a syllabus change in maths. A questionnaire was sent to a large number of maths teachers asking for their opinions. Of the 180 replies received, 134 were in favour of the change.

Investigate if the NCCB's beliefs were borne out at the 95% level of confidence.

10. The owner of a large apple-orchard states that 10% of the apples on the trees in his orchard have been attacked by birds. A random sample of 2500 apples is picked and 274 apples are found to have been attacked by birds.

    (i) At the 95% level of confidence, what is the margin of error?

    (ii) Calculate $\hat{p}$, the sample proportion.

    (iii) Investigate if the orchard owner's claim is justified at the 95% confidence level.

C – questions

1. The lengths of roofing nails are normally distributed with a mean of 20 mm and a standard deviation of 3 mm.
   - (i) What percentage of nails lie between
     - (a) 17 mm and 23 mm
     - (b) 14 mm and 23 mm?
   - (ii) If 10 000 nails were measured, how many would have a length between 17 mm and 26 mm?
   - (iii) What is the probability that a roofing nail, selected at random, is more than 23 mm long?

2. A class of students takes examinations in both mathematics and physics. The marks that they obtain are as follows:

Student	1	2	3	4	5	6	7	8	9	10
Mathematics	65	45	40	55	60	50	80	30	70	65
Physics	60	60	55	70	80	40	85	50	70	80

   - (i) Plot the data on a scatter diagram and draw the line of best fit by eye.
   - (ii) Find the equation of the line of best fit.
   - (iii) Determine the value of the correlation coefficient, using your calculator.
   - (iv) Interpret this value in the context of the question.

3. A large supermarket chain commissioned a survey to find out whether people favoured extended opening hours at the weekend. Four hundred people were surveyed in Cork and 88% said that they were in favour of extended opening hours.
   At the 95% confidence level,
   - (i) calculate the margin of error
   - (ii) calculate the confidence interval.

   In Dublin, 1000 people were surveyed and 810 said that they were in favour of the extended opening hours.
   The company claimed that there was no difference in opinion between the Cork and Dublin samples.
   Is the company's claim justified at the 95% confidence level?
   Justify your answer.

4. The average age of a sample of Bingo players is 60 years with a standard deviation of 8 years. The distribution is found to be normally distributed.
   - (i) If the ages were standardised, what would the z-scores be for
     - (a) Abdul: 70   (b) Marie: 52   (c) George: 60   (d) Elsie: 92?
   - (ii) What percentage of people in the sample are more than 76 years old?
   - (iii) Ezra has a z-score of 2.5. How old is she?
   - (iv) Comment on the likelihood of a 40-year-old being in the sample.

5. A person's *maximum heart rate* is the highest rate at which their heart beats during certain extreme kinds of exercise. It is measured in beats per minute (bpm). It can be measured under controlled conditions. As part of a study in 2001, researchers measured the maximum heart rate of 514 adults and compared it to each person's age.
    A representative sample of the results are shown in the scatter diagram below.

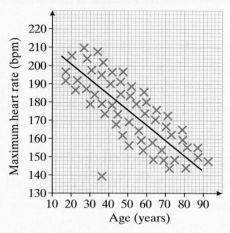

   (i)   From the diagram, estimate the correlation coefficient.
   (ii) Circle the *outlier* on the diagram and write down the person's age and maximum heart rate.
   (iii) The line of best fit is shown on the diagram.
         Use the line of best fit to estimate the maximum heart rate of a 44-year-old person.
   (iv) By taking suitable readings from the diagram, calculate the slope of the line of best fit.
   (v)   Find the equation of the line of best fit and write it in the form:
         $MHR = a - b \times$ (age), where MHR is the maximum heart rate.
   (vi) The researchers compared their new rule for estimating maximum heart rate to an older rule. The older rule is: $MHR = 220 -$ age. The two rules can give different estimates of a person's maximum heart rate. Describe how the level of agreement between the two rules varies according to the age of the person. Illustrate your answer with two examples.
   (vii) A particular exercise programme is based on the idea that a person will get most benefit by exercising at 75% of their estimated MHR. A 65-year-old man has been following this programme, using the old rule for estimating MHR. If he learns about the researchers' new rule for estimating MHR, how should he change what he is doing?

Key words

sampling distribution   **Central Limit Theorem**   **parameter**   **statistic**
standard error   **confidence interval**   **proportion**   **hypothesis**
null hypothesis   **critical region**   **test statistic**   **p-value**

Section 5.1 The sampling distribution of the mean – The Central Limit Theorem

In Section 4.4 it was stated that the purpose of sampling is to obtain information about a whole population by surveying a small part of the population. This small part is called a **sample**.

When we select a sample from a population, and study it, we hope that it is representative of the population as a whole. To ensure that it is representative, it must be a *random* sample. By a random sample we mean that

 (i) every member of the population has an equal chance of being selected
(ii) the selections are made independently.

A very important part of the work of a statistician involves drawing conclusions about a population based on evidence gathered from the sample. This process is known as **statistical inference**.

Parameters – Statistics

It is known that the mean height of men in Ireland is 176 cm.
The mean height of a sample of Munster rugby players is 186 cm.
The value 176 cm is called a **parameter** as it is a numerical property of a **population**.
The value 186 cm is called a **statistic** as it is a numerical property of a **sample**.

Parameter   A **parameter** is a numerical property of a **population**.
Statistic   A **statistic** is a numerical property of a **sample**.

The sampling distribution of the mean

If we are interested in the weights, for example, of all sixteen-year-olds in Ireland, we generally require the mean and standard deviations of these weights. We use the symbols

 (i) μ to denote the **population mean**
(ii) σ to denote the **population standard deviation**.

In such a large population it would be impossible to obtain the weight of each person and so the values of μ and σ will not be known. However, if we take a random sample of this population, we can get approximate values for μ and σ. Obviously, the larger the sample, the more accurate we would expect the approximations to be.

If we take a large number of different random samples of size n, each sample will have its own mean, $\bar{x}$, and standard deviation, $\sigma_{\bar{x}}$.

Some of these samples are illustrated on the right.

The different means of these samples are called the **sample means**.

| Sample 1 $\bar{x}_1$ $\sigma_{\bar{x}_1}$ | Sample 2 $\bar{x}_2$ | Sample 3 $\bar{x}_3$ |
| Sample 4 $\bar{x}_4$ | Sample 5 $\bar{x}_5$ | Sample 6 $\bar{x}_6$ |

If a large number of samples of the same size are taken, you get a correspondingly large number of means.

These means form their own distribution giving us the **distribution of sample mean**.

This distribution is also called **the sampling distribution of the mean**.

The following example illustrates the shape a distribution might take when different samples (of the same size) from a population are selected.

Example 1

A population consists of five digits 2, 4, 6, 8, 10.

(i) Write down all the possible samples of 2 different digits that can occur if random samples are taken.

(ii) Find the mean of each sample and plot the distribution of the sample means.

(iii) Compare the value of the mean of the sample means with the value of the population mean.

(i) The possible samples are:
(2, 4), (2, 6), (2, 8), (2, 10), (4, 6), (4, 8), (4, 10), (6, 8), (6, 10), (8, 10)

(ii) Their means are: 3, 4, 5, 6, 5, 6, 7, 7, 8, 9
The distribution of the sample means is plotted below.

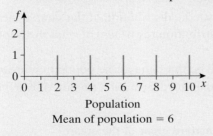

Population
Mean of population = 6

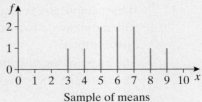

Sample of means
Mean of sample means = $\frac{60}{10}$ = 6

(iii) The mean of the population is 6.
The mean of the sample means is also 6.
Thus the mean of the sample means and the population mean are equal.

If you examine the distribution of the sample means plotted on the right in the worked example above, you will notice that it begins to approximate to a normal distribution. In this case the sample size was only 2.

However, as the sample size n increases the closer the distribution will approximate to a normal distribution. Also the mean of the sampling distribution will be the same as the mean of the population.

The successive diagrams below illustrate the **shape** of the **sampling distribution of means** resulting from different-sized samples from a given population with a normal distribution.

Distribution when $n = 2, 5$ and 25.

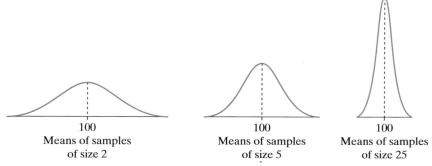

| 100 | 100 | 100 |
| Means of samples of size 2 | Means of samples of size 5 | Means of samples of size 25 |

From the diagrams, you can see that if samples are taken from a normal population, the sampling distribution of means is normal for any sample size.

As n increases, the curve representing the sampling distribution of the mean gets taller and narrower. These diagrams also show how the standard deviation decreases as n increases. The sample means will be packed tightly around the population mean. The larger the samples become, the tighter the means will be packed.

From the worked example and from the three diagrams shown above, we can see that when samples are taken from a population, the sampling distribution of the mean takes on the characteristics of a normal curve as the sample size increases. This observation leads us to one of the most important theorems in statistics that is widely used in sampling. It is called the **Central Limit Theorem** and is stated more formally below.

The Central Limit Theorem

If a random sample of size n with mean $\bar{x}$ is taken from a population with mean μ and standard deviation σ, then

> If the sample size is large ($n \geqslant 30$), the distribution of the sample means will approximate to a normal distribution regardless of what the population distribution is.

> The mean of the distribution will be the same as the population mean μ.

> The standard deviation of the sampling distribution (denoted by $\sigma_{\bar{x}}$) is given by $\dfrac{\sigma}{\sqrt{n}}$.

$\left[\dfrac{\sigma}{\sqrt{n}} \text{ is often referred to as the } \textbf{standard error of the mean.} \right]$

As n increases, the standard error gets smaller.

> If the underlying population is normal, the sampling distribution of the mean will always have a normal distribution even if the sample size is small (<30).

The diagram on the right illustrates how the distribution of the sample mean approximates to a normal distribution even when the underlying population is skewed.

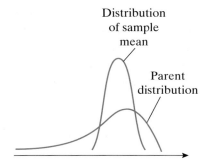

Distribution of sample mean

Parent distribution

When dealing with the sampling distribution of the mean, we convert the given units to standard units using the formula given on the right.

$$z = \frac{\bar{x} - \mu}{\sigma_{\bar{x}}} = \frac{\bar{x} - \mu}{\frac{\sigma}{\sqrt{n}}}$$

Example 2

A random sample of 250 is selected from a population having mean 30 and standard deviation 5.
Find the probability that the sample mean is greater than 30.5.

Since $n = 250$, the sample mean is normally distributed since $n \geqslant 30$.
Changing to standard units we get:

$$z = \frac{\bar{x} - \mu}{\frac{\sigma}{\sqrt{n}}} = \frac{30.5 - 30}{\frac{5}{\sqrt{250}}} = \frac{0.5}{0.3162} = 1.581$$

$z = 1.581$

Now
$$\begin{aligned} P(x > 30.5) &= P(z > 1.581) \\ &= 1 - P(z \leqslant 1.581) \\ &= 1 - 0.9429 \\ &= 0.0571 \end{aligned}$$

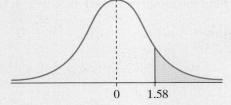

The probability that the mean is greater than 30.5 is 0.571.

Example 3

A normal distribution has a mean of 40 and a standard deviation of 4.
If 25 items are drawn at random, find the probability that their mean lies between 38 and 40.5.

Converting the given units to standard units we get:

$$z = \frac{\bar{x} - \mu}{\frac{\sigma}{\sqrt{n}}}$$

For $x = 38$, $z = \dfrac{38 - 40}{\frac{4}{\sqrt{25}}} = \dfrac{-2}{0.8} = -2.5$

For $x = 40.5$, $z = \dfrac{40.5 - 40}{\frac{4}{\sqrt{25}}} = \dfrac{0.5}{0.8} = 0.625$

$$
\begin{aligned}
P(38 < x < 40.5) &= P(-2.5 < z < 0.625) \\
&= P(z < 0.625) - P(z < -2.5) \\
&= P(z \leqslant 0.625) - [1 - P(z \leqslant 2.5)] \\
&= 0.7324 - [1 - 0.99379] \\
&= 0.7324 - [0.00621] \\
&= 0.7262
\end{aligned}
$$

$\Rightarrow$ P(mean lies between 38 and 40.5) = 0.7262.

Example 4

A population is normally distributed with mean 12 and standard deviation 3.
Find the sample size such that $P(\bar{x} > 12.5) = 0.05$, where $\bar{x}$ is the sample mean.

$$
\begin{aligned}
P(z > z_1) &= 0.05 \\
\Rightarrow P(z \leqslant z_1) &= 0.95 \\
\Rightarrow z_1 &= 1.645
\end{aligned}
$$

$$z_1 = \frac{\bar{x} - \mu}{\frac{\sigma}{\sqrt{n}}} \Rightarrow 1.645 = \frac{12.5 - 12}{\frac{3}{\sqrt{n}}}$$

$$\Rightarrow 1.645 = \frac{\sqrt{n}(12.5 - 12)}{3}$$

$$\Rightarrow \sqrt{n} = \frac{(1.645)3}{0.5}$$

$$\Rightarrow n = 97.42 \quad \text{i.e. } 98 \quad \text{... round up}$$

The required sample size is 98.

Example 5

A company installs new machines for packing peanuts.
The company claims that the machines fill packets with a mean mass of 500 g and a standard deviation of 18 g.
To test the company's claim several samples of size 40 packets are taken and their mean masses, $\bar{x}$ grams, are recorded.

(i) Describe the sampling distribution of $\bar{x}$ and explain your answer, referring to the theorem you have used.

(ii) Write down the mean and standard deviation of the distribution of $\bar{x}$.

(iii) Draw a rough sketch of the sampling distribution of $\bar{x}$.

(iv) Find the probability that the mean of the distribution of $\bar{x}$ is less than 496.

(v) What sample size n is required so that $P(\bar{x}) > 503 = 0.06$?

(i) The sampling distribution of $\bar{x}$ is approximately normal as the sample size of 40 is sufficiently large (i.e. $\geqslant 30$) to apply **The Central Limit Theorem**.

(ii) The mean of the distribution of the sample means is 18 g, the same as the population mean.
The standard deviation (or standard error) is $\dfrac{\sigma}{\sqrt{n}} = \dfrac{18}{\sqrt{40}} = 2.846$
$= 2.85$

(iii) A sketch of the distribution of $\bar{x}$ is shown below.

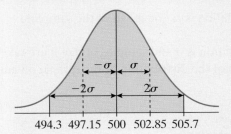

$$\mu = 500$$
$$\sigma = 2.85$$

494.3 497.15 500 502.85 505.7

(iv) Converting the given units to z-scores, we use $z = \dfrac{\bar{x} - \mu}{\dfrac{\sigma}{\sqrt{n}}}$.

For $x = 496$, $z = \dfrac{496 - 500}{\dfrac{18}{\sqrt{40}}} = \dfrac{-4}{2.846} = -1.405$

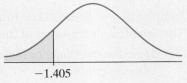

$P(\bar{x} < 496) = P(z < -1.405)$
$= 1 - P(z \leqslant 1.405)$
$= 1 - 0.9265$
$= 0.0735$

The probability that $\bar{x} < 496 = 0.0735$ or 7.35%.

(v) $P(z > z_1) = 0.06$

$\quad P(z \leqslant z_1) = 1 - 0.06 = 0.94$

$\quad \Rightarrow z_1 = 1.56$

$$z_1 = \frac{\overline{x} - \mu}{\frac{\sigma}{\sqrt{n}}} \Rightarrow 1.56 = \frac{503 - 500}{\frac{18}{\sqrt{n}}} = \frac{3\sqrt{n}}{18} = \frac{\sqrt{n}}{6}$$

$$\Rightarrow 1.56 = \frac{\sqrt{n}}{6}$$

$$\Rightarrow \sqrt{n} = 6(1.56) = 9.36$$

$$\Rightarrow n = (9.36)^2$$

$$\Rightarrow n = 87.6 = 88 \quad \text{… round up}$$

The sample size required is 88.

Exercise 5.1

1. Fill in the correct word or symbol to complete the following statements:

   (i) When a large number of samples of size n are taken from a population, then the distribution of $\overline{x}$, the sample mean, is known as the _____ _____ of the mean.

   (ii) As the sample size increases, the standard deviation of the sampling distribution of the sample means will _____.

   (iii) If the mean of the underlying population is μ, the mean of the sampling distribution of the means is _____.

   (iv) If the standard deviation of a population is σ and samples of size n are taken from it, then the standard deviation of the distribution of the sample means is

   _____.

2. The diagram on the right shows two curves. One of these curves represents a distribution and the other represents the distribution of the sample means of size n taken from this distribution. Which curve represents the distribution of the sample means?

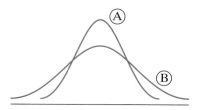

3. Samples of size 36 are taken from a population with mean 12 and standard deviation 2. The sampling distribution of the means are plotted in a curve.

   (i) Describe the shape of this curve naming the theorem you have used to support your description.

   (ii) Explain why the theorem you have mentioned can be applied when the shape of the underlying population is unknown.

   (iii) Write down the mean and standard deviation of the sampling distribution of the mean.

4. A population consists of the elements {4, 6, 8, 10}.
    (i) Write down all possible samples of size 2 (chosen without replacement) from this population.
    (ii) Give the sample mean, $\bar{x}$, for each pair.
    (iii) Are each of the values you have found a statistic or a parameter?
    (iv) Show that the mean of all possible samples of size 2 equals the mean of the population.

5. Explain the difference between a *parameter* and a *statistic*.

6. The diagram on the right shows two curves Ⓐ and Ⓑ. Diagram Ⓐ represents the distribution of a population and diagram Ⓑ represents the distribution of the means from a large number of samples of size 40.

    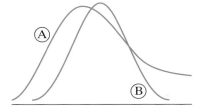

    (i) Is distribution Ⓐ skewed positively or negatively?
    (ii) Describe distribution Ⓑ.
    (iii) Explain why the *Central Limit Theorem* can be used to describe distribution Ⓑ even though the underlying population is not normally distributed.

7. A random sample of size 36 is chosen from a population with a mean of 12 and a standard deviation of 3.
    Find the probability that the sample mean is greater than 13.

8. A random sample of size 15 is taken from a normal distribution with mean 60 and standard deviation 4.
    Find the probability that the mean of the sample is less than 58.

9. Men have a mean height of 176 cm with standard deviation 11 cm.
    Find the probability that the mean of a random sample of 80 men
    (i) exceeds 177 cm   (ii) is less than 174.8 cm.

10. At a certain college, students spend on average 4.2 hours per week at a computer terminal, with a standard deviation of 1.8 hours.
    (i) Find the standard error for a random sample of 36 students.
    (ii) Find the probability that the average time spent using a computer terminal is
        (a) greater than 4.8 hours
        (b) between 4.1 and 4.5 hours.

11. The sugar content per litre bottle of a soft drink is known to be distributed with mean 5.8 and standard deviation 1.2. A sample of 900 bottles is taken at random and the sugar content of each bottle is measured.
    Estimate to 3 decimal places the probability that the mean sugar content of the 900 bottles will be less than 5.85.

12. A firm produces alternators for cars. The alternators are known to have a mean lifetime of 8 years with standard deviation 6 months.
   Forty samples of 144 alternators produced by the firm are tested.
   Estimate the number of samples which would be expected to have a mean lifetime of more than 8 years and 1 month.

13. A random sample of size 10 is taken from a normal distribution with mean 200 and standard deviation 10.
   Find the probability that the sample mean lies outside the range 198 to 205.

14. In the given diagram, curve Ⓐ represents a normal distribution.
   Curve Ⓑ represents the sampling distribution of means taken from samples of size 36.
   The distribution represented by Ⓐ has mean $\mu = 80$ and standard deviation $\sigma = 8$.
   The point C represents the mean of both distributions.
   The point D represents the value of the variable that is two standard deviations from C in distribution Ⓐ.
   The point E represents the value of the variable that is one standard error from C in distribution Ⓑ.
   Write down the values of C, D and E.

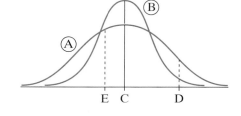

15. A normal distribution has mean 75 and standard deviation 9.
   A sample of size n is selected at random and the mean of this sample is $\bar{x}$.
   Find n if $P(\bar{x} > 73) = 0.8708$.

16. A normal distribution has a mean of 30 and a standard deviation of $\sqrt{5}$.
   (i) Find the probability that the mean of a random sample of 40 exceeds 30.5.
   (ii) Find the value of n such that the probability that the mean of a sample of size n exceeds 30.4 is less than 0.01.

17. Free-range eggs supplied by a health food cooperative have a mean weight of 52 g with a standard deviation of 4 g.
   Assuming the weights are normally distributed find the probability that:
   (i) a randomly selected egg will weigh more than 60 g
   (ii) the mean weight of five randomly selected eggs will be between 50 g and 55 g
   (iii) the mean weight of 90 randomly selected eggs will be between 52.1 g and 52.2 g.
   Which of your answers would be unchanged if the weights are not normally distributed?

Section 5.2 Confidence interval for a mean

In Section 5.1, the Central Limit Theorem was used to show that the sampling distribution of the mean approximates to a normal distribution for large n ($n \geqslant 30$). In this section we introduce a different way of presenting information provided by a sample mean to estimate the mean of the population from which the sample came.

If samples of size n are taken from a population, the means of the samples will vary. To accommodate this variety, we introduce the concept of a **confidence interval**. This interval will produce a range of values in which we are 'quite confident' the population mean μ lies. The endpoints of this interval are called **confidence limits**.
But how do we measure this **confidence**?
The **degree of confidence** is generally given as a percentage.
These percentages are generally 90%, 95% and 99%.
The most commonly used measure of confidence is a **95% confidence level**.
This means that there is a 95% probability that the population mean lies in the given interval.

In the standard normal distribution, we require the values of z such that 95% of the population lies in the interval $-z_1 \leqslant z \leqslant z_1$.
The work involved in finding the value of z, is shown below.
We use the standard normal tables on pages 36 and 37 of *Formulae and Tables*.

From the given diagram,

$$P(z \leqslant z_1) = 0.95 + 0.025$$
$$= 0.975$$

From the tables

$$z_1 = 1.96$$
$$\Rightarrow -z_1 = -1.96$$

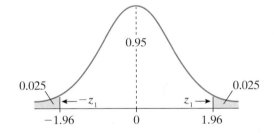

Thus in the normal distribution, 95% of the population lies within 1.96 standard deviations of the mean. Since the sample mean is normally distributed, 95% of the population will lie in the interval

$$\bar{x} \pm 1.96\sigma_{\bar{x}},$$

$$\sigma_{\bar{x}} = \frac{\sigma}{\sqrt{n}}$$

where $\sigma_{\bar{x}}$ is the standard error of the mean.

If μ is the population mean, then 95% of the sample means lie in the interval

$$\bar{x} - 1.96\sigma_{\bar{x}} < \mu < \bar{x} + 1.96\sigma_{\bar{x}}$$

where $\sigma_{\bar{x}} = \frac{\sigma}{\sqrt{n}}$, σ being the standard deviation of the population.

This can be written as $\bar{x} \pm 1.96\dfrac{\sigma}{\sqrt{n}}$, which are the end-points (or confidence limits) of the mean.

If $\bar{x}$ is the mean of a random sample of size n taken from a population with a normal distribution with known standard deviation σ, then the end-points of the 95% confidence interval for μ, the population mean, are given by

$$\bar{x} \pm 1.96 \frac{\sigma}{\sqrt{n}}$$

Note: If σ, the standard deviation of the population, is not given, use the standard deviation of the sample as an approximation.

Example 1

A random sample of 400 oranges was taken from a large consignment with unknown mean μ and standard deviation 15 grams.
The mean weight of the random sample was 81.4 grams.

Find a 95% confidence interval for the mean weight of the oranges in the consignment.

The 95% confidence interval for μ is $\bar{x} \pm 1.96 \frac{\sigma}{\sqrt{n}}$.

$$\bar{x} \pm 1.96 \frac{\sigma}{\sqrt{n}} = 81.4 \pm 1.96 \left(\frac{15}{\sqrt{400}} \right) \quad \dots \sigma = 15 \text{ and } n = 400$$

$$= 81.4 \pm 1.96(0.75)$$
$$= 81.4 \pm 1.47$$
$$= 79.93, 82.87$$
$$\Rightarrow 79.93 < \mu < 82.87$$

The mean of the consignment lies between 79.93 g and 82.87 g.

Example 2

A certain type of tennis ball is known to have a height of bounce which is normally distributed with standard deviation 2 cm.
A sample of 60 such tennis balls is tested and the mean height of the bounce of the sample is 140 cm.

  (i) Find a 95% confidence interval for the mean height of the bounce of this type of tennis ball.
 (ii) Explain what is meant by a "95% confidence interval".
(iii) If a tennis ball is selected at random, what is the probability that its bounce is outside the confidence interval found in (i) above?

(i) The 95% confidence interval is given by

$$\bar{x} \pm 1.96 \frac{\sigma}{\sqrt{n}}$$

$$= 140 \pm 1.96\left(\frac{2}{\sqrt{60}}\right)$$

$$= 140 \pm 1.96(0.258)$$

$$= 140 \pm 0.506$$

$$= 140.506, \ 139.494$$

The 95% confidence interval is $140.506 < \mu < 139.494$.

(ii) A "95% confidence interval", means that on 95 occasions out of 100 the interval will contain the true population mean.

(iii) P(ball bounce lies outside 95% confidence interval) $= \frac{5}{100} = \frac{1}{20}$.

Example 3

The heights of people have a standard deviation of 11.5 cm.
It is required to estimate the mean height of people, with 95% confidence, to within ±0.4 cm.
What sample size should be taken in order to achieve this estimate?

Let μ be the mean height of people.

The 95% confidence limits for μ are $\bar{x} \pm 1.96 \frac{\sigma}{\sqrt{n}}$.

$$\Rightarrow \ \pm 1.96 \frac{\sigma}{\sqrt{n}} = \pm 0.4 \ldots \text{ standard error is } \pm 0.4 \text{ cm}$$

$$\Rightarrow \ 1.96\left(\frac{11.5}{\sqrt{n}}\right) = 0.4$$

$$\Rightarrow \ \sqrt{n} = \frac{11.5(1.96)}{0.4}$$

$$\Rightarrow \ \sqrt{n} = 56.35$$

$$\Rightarrow \ n = (56.35)^2 = 3175.3$$

Therefore, a sample of at least 3176 should be taken.

Example 4

On the basis of the results obtained from a random sample of 100 men from a particular district, the 95% confidence interval for the mean height of the men in the district is found to be (177.22 cm, 179.18 cm).
Find the value of $\bar{x}$, the mean of the sample, and σ, the standard deviation of the normal population from which the sample is drawn.

The 95% confidence interval is given by

$$\bar{x} \pm 1.96\frac{\sigma}{\sqrt{n}} = (177.22, 179.18)$$

$$\Rightarrow \bar{x} + 1.96\frac{\sigma}{10} = 179.18 \ldots ①$$

$$\text{and} \quad \bar{x} - 1.96\frac{\sigma}{10} = 177.22 \ldots ②$$

Adding ① and ②: $2\bar{x} = 356.4$
$$\bar{x} = 178.2$$

Subtracting ① and ②:

$$2(1.96)\frac{\sigma}{10} = 1.96$$

$$\frac{2\sigma}{10} = 1 \Rightarrow \sigma = 5$$

The sample mean $\bar{x} = 178.2$ cm.
The population standard deviation is 5 cm.

Exercise 5.2

1. A population has mean μ and standard deviation 12.
   A random sample of 800 from this population has mean 63.
   Find a 95% confidence interval for μ.

2. The weights of dairy cows are known to have a standard deviation of 42 kg.
   A random sample of 280 dairy cows has a mean weight of 284 kg.
   Find a 95% confidence limit for the mean weight of all the cows.

3. Seventy packs of butter, selected at random from a large batch delivered to a supermarket, are weighed. The mean weight is found to be 227 g and the standard deviation is found to be 7.5 g.
   (i) Calculate a 95% confidence interval for the mean weight of all packs in the batch.
   (ii) If one pack is selected at random from the seventy packs, find the probability that its weight is not in the given interval.

4. In a random sample of 100 students taking a state examination, it was found that the mean mark was 62.7 with a standard deviation of 9.2 marks.
   Find the 95% confidence limits for the mean score of all the students who took the examination.

5. The weight of vitamin E in a capsule manufactured by a drug company is normally distributed with standard deviation 0.04 mg.
   A random sample of 12 capsules was analysed and the mean weight of vitamin E was found to be 5.12 mg.
   (i) Calculate a 95% confidence interval for the population mean weight of vitamin E per capsule.
   (ii) Give the values of the end-points of the interval, correct to three significant figures.
   (iii) Explain what is meant by "95% confidence"?

6. A bank selected a random sample of 400 customers and found that they had a mean credit of €280 with a standard deviation of €105 in their accounts.
   Calculate a 95% confidence interval for the mean credit of all the bank's customers.

7. Shoe shop staff routinely measure the lengths of their customers' feet. Measurements of the length of one foot (without shoes) from each of 180 adult male customers yielded a mean length of 29.2 cm and a standard deviation of 1.47 cm.
   (i) Calculate a 95% confidence interval for the mean length of male feet.
   (ii) Why was it not necessary to assume that the lengths of feet are normally distributed in order to calculate the confidence interval in (i) above?

8. A random sample of 64 sweets is selected from a large batch.
   The sweets are found to have a mean weight of 0.932 grams and a standard deviation of 0.1 grams.
   (i) Calculate the standard error of the mean.
   (ii) What is the best estimate for μ, the mean of the large batch?
   (iii) Construct a 95% confidence interval for μ.
   (iv) What would happen if a sample size of 100 was selected rather than a sample of 64?
   (v) What conclusion can you draw from your result in part (iv)?

9. A random sample of 240 cars had a mean age of 4.6 years with a standard deviation of 2.5 years.
   (i) Give a 95% confidence interval for the mean age of all cars.
   (ii) What size of sample would be needed to estimate the mean age, with 95% confidence, to within ±0.2 years?

10. 150 boxes of cereal of a certain brand are weighed and the mean weight is 748 grams with standard deviation 3.6 grams.
    (i) Find a 95% confidence interval for the mean weight of all boxes of cereal of that brand.
    (ii) What size of sample would be needed to estimate the mean weight, with 95% confidence, to within ±1.5 grams?

11. Eighty people were asked to measure their pulse rates when they woke up in the morning. The mean was 69 beats per minute and the standard deviation 4 beats.
    (i) Find a 95% confidence interval for the population mean.
    (ii) What size of sample would be needed to estimate the mean number of beats, with 95% confidence, to within ±1.5 beats?

12. The weights of pebbles on a beach are distributed with mean 48.6 g and standard deviation 8.5 g.
    A random sample of 50 pebbles is chosen.
    (i) Find the probability that the mean weight will be less than 49 g.
    (ii) Find the limits within which the central 95% of such sample means would lie.
    (iii) How large a sample would be needed in order that the central 95% of sample means would lie in an interval of width at most 4 g?

13. The 95% confidence interval for the mean mark of a group of students is (54.09, 60.71). This interval is based on the results from a random sample of 80 students.
    (i) Find $\bar{x}$, the mean of the sample.
    (ii) Find σ, the standard deviation of the normal population from which the sample is taken.

Section 5.3 Confidence interval for a proportion

In Section 4.4 of Chapter 4 it was shown how to find the confidence interval for a population proportion using the margin of error $\dfrac{1}{\sqrt{n}}$, where n is the sample size.

This confidence interval is shown again on the right.

> The 95% confidence interval for a proportion p is
> $$\hat{p} - \frac{1}{\sqrt{n}} < p < \hat{p} + \frac{1}{\sqrt{n}}$$

Here is a reminder of what a **proportion** is!
If 150 television viewers are interviewed in a sample survey and 63 say they like a new situation comedy, then $\frac{63}{150} = 0.42$ is the proportion of the sample who like the new show. This sample proportion, $\hat{p}$, is used as an estimate of the true population proportion p of television viewers who like the new show.

> The notation $\hat{p}$ is used to denote **sample proportion**.
> The notation p is used to denote **population proportion**.
>
> Since p is generally not known, $\hat{p}$ is used as an estimator for the true population proportion, p.

If many samples of the same size are taken from a population, each sample will produce a different (but similar) proportion. All these proportions form their own distribution called the **sampling distribution of the proportion**.

The **standard error**, $\sigma_{\hat{p}}$, of this distribution is given on page 34 of *Formulae and Tables* and is shown on the right.

$$\sigma_{\hat{p}} = \sqrt{\frac{p(1-p)}{n}}$$

In this section we will use the Standard Normal Tables $\left(\text{rather than the margin of error, } \dfrac{1}{\sqrt{n}}\right)$ to get a more accurate confidence interval for a population proportion.

Since the 95% level of confidence will be used, the diagram on the right will remind us that 95% of a normal distribution lies within 1.96 standard deviations of the mean.

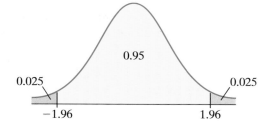

If $\hat{p}$ is the sample proportion and p is the population proportion, then the 95% confidence interval for p is given by

$$\hat{p} - 1.96\sqrt{\frac{p(1-p)}{n}} \leqslant p \leqslant \hat{p} + 1.96\sqrt{\frac{p(1-p)}{n}}$$

This can be written more concisely as $\hat{p} \pm 1.96\sqrt{\dfrac{p(1-p)}{n}}$.

> *The 95% confidence interval for a population proportion*
>
> $$\hat{p} \pm 1.96\sqrt{\frac{p(1-p)}{n}}$$

Note: An increase in confidence levels results in an increase in the interval width.

Example 1

In a survey carried out in a large city, 170 households out of a random sample of 250 owned at least one pet.
  (i) Find the standard error of the sampling distribution of the proportion at the 95% confidence level.
  (ii) Find the 95% confidence interval for the proportion of households in the city who own at least one pet.

(i) The sample proportion $\hat{p} = \dfrac{170}{250} = 0.68$

Standard error $\sigma_{\hat{p}} = \sqrt{\dfrac{p(1-p)}{n}}$

$$= \sqrt{\frac{0.68(1-0.68)}{250}}$$

$$\sigma_{\hat{p}} = 0.029$$

(ii) The 95% confidence interval is given by

$$\hat{p} \pm 1.96\sqrt{\frac{p(1-p)}{n}}$$

$$= 0.68 \pm 1.96(0.029) \ldots \text{ from (i) above}$$

$$= 0.68 \pm 0.0568$$

$$= (0.6232, 0.7368) \text{ or about } (62\%, 74\%)$$

Example 2

A random sample of 250 cars were surveyed passing a certain junction and 36 were found to have K registrations.
  (i) Determine a 95% confidence interval for the proportion of cars in that area that have a K registration.
 (ii) What sample size would have to be taken in order to estimate the percentage to within $\pm 2\%$?

(i) The sample proportion $\hat{p} = \dfrac{36}{250} = 0.144$.

The 95% confidence interval is given by

$$\hat{p} \pm 1.96\sqrt{\frac{p(1-p)}{n}}$$

$$= 0.144 \pm 1.96\sqrt{\frac{0.144(1-0.144)}{250}}$$

$$= 0.144 \pm 1.96(0.0222)$$

$$= 0.144 \pm 0.0435$$

$$= 0.100, 0.1875$$

The 95% confidence interval is $(0.100, 0.1875)$.

(ii) Let n be the sample size.

We require n such that $\hat{p} \pm \sqrt{\dfrac{p(1-p)}{n}} = \hat{p} \pm 0.02 \ldots 2\% = 0.02$

$$\therefore \quad \sqrt{\frac{0.144(1-0.144)}{n}} = 0.02$$

$$\sqrt{\frac{(0.144)(0.856)}{n}} = 0.02$$

$$\frac{0.123264}{n} = (0.02)^2$$

$$n = \frac{0.123264}{(0.02)^2} = 308.16$$

So a sample size of 309 would have to be taken.

Exercise 5.3

1. A manufacturer wants to assess the proportion of defective items in a large batch produced by a particular machine.
   He tests a random sample of 300 items and finds that 45 are defective.
   Calculate a 95% confidence interval for the proportion of defective items in the complete batch.

2. In order to assess the probability of a successful outcome, an experiment is performed 200 times and the number of successful outcomes is found to be 72.
   Find a 95% confidence interval for p, the probability of a successful outcome.

3. A market researcher carries out a survey in order to determine the popularity of SUDZ washing powder in the Cork area.
   He visits every house in a large housing estate in Cork and asks the question:
   "Do you use SUDZ washing powder?"
   Of 235 people questioned, 75 answered "YES".
   Treating the sample as being random, calculate a 95% confidence interval for the proportion of households in the Cork area which use SUDZ.

4. An importer has ordered a large consignment of tomatoes.
   When it arrives, he examines a randomly chosen sample of 50 boxes and finds that 12 contain at least one bad tomato.
   Assuming that these boxes may be regarded as being a random sample from the boxes in the consignment, obtain an approximate 95% confidence interval for the proportion of boxes containing at least one bad tomato, giving your confidence limits correct to three decimal places.

5. If 400 persons, constituting a random sample, are given a flu vaccine and 136 of them experienced some discomfort, construct a 95% large-sample confidence interval for the corresponding true proportion.

6. A random sample of 120 library books is taken as they are borrowed.
   They are classified as fiction or non-fiction, and hardback or paperback.
   88 books are found to be fiction, and of these, 74 are paperback.
   Find a 95% confidence limit for:
   (i) the proportion of books borrowed that are fiction
   (ii) the proportion of fiction books borrowed that are paperback.

7. In a sample of 400 shops taken in 2012, it was discovered that 136 of them sold carpets at below the list prices which had been recommended by manufacturers.
   (i) Estimate the percentage of all carpet-selling shops selling below list price.
   (ii) Calculate the 95% confidence limits for this estimate, and explain briefly what these mean.
   (iii) What size sample would have to be taken in order to estimate the percentage to within $\pm 2\%$?

8. In a random sample of 1,200 voters interviewed nationwide, only 324 felt that the salaries of certain government officials should be raised.
   Construct a 95% confidence interval of the corresponding true proportion.

9. In a market research survey, 15 people out of a random sample of 100 from a certain area said that they used a particular brand of soap.
   (i) Calculate a 95% confidence interval for the proportion of people who use this brand of soap.
   (ii) What size sample would need to be taken in order to estimate the percentage to within $\pm 1\frac{1}{2}\%$? Give your answer correct to the nearest 10.

Section 5.4 Hypothesis testing for a population mean ——

Hypothesis testing

In Sections 5.2 and 5.3 we dealt with confidence intervals, one of the two most common types of statistical inference.

The second type of statistical inference has a different objective. It is called **hypothesis testing**. Its purpose is to test the truth or otherwise of a claim, statement or **hypothesis** made about a population parameter.

An **hypothesis** is a statement or conjecture made about some characteristic or parameter of a population.

Here is an example of an hypothesis:

   'The mean age of men on their wedding day is 32 years.'

An **hypothesis test** is a statistical method of proving the truth or otherwise of this statement.

It has already been shown that in any normal distribution 95% of the population lies within 1.96 standard deviations of the mean, that is, 95% of the population will be in the interval $\mu \pm 1.96\sigma$.

If we are dealing with a normal distribution and an experiment produces a result which is outside the interval $\mu \pm 1.96\sigma$, we would be inclined to suspect that factors other than chance are involved in the result. For example, some form of bias may be present. If we toss a coin 100 times we would 'expect' heads to occur 50 times.
Do we conclude that the coin is biased if heads occur 60 times?
Is the unexpected result more than mere chance?

To answer this question we start with the assumption, or hypothesis, that the coin is not biased.
This assumption is called the **null hypothesis**, denoted by **H_0**.
Usually the null hypothesis is a statement of "**no** difference", "**no** effect" or "**no** change".
An hypothesis test is then carried out to accept or reject the null hypothesis.
In this test, we speak of rejecting the null hypothesis 'at a certain level'.
This 'certain level' is called the **level of significance**.
The 5% level of significance is by far the most commonly-used one.
It is the only one that we deal with in our course.

The 5% level of significance means that the result obtained is likely to occur on only 5 occasions out of 100.

At the 5% level of significance, the set of values, $z > 1.96$ or $z < -1.96$, is known as the **critical region** and the boundaries of the critical region are called the **critical values**.

If the values of z are in the critical region (i.e. $z > 1.96$ or $z < -1.96$), we reject the null hypothesis and conclude that factors other than chance are involved.

The critical regions at the 5% level of significance are shown below.

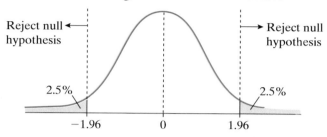

Hypothesis Testing

At the 5% level of significance, the null hypothesis is rejected if

$$z < -1.96 \quad \text{or} \quad z > 1.96$$

Hypothesis testing for a population mean

When a population is very large, it is generally not practical to find the true mean and standard deviation of the total population. However, assumptions are often made about these values and their validity is tested based on observations made from random samples taken from the population.

Take, for example, machines designed to produce batteries which last for 120 hours with a standard deviation 4 hours. What conclusions can we come to about one of these machines if a random sample of 50 batteries produced by it had a mean life of 121 hours?

We now begin the process of investigating whether these machines are producing the type of battery they were designed to produce. This process is called hypothesis testing.

Here are the basic steps of a hypothesis test:

1. Write down H_0, the **null hypothesis**, and H_1, the **alternative hypothesis**.
   H_0: The mean life of a battery is 120 hours.
   H_1: The mean life of a battery is **not** 120 hours.

2. State the **significance level**, α.
   The significance level on our course is 5% ($\alpha = 0.05$).
   This means that if $z < -1.96$ or $z > 1.96$, we **reject** the null hypothesis and **accept** the alternative hypothesis.

3. Calculate the value of the **test statistic**.
   This involves converting the given units to z-units.

To convert the given units to standard units we use

$$z = \dfrac{\bar{x} - \mu}{\dfrac{\sigma}{\sqrt{n}}}, \text{ where }$$

$\bar{x}$ = the sample mean
μ = population mean
σ = population standard deviation
n = size of sample

For the machine mentioned above,

$$z = \dfrac{\bar{x} - \mu}{\dfrac{\sigma}{\sqrt{n}}} = \dfrac{121 - 120}{\dfrac{4}{\sqrt{50}}} = \dfrac{1}{0.566} = 1.767$$

The test statistic is $z = 1.767$.

4. Come to a **conclusion**.
   Since $z = 1.767$ does not lie outside the range $-1.96 < z < 1.96$ it is **not** in the **critical region**. So we accept the null hypothesis which states that the mean life of a battery is 120 hours.

Note: If σ, the standard deviation of the population is not given, use $\sigma_{\bar{x}}$ the standard deviation of the sample instead.

Example 1

Over the years, a market gardener found that the mean yield from his tomato plants was 1.83 kg per plant with a standard deviation of 0.35 kg per plant. One year he planted 600 of a new variety and these yielded 1.87 kg per plant. At the 5% level of significance, test whether the mean yield from the new plants is different from his normal variety.

1. H_0: The mean μ is 1.83.
   H_1: The mean μ is **not** 1.83.

2. The level of significance is 5%.
   The critical region is $z < -1.96$ or $z > 1.96$.

3. Calculate the test statistic by converting to standard units.

$$z = \dfrac{\bar{x} - \mu}{\dfrac{\sigma}{\sqrt{n}}} \dots \quad \begin{array}{ll} \bar{x} = 1.87 & \mu = 1.83 \\ n = 600 & \sigma = 0.35 \end{array}$$

$$= \dfrac{1.87 - 1.83}{\left(\dfrac{0.35}{\sqrt{600}}\right)} = \dfrac{0.04}{0.0143} = 2.797$$

$$z = 2.797$$

Since $z = 2.797$ and $2.797 > 1.96$, we reject the null hypothesis and conclude that the new variety is different from the normal variety.

Using p-values

Suppose we carry out an hypothesis test and find the test statistic to be $z = 2.16$.
Since 2.16 is greater than 1.96, we reject the null hypothesis at the 5% level of significance
($\alpha = 0.05$).

Instead of comparing $z = 2.16$ with $z = 1.96$ (and $z = -1.96$), we compare the total area of
the two coloured regions below with the specific level of significance, $\alpha = 0.05$.

We use pages 36 and 37 of *Formulae
and Tables* to find the probability
that $z \leqslant -2.16$ or $z \geqslant 2.16$.

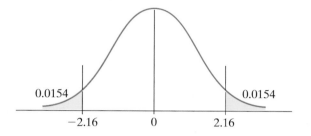

$$P(z \leqslant -2.16) + P(z \geqslant 2.16)$$
$$= 2P(z \geqslant 2.16)$$
$$= 2[1 - P(z \leqslant 2.16)]$$
$$= 2[1 - 0.9846]$$
$$= 2[0.0154]$$
$$= 0.0308$$

The shaded areas above are referred to as the **p-value**, or probability-value corresponding to
the observed value of the test statistic.
The value 0.0308 found above is the p-value that corresponds to the test statistic $z = |2.16|$.
The p-value 0.0308 is interpreted as the **lowest level of significance** at which the null
hypothesis could have been rejected.

With a test statistic of $z = 2.16$, we would certainly have rejected the null hypothesis at the
specified level of significance ($\alpha = 0.05$).
The p-value of 0.0308 gives us a **specific** or more precise level of significance.
The **smaller** the p-value is, the **stronger** is the evidence against H_0 provided by the data.

*The p- alue of a
Test Statistic*

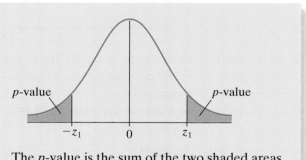

The p-value is the sum of the two shaded areas.
$$p\text{-value} = 2 \times P(z > |z_1|),$$
where z_1 is the test statistic.

Example 2

Calculate the p-value for the sample statistic $z = -2.08$.

Sample statistic is $z = -2.08$.
The sum of the probabilities that

$$z > 2.08 \quad \text{and} \quad z < -2.08$$

is the p-value.

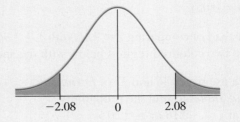

$$p\text{-value} = 2 \times P(z > |2.08|)$$
$$= 2 \times [1 - P(z \leqslant 2.08)]$$
$$= 2 \times [1 - 0.9812]$$
$$= 2(0.0188)$$
$$p\text{-value} = 0.0376$$

Steps involved in a Test of Significance using a p-value

1. Write down the **null hypothesis H_0** and the **alternative hypothesis H_1**.

2. State the **significance level** α. (On our course $\alpha = 0.05$.)

3. Calculate the **test statistic**.

4. Find the p-value that corresponds to the test statistic.

5. If the p-value > 0.05, the result is not significant and we do **not** reject the null hypothesis H_0.

   If the p-value $\leqslant 0.05$, we reject the null hypothesis H_0 in favour of the alternative hypothesis H_1.

Example 3

A random sample of 36 observations is to be taken from a distribution with standard deviation 10. In the past, the distribution has had a mean of 83, but it is believed that the mean may have changed.
When the sample was taken it was found to have a mean of 86.2.

   (i) State H_0 and H_1.

   (ii) Calculate the value of the test statistic.

   (iii) Calculate the p-value for the test statistic.

   (iv) Use the p-value to state if the result is significant at the 5% level of significance.
   Explain your conclusion.

(i) H_0: Mean $\mu = 83$
H_1: Mean $\mu \neq 83$

(ii) Test statistic $z = \dfrac{\bar{x} - \mu}{\dfrac{\sigma}{\sqrt{n}}}$

$$z = \frac{86.2 - 83}{\dfrac{10}{\sqrt{36}}} = \frac{3.2 \times \sqrt{36}}{10} = 1.92$$

The test statistic is $z = 1.92$

(iii) The p-value $= 2 \times P(z > 1.92)$
$$= 2 \times [1 - P(z \leqslant 1.92)]$$
$$= 2 \times [1 - 0.9726]$$
$$= 2(0.0274) = 0.0548$$

(iv) As the p-value is not less than or equal to 0.05, the result is not significant; we do not reject the null hypothesis.

Exercise 5.4

1. A normal distribution is thought to have a mean of 50.
   A random sample of 100 gave a mean of 52.4 and a standard deviation of 14.3.
   Is there evidence to suggest that the true mean is different from the assumed mean at the 5% level of significance?

2. Over a long period the scores obtained in a particular intelligence test were normally distributed with mean score 70 and standard deviation 6.
   When a test was taken by a random sample of 64 students, the mean score was 68.
   Is there sufficient evidence, at the 5% level of significance, that these students differ from the normal students?

3. The management of a large hospital states that the mean age of its patients is 45 years.
   The HSE statistics department decides to test this claim about the mean age of the patients.
   It took a random sample of 100 patients and found that the mean age was 48.4 years with a standard deviation of 18 years.
   (i) What is the null hypothesis?
   (ii) State the alternative hypothesis.
   (iii) Work out the test statistic for the sample mean.
   (iv) At the 5% level of significance, is there evidence to show that the mean age of the patients is not 45 years?
   Give a reason for your conclusion.

4. A particular machine produces metal rods which are normally distributed with a mean length of 210 cm and with a standard deviation of 6 cm.
   The machine is serviced and a sample is taken to investigate if the mean length has changed.
   The sample of 100 rods gave a mean length of 211.5 cm.
   (i) What is the null hypothesis?
   (ii) What is the alternative hypothesis?
   (iii) Work out the test statistic for the sample mean.
   (iv) At the 5% level of significance, is there evidence of a change in the mean length of rods produced by the machine?
   Explain your conclusion.

5. Mice kept under laboratory conditions have a mean lifespan of 258 days and a standard deviation of 45 days.
   64 of these mice, selected at random, were each given a measured dose of a certain drug each day, and the mean lifespan for this group was 269 days.
   At the 5% level of significance, is there evidence to suggest that the drug has altered the mean lifespan of the mice?

6. In 1970 the average number of children per family in a certain town was 3.8 with a standard deviation of 0.6. In 1980 a random sample of 40 families had a total of 144 children.
   At the 5% level of significance, is there evidence to conclude that the mean number of children per family had changed?

7. The mean mark for all students taking a certain Leaving Certificate subject was 48.7.
   In a particular town, 120 students took this examination.
   The mean mark of these students was 46.5 with a standard deviation of 9.5.
   At the 5% level of significance, is there evidence to suggest that the mean mark of the students of this town differs from the rest of the population?

8. In each of the following, the z-score for a sample mean is given.
   Work out the corresponding p-value for each test statistic.
   (i) $z = 1.73$ (ii) $z = -1.91$ (iii) $z = -1.65$ (iv) $z = -2.06$

9. 'Standard' batteries have a mean lifetime of 85 hours with a standard deviation 12 hours. A sample of 200 'long-life' batteries had a mean lifetime of 86.5 hours.
   (i) Calculate the sample statistic for this sample.
   (ii) Work out the corresponding p-value for this sample statistic.
   (iii) Is the result significant at the 5% level of significance?

10. Experience has shown that the scores obtained in a particular test are normally distributed with mean score 70 and standard deviation 6.
    When the test is taken by a random sample of 36 students, the mean is 68.5.

(i) Calculate the sample statistic for this sample.

(ii) Calculate the p-value for this sample statistic.

(iii) Use the p-value you have found to investigate if the mean score of the sample differs from the mean score of the population at the 5% level of significance.

11. The security department of a warehouse wants to know whether the average time required by the night watchman to walk his round is 12.0 minutes.
In a random sample of 36 rounds, the night watchman averaged 12.3 minutes with a standard deviation of 1.2 minutes.

(i) Calculate the test statistic for this sample.

(ii) Can we reject the null hypothesis that $\mu = 12.0$ minutes at the 5% level of significance?

(iii) Work out the p-value that corresponds to the test statistic found in (i) above.

(iv) If this p-value is used, do you reach the same conclusion with regard to significance at the 5% level?

12. The lengths of metal bars produced by a particular machine are normally distributed with mean length 420 cm and standard deviation 12 cm.
The machine is serviced, after which a sample of 100 bars gives a mean length of 423 cm.

(i) Calculate the sample statistic for this sample.

(ii) Work out the p-value for this sample statistic.

(iii) Use this p-value to determine if there is evidence, at the 5% level, of a change in the mean length of the bars produced by the machine, assuming that the standard deviation remains the same.

13. A machine is designed to produce screws with a stated mean length of 5 mm.
A random sample of 400 screws produced by the machine is found to have a mean length of 5.008 mm and a standard deviation of 0.072 mm.
Estimate the standard error of the mean, and obtain an approximate 95% confidence interval for the mean of the whole output of this machine.

Investigate if the mean of the sample differs significantly from the stated mean at the 5% level of significance.

Test yourself 5

A – questions

1. The weights of a large collection of bags of potatoes have a mean of 25 kg and a standard deviation of $\sqrt{5}$ kg.
   Estimate, to 2 decimal places, the probability that a random sample of 50 bags will have a mean weight of between 24.5 kg and 25.5 kg.

2. A random sample of size 20 is taken from a population of size 80 (with replacement). Find the mean and standard error of the sample if the population is normally distributed with mean 2.85 and standard deviation 0.07.

3. The pulse-rate of a sample of 32 people was measured.
   The mean was found to be 26.2 with standard deviation $\sigma_{\bar{x}} = 5.15$.
   Calculate the 95% confidence interval for the population mean.

4. A machine is regulated to dispense liquid into cartons in such a way that the amount of liquid dispensed on each occasion is normally distributed with a standard deviation of 20 ml.
   Find the confidence limits for the mean amount of liquid dispensed if a random sample of 40 cartons had an average content of 266 ml.

5. Among the first 150 customers at a new snack bar, 90 order coffee.
   Assuming that this is a random sample from the population of future customers, estimate a 95% confidence interval for the proportion of future customers who will order coffee.

6. A sample poll of 100 voters chosen at random from all voters in a given constituency indicated that 55% of them were in favour of candidate A.
   Find the 95% confidence interval for the proportion of all the voters in the district in favour of this candidate.

7. Irish third-level students are known to have a mean height of 176 cm with a standard deviation 11 cm.
   A random sample of 60 equivalent German students had a mean height of 179 cm.
   Does this suggest that the mean height of German students differs from that of Irish students at the 95% confidence level?

8. Jars of honey are filled by a machine.
   It has been found that the quantity of honey in a jar has a mean of 460.3 g with a standard deviation of 3.2 g.
   It is believed that the machine controls have been altered in such a way that, although the standard deviation is unaltered, the mean quantity may have changed.
   A random sample of 60 jars is taken and the mean quantity of honey per jar is found to be 461.2 g.

(i) State the null and alternative hypotheses.

(ii) Calculate the sample statistic for the mean.

(iii) Is there evidence, at the 5% level of significance, that the sample mean is different from the population mean?

9. A firm produces batteries which are known to have a mean lifetime of 96 hours. Forty samples of 36 batteries each are tested.

(i) Describe the sampling distribution of the means of these samples, mentioning the theorem you have used to justify your answer.

(ii) Explain why the theorem you have mentioned can be applied when the shape of the underlying population is not known.

(iii) Estimate the number of samples in which the average lifetime of the 36 batteries is greater than 98 hours if the standard deviation of the batteries is 6 hours.

10. Draw a rough sketch of the normal curve showing the critical regions, at the 5% level of significance, of a hypothesis test.

(i) Clearly indicate the rejection regions.

(ii) What are the critical z-values for the limits of these rejection regions?

(iii) For a z-value of 1.6, estimate the corresponding p-value for this statistic.

B – questions

1. A large number of random samples of size n are taken from a normal distribution with a mean of 74 and a standard deviation of 6.
The means, $\bar{x}$, of these samples are calculated.
Find the sample size n required to ensure that the probability of $\bar{x} > 72$ is 0.854.

2. The weights of bags of fertiliser may be modelled by a normal distribution with mean 12.1 kg and standard deviation 0.4 kg.
Find the probability that:

(i) a randomly selected bag will weigh less than 12.0 kg,

(ii) the mean weight of four bags selected at random will weigh more than 12.0 kg,

(iii) the mean weight of 100 bags will be between 12.0 and 12.1 kg.

How would your answer to (iii) be affected if the normal distribution was not a good model for the weights of the bags?
Explain your answer.

3. A plant produces steel sheets whose weights are known to be normally distributed with a standard deviation of 2.4 kg.
A random sample of 36 sheets had a mean weight of 31.4 kg.
Find a 95% confidence interval for the mean weight of sheets produced by the plant.

4. The residents of a rural area are being asked for their views on a plan to build a wind farm in their area.
   Environmental campaigners claim that 20% of the residents are against the plan.

   (i) State one reason why surveying a random sample of 30 residents will allow reliable conclusions to be drawn.

   (ii) Using a 5% significance level, calculate a 95% confidence interval for the population proportion against the plan.

5. (i) Explain briefly what is meant by the term "95% confidence interval".

   (ii) A car manufacturing company tested a random sample of 150 cars of the same model to estimate the mean number of kilometres travelled per litre of petrol consumption for all cars of that model.
   The sample mean of kilometres travelled per litre consumed was 13.52 and the standard deviation was 2.23.

   Form a 95% confidence interval for the mean number of kilometres travelled per litre of petrol consumed for all cars of that make.
   Give all calculations correct to two places of decimal.

6. A neurologist wants to test the effect a new drug has on response times. 100 rats are injected with a unit dose of this drug and the response times are recorded.
   The neurologist knows that the mean response time for rats not injected with the drug is 1.2 seconds.
   The mean response time of the 100 rats injected with the drug is 1.05 seconds with a sample standard deviation of 0.5 seconds.

   (i) State the null and alternative hypotheses for this test.

   (ii) Determine the critical region at the 5% level of significance and illustrate your answer with a sketch.

   (iii) Calculate the test statistic and answer the question "Do you think that the drug has an effect on the response time at the 5% level of significance?"

   (iv) Calculate the p-value for the test statistic and interpret this value.

7. A school of motoring claims that 80% of its clients are successful in their first driving test. A person who did not believe this claim took a random sample of 72 clients and found that 50 of these had been successful in their first driving test.

   (i) Using $\dfrac{1}{\sqrt{n}}$, write down the margin of error.

   (ii) Calculate the sample proportion as a decimal correct to two decimal places.

   (iii) Write down the confidence interval, at the 95% level of confidence, in terms of $\hat{p}$ and n.

   (iv) Can the school's claim be upheld at the 95% level of confidence?
   [Note: See Section 4.4, page 166.]

8. A market gardener sells carrots in 25 kg sacks.
   The wholesaler suspects that the true mean weight is not 25 kg.
   He weighs a random sample of 50 sacks and finds that the mean weight is 24.5 kg with a standard deviation of 1.5 kg.
   (i) State the null and alternative hypotheses.
   (ii) Calculate the sample statistic for the sample.
   (iii) Calculate the p-value for this statistic.
   (iv) Is the wholesaler's suspicion justified at the 5% level of significance?
   (v) Complete the following sentence:
       "The p-value is the _____ level of significance at which the null hypothesis could have been _____".

9. The weights of male students at a large university are normally distributed with a mean of 68 kg and a standard deviation of 3 kg.
   Eighty samples of 25 students are picked at random (with replacement).
   (i) Find the mean and standard error of the resulting sampling distribution.
   (ii) In how many of the samples would you expect the sample mean to be less than 67.5 kg?

C – questions

1. A company instals a new machine in a factory.
   The company claims that the machine will fill bags with wholemeal flour having a mean weight of 500 g and a standard deviation of 18 g.
   36 bags are checked in a random sample to test this claim.
   Their mean weight is 505 g.
   (i) State the null and the alternative hypotheses.
   (ii) Calculate the test statistic for the sample mean.
   (iii) Find the p-value that corresponds to the test statistic.
   (iv) Is the result significant at the 5% level of significance?
       Explain your answer.

2. Among 80 fish caught in a certain lake, 28 were inedible as a result of the chemical pollution of their environment.
   (i) Work out the standard error for this proportion.
   (ii) Construct a 95% confidence interval for the true proportion of fish in this lake which are inedible as a result of chemical pollution.

3. The 95% confidence interval for the mean weight, in grams, of a consignment of oranges is (79.93, 82.87). This result is based on a random sample of 400 oranges.
   Using this confidence interval, find
   (i) $\bar{x}$, the mean of the sample
   (ii) σ, the standard deviation of the normal population from which the sample is taken.

4. The masses of loaves from a certain bakery are normally distributed with mean 500 grams and standard deviation 20 grams.
   (i) Determine what percentage of the output would fall below 475 grams and what percentage would be above 530 grams.
   (ii) A sample of 40 loaves yielded a mean mass of 495 grams.
       Calculate the sample statistic for the mean.
   (iii) Calculate the p-value for this sample statistic.
   (iv) Does the p-value found above provide evidence that the mean weight of loaves from this sample is different from the mean of 500 g at the 5% level of significance?

5. (a) Write down the mean and standard deviation of the distribution of the means of all possible samples of size n taken from an infinite population having mean μ and standard deviation σ.

   Describe the shape of this distribution of sample means when
   (i) n is large
   (ii) the distribution of the population is normal.
   Explain briefly how the Central Limit Theorem can be applied to (i) and (ii) above.

   (b) The standard deviation of all till receipts at a supermarket during 2013 was €8.50 and the mean of the receipts was €37.

   (i) Find the probability that the mean of a random sample of 100 till receipts is greater than €37.50.
   (ii) Find the value of n such that the probability that the mean of the sample of size n exceeds €37.50 is less than 0.06.

6. The distribution of the hourly earnings of all employees in Ireland in October 2009 is shown in the diagram. It can be seen that the distribution is positively skewed.

   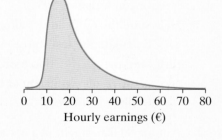
   Hourly earnings (€)

   The mean is €22.05.
   The median is €17.82.
   The standard deviation is €10.64.
   The lower quartile is €12.80.
   The upper quartile is €26.05.

   (i) If an employee is selected at random from this population, what is the probability that the employee earns more than €12.80?
   (ii) If six employees are selected at random from this population, what is the probability that exactly four of them had hourly earnings of more than €12.80?

   In a computer simulation, random samples of size 200 are repeatedly selected from this population and the mean of each sample is recorded. A thousand such sample means are recorded.

   (iii) Describe the expected distribution of these sample means. Your description should refer to the shape of the distribution and to its mean and standard deviation.
   (iv) How many of the sample means would you expect to be greater than €23?

7. The contents of a bag of oats are normally distributed with mean 3.05 kg and standard deviation 0.08 kg.
   (i) What proportion of bags contains less than 3.11 kg?
   (ii) What proportion of bags contains between 3.00 kg and 3.15 kg?
   (iii) Without using tables, write down the weight that is exceeded by 97.5% of the bags. (Use the Empirical Rule.)
   (iv) If 6 bags are selected at random, what is the probability that the mean weight of the contents will be between 3.00 kg and 3.15 kg?

8. A gas supplier maintains a team of engineers who are available to deal with leaks reported by customers. Most reported leaks can be dealt with quickly, but some require a long time. The time (excluding travelling time) taken to deal with reported leaks is found to have a mean of 65 minutes and a standard deviation of 60 minutes.
   (a) Assuming that the times may be modelled by a normal distribution, estimate the probability that:
      (i) it will take more than 185 minutes to deal with a reported leak,
      (ii) it will take between 50 minutes and 125 minutes to deal with a reported leak,
      (iii) the mean time to deal with a random sample of 90 reported leaks is less than 70 minutes.
   (b) A statistician, consulted by the gas supplier, stated that, as the times had a mean of 65 minutes and a standard deviation of 60 minutes, the normal distribution would not provide an adequate model.
      (i) Explain the reason for the statistician's statement.
      (ii) Give a reason why, despite the statistician's statement, your answer to (a) (iii) is still valid.

9. Hens' eggs have masses which may be said to have a normal distribution about a mean mass of 60 g and a standard deviation of 15 g.
   Eggs of mass less than 45 g are classified as *small*. The remainder are classified into two further divisions called *standard* and *large*.
   (i) If an egg is picked at random from the batch, find the probability that it is *small*.
   (ii) A sample of 50 eggs are selected at random.
       Find the probability that the mean of the sample is less than 58 g.
   (iii) It is desired that the *standard* and *large* classes should have about the same number of eggs in each. Estimate the mass at which the division should be made. Give your answer to the nearest gram.

Appendix 1

Using a calculator to find the correlation coefficient, *r*.

Different models of calculator require different input commands to find the correlation coefficient, *r*. You should use the instruction booklet that accompanies your calculator to familiarise yourself with the sequence of inputs to find *r*.

The general steps are as follows:
  (i)   Place the calculator in **STAT LINEAR MODE** .
  (ii) Input the PAIRED DATA.
  (iii) Follow the input instructions to find *r*, the correlation coefficient.

Example

We will now use a **Casio fx-83 ES** to find the correlation coefficient *r*, for the following paired data:

    (150, 65),   (148, 68),   (172, 75)

  (i)   Put the calculator in STAT LINEAR MODE, by keying in

           MODE 2 (STAT) 2 (A + Bx)

  (ii) Input paired data

           1 5 0 = 1 4 8 = 1 7 2 = ↓ →
              6 5 =   6 8 =   7 5 =

  (iii) To calculate *r*, key in

           AC SHIFT 1 (STAT) 7 (REG) 3 *r* =

The answer is 0.93167406

    ∴   *r* = 0.932, correct to three decimal places.

Note: **1.** Ensure you **clear** calculator memory before **each** question.

           2. When you have entered the paired data, you can continue on and find $\bar{x}$, $\bar{y}$ and also the equation of the line of best fit.

Appendix 2

Using a calculator to find the standard deviation of a frequency distribution

We will use a **Casio fx-83 ES** to find the standard deviation of a frequency distribution.

The following frequency distribution table shows the number of birdies scored per round of golf.

No. of birdies	0	1	2	3	4	5	6
Frequency	5	6	4	6	3	1	0

Find the mean and standard deviation, correct to one decimal place.

Key in MODE and select 2 for statistics mode.

Then select 1 for 1 − VAR and input variables.

0	=		5	=
1	=	◀ REPLAY ▶	6	=
2	=		4	=
3	=		6	=
4	=		3	=
5	=		1	=
6	=		0	=

CASIO *fx-83ES*

	X	FREQ
1	0	5
2	1	6
3	2	4
4	3	6
5	4	3
6	5	1
7	6	0

For answers key in

AC SHIFT 1 5 2 = $1.96 = 2.0 =$ mean (birdies per round)

AC SHIFT 1 5 3 = $1.4554\ldots = 1.5 =$ standard deviation

$\therefore$ Mean = 2.0 and standard deviation = 1.5

Answers

Chapter 1: Probability 1

Exercise 1.1
1. 60
2. 42
3. 1872
4. 240
5. 720
6. 5040; 1440
7. 120; (i) 24 (ii) 6
8. 5040; (i) 1440 (ii) 1440
9. (i) 480 (ii) 240 (iii) 240
10. (i) 720 (ii) 1440
11. 5040; 720
12. (i) 720 (ii) 144
13. 840
14. 360
15. 336
16. 1440
17. (i) 504 (ii) 648
18. 24; (i) 6 (ii) 6 (iii) 12
19. 4536; (i) 1008 (ii) 504
20. 72; 24
21. 100; (i) 60 (ii) 20
22. (i) 300 (ii) 60
23. 36
24. 60 480
25. 5040; (i) 1440 (ii) 3600
26. (i) 720 (ii) 336 (iii) 48

Exercise 1.2
1. (i) 15 (ii) 35 (iii) 45
   (iv) 66 (v) 153
3. 56
4. 364; 286
5. 126; (i) 70 (ii) 35
6. 126; 70
7. 22 100; 286
8. (i) 56 (ii) 126 (iii) 35
9. 40
10. (i) 26 400 (ii) 22 275
11. 20; (i) 12 (ii) 16
12. 28; 6
13. (i) 15 (ii) 18
14. 360
15. (i) 70 (ii) 15 (iii) 15
16. 10; 3
17. (i) 15 (ii) 6
18. (i) 35 (ii) 70 (iii) 120
19. 560
20. 288
21. (i) $n = 5$ (ii) $n = 10$ (iii) $n = 7$

Exercise 1.3
1. (i) Impossible (ii) V. likely
   (iii) V. unlikely (iv) V. unlikely
   (v) Evens (vi) Certain
   (vii) Unlikely
2. (i) 6 (ii) 4 (iii) 0 (iv) 2
3. (i) 6 (ii) 8 (iii) 2
4. (i) $\frac{1}{6}$ (ii) $\frac{1}{3}$ (iii) $\frac{1}{2}$ (iv) $\frac{1}{2}$
   (v) $\frac{1}{3}$ (vi) $\frac{1}{2}$
5. (i) $\frac{1}{13}$ (ii) $\frac{1}{4}$ (iii) $\frac{3}{13}$ (iv) $\frac{1}{26}$
   (v) $\frac{5}{13}$
6. (i) $\frac{9}{17}$ (ii) $\frac{8}{17}$ (iii) $\frac{5}{17}$ (iv) $\frac{4}{17}$
7. (i) $\frac{1}{8}$ (ii) $\frac{1}{4}$ (iii) $\frac{3}{8}$ (iv) $\frac{1}{2}$
8. (i) $\frac{1}{2}$ (ii) $\frac{1}{6}$ (iii) $\frac{2}{3}$ (iv) $\frac{1}{2}$
9. (i) $\frac{1}{12}$ (ii) $\frac{1}{4}$ (iii) $\frac{1}{6}$ (iv) $\frac{1}{3}$
10. (i) $\frac{1}{36}$ (ii) $\frac{1}{12}$ (iii) $\frac{1}{9}$
11. $\frac{2}{5}$
12. (i) $\frac{3}{5}$ (ii) 3 (iii) 3
13. (i) $\frac{1}{12}$ (ii) $\frac{1}{6}$ (iii) $\frac{1}{2}$; 9 most often; $\frac{1}{4}$
14. (i) $\frac{2}{9}$ (ii) $\frac{1}{9}$
15. (i) $\frac{1}{8}$ (ii) $\frac{1}{8}$ (iii) $\frac{3}{8}$
16. (i) $\frac{1}{2}$ (ii) $\frac{8}{25}$ (iii) $\frac{8}{25}$; $\frac{16}{25}$
17. (i) $\frac{1}{6}$ (ii) $\frac{7}{12}$

Exercise 1.4
1. (i) 150 (ii) 150 (iii) 300
2. (i) $\frac{1}{2}$ (ii) (a) 200 (b) 150
3. (i) $\frac{17}{50}$
   (ii) No; as 34 is well below the expected value of 50
4. (i) (a) $\frac{1}{5}$ (b) $\frac{2}{15}$
   (ii) (a) $\frac{1}{6}$ (b) $\frac{1}{6}$ (iii) No
5. (i) $\frac{77}{150}$
   (ii) No; far more red than one would expect
6. No; after 300 spins the results should be close to the expected value
7. (i) $x = 0.1$ (ii) 0.6 (iii) 200
8. $\frac{7}{10}$

9. $\frac{33}{200}$; largest no. of trials

10. (i) Bill's   (ii) Biased
   (iii) $\frac{63}{290}$ (v) 322

11. (i) $\frac{1}{3}$ (ii) 1, 2, 2, 3, 3, 4

Exercise 1.5

1. (i) $\frac{1}{2}$ (ii) $\frac{1}{4}$ (iii) $\frac{3}{4}$

2. (i) $\frac{1}{4}$ (ii) $\frac{3}{26}$ (iii) $\frac{19}{52}$

3. (i) $\frac{1}{3}$
   (ii) $\frac{1}{5}$; As 15 and 30 are multiples of both 3 and 5; $\frac{7}{15}$

4. (i) $\frac{1}{2}$ (ii) $\frac{1}{3}$ (iii) $\frac{2}{3}$

5. (i) $\frac{1}{4}$ (ii) $\frac{1}{13}$ (iii) $\frac{4}{13}$
   (iv) $\frac{1}{2}$ (v) $\frac{1}{13}$ (vi) $\frac{7}{13}$

6. (i) $\frac{1}{6}$ (ii) $\frac{5}{36}$ (iii) $\frac{5}{18}$

7. (i) $\frac{1}{2}$ (ii) $\frac{3}{4}$ (iii) $\frac{2}{7}$
   (iv) $\frac{11}{14}$ (v) $\frac{3}{4}$ (vi) 0

8. (i) $\frac{4}{25}$ (ii) $\frac{1}{2}$ (iii) $\frac{53}{100}$

9. (i) $\frac{1}{4}$ (ii) $\frac{1}{4}$ (iii) $\frac{7}{16}$
   (iv) $\frac{3}{4}$ (v) $\frac{1}{4}$ (vi) $\frac{7}{8}$
   (vii) $\frac{5}{8}$

10. 5

11. (i) $\frac{2}{5}$ (ii) $\frac{7}{10}$ (iii) $\frac{7}{10}$

12. (i) $\frac{1}{25}$ (ii) $\frac{13}{100}$ (iii) $\frac{16}{25}$

13. (i) (a) N (b) N (c) N (d) Y (e) Y
   (ii) $\frac{1}{2}$
   (iii) No; not mutually exclusive events

14. (i) $\frac{2}{5}$ (ii) $\frac{11}{20}$ (iii) $\frac{17}{20}$

15. (i) 0.6   (ii) 0.5   (iii) 0.9
   (iv) 0.2

16. (i) 12   (ii) $\frac{3}{5}$ (iii) $\frac{1}{10}$
   (iv) $\frac{21}{25}$ (v) $\frac{37}{50}$

17. (i) 40   (ii) $\frac{3}{40}$ (iii) $\frac{3}{11}$
   (iv) $\frac{5}{24}$ (v) $\frac{2}{3}$

18. (ii) 52%   (iii) 26%

19. $\frac{1}{2}$ **20.** $\frac{1}{5}$

21. 0.5   **22.** 1

23. (i) $\frac{13}{15}$ (ii) No

24. $\frac{22}{35}$

Exercise 1.6

1. (i) $\frac{4}{25}$ (ii) $\frac{1}{25}$ (iii) $\frac{4}{25}$ (iv) $\frac{2}{25}$

2. (i) $\frac{1}{36}$ (ii) $\frac{1}{12}$ (iii) $\frac{1}{6}$

3. (i) $\frac{1}{12}$ (ii) $\frac{1}{4}$

4. (i) $\frac{1}{4}$ (ii) $\frac{1}{169}$ (iii) $\frac{1}{104}$

5. (i) $\frac{4}{25}$ (ii) $\frac{6}{25}$ (iii) $\frac{6}{25}$ (iv) $\frac{9}{25}$
   (v) $\frac{13}{25}$

6. $\frac{1}{2}$

7. (i) $\frac{1}{4}$ (ii) $\frac{1}{16}$ (iii) $\frac{3}{169}$
   (iv) $\frac{1}{676}$ (v) $\frac{1}{2704}$

8. $\frac{1}{72}$

9. (i) 0.04   (ii) 0.32

10. (i) 0.504 (ii) 0.006 (iii) 0.994

11. (i) $\frac{1}{3}$ (ii) $\frac{1}{6}$ (iii) $\frac{1}{2}$

12. (i) 0.336 (ii) 0.788

13. (i) $\frac{125}{216}$ (ii) $\frac{91}{216}$ (iii) $\frac{25}{72}$; $\frac{1}{36}$

14. (i) $\frac{1}{49}$ (ii) $\frac{1}{7}$ (iii) $\frac{6}{7}$ (iv) $\frac{13}{49}$

15. (i) $\frac{216}{343}$ (ii) $\frac{108}{343}$ (iii) $\frac{127}{343}$

Exercise 1.7

1. (i) $\frac{1}{2}$ (ii) $\frac{1}{13}$ (iii) $\frac{1}{3}$

2. (i) $\frac{7}{9}$ (ii) $\frac{4}{5}$ (iii) $\frac{19}{25}$

3. (i) $\frac{1}{6}$ (ii) $\frac{2}{3}$

4. (i) $\frac{3}{8}$ (ii) $\frac{7}{11}$ (iii) $\frac{5}{9}$

5. (i) $\frac{5}{8}$ (ii) $\frac{5}{14}$ (iii) $\frac{3}{28}$ (iv) $\frac{13}{28}$

6. (i) $\frac{2}{11}$ (ii) $\frac{3}{11}$ (iii) $\frac{3}{11}$ (iv) $\frac{5}{11}$
   (v) $\frac{5}{11}$

7. (i) $\frac{1}{20}$ (ii) $\frac{1}{10}$ (iii) $\frac{2}{5}$

8. $\frac{1}{14}$

9. (i) $\frac{20}{33}$ (ii) $\frac{4}{13}$ (iii) $\frac{1}{13}$ (iv) $\frac{3}{8}$

10. (i) 0.48   (ii) 0.52

11. $\frac{3}{5}$

12. (i) 0.6   (ii) 0.2   (iii) 0.9   (iv) 0.4
   (v) $0.3\dot{3}$

13. (i) $\frac{2}{5}$ (ii) $\frac{2}{15}$ (iii) $\frac{4}{5}$ (iv) $\frac{1}{4}$; No

14. (i) 0.35 (ii) 0.4   (iii) 0.5

15. (i) 0.3   (ii) 0.7   (iii) 0.7   (iv) 0.3
   (v) 0.4   (vi) $0.3\dot{3}$

16. (ii) 0.2   (iii) 0.2   (iv) No

17. (i) 0.5   (ii) 0.35 (iii) 0.375 (iv) 0.4

18. (i) 0.7   (ii) $0.6\dot{6}$ (iii) 0.8   (iv) 0.1

19. (i) $\frac{1}{20}$ (ii) $\frac{3}{20}$

20. (i) 0.42   (ii) 0.1
   (iii) 0.476 (or $\frac{10}{21}$)   (iv) $0.16\dot{6}$ (or $\frac{1}{6}$)
   (v) 0.48   (vi) 0.2

Test yourself 1

A – questions

1. 60;   (i) 12   (ii) 36
2. (i) 330   (ii) 150
3. (i) $\frac{1}{36}$ (ii) $\frac{1}{6}$ (iii) $\frac{1}{6}$
4. (i) 0.15   (ii) '1'   (iii) 50
5. (i) 720   (ii) 240
6. (i) (a)   (ii) $\frac{11}{15}$
7. (i) $\frac{1}{3}$ (ii) $\frac{1}{9}$ (iii) $\frac{4}{27}$
8. $\frac{12}{143}$
9. (i) 0.3   (ii) $\frac{1}{2}$ (iii) $\frac{19}{20}$
10. (i) $\frac{11}{25}$ (ii) $\frac{7}{13}$ (iii) $\frac{1}{30}$

B – questions

1. (i) $\frac{1}{6}$ (ii) $\frac{5}{36}$ (iii) $\frac{11}{36}$
2. (i) 70   (ii) 35   (iii) 40
3. (i) 5040   (ii) 120   (iii) 1440
4. (i) $\frac{2}{9}$ (ii) $\frac{1}{18}$ (iii) $\frac{4}{9}$
5. (ii) (a) 7315   (b) 1330   (c) $\frac{2}{11}$
6. (i) $\frac{4}{15}$ (ii) $\frac{8}{15}$ (iii) $\frac{2}{5}$
7. (i) 0.4   (ii) 0.5   (iii) 0.9
   (iv) $\frac{3}{7}$
8. (i) $\frac{4}{7}$ (ii) $\frac{26}{35}$ (iii) $\frac{8}{13}$
   (iv) $\frac{16}{35}$ (v) $\frac{6}{7}$; Not mutually exclusive
9. (i) $\dfrac{x(x-1)}{(x+6)(x+5)}$
   (ii) 14   (iii) $\frac{15}{91}$
10. (i) $\frac{1}{3}$ (ii) $\frac{1}{3}$
    (iii) (a) {3, 4, 5} or {5, 4, 3} or {2, 6, 4} or …
    (b) 10
    (iv) (a) 3   (b) $\frac{1}{216}$

C – questions

1. (i) $\frac{1}{6}$ (ii) $\frac{20}{21}$ (iii) $\frac{25}{42}$
2. (i) 0.8%   (ii) 7.2%   (iii) 9.2%
3. (i) Equally likely outcomes
   (ii) $\dfrac{P(A \cap B)}{P(B)}$
   (iii) (a) $\frac{1}{15}$ (b) $\frac{4}{5}$ (c) $\frac{1}{5}$
4. (i) $\frac{4}{5}$ (ii) $\frac{2}{25}$; $\frac{32}{625}$
5. (ii) $\frac{1}{5}$ (iii) 36
6. (i) 0.030   (ii) 0.146   (iii) 0
7. $\frac{7}{10}$
8. (i) $x = 0.2, y = 0.2, z = 0.05$
   (ii) $\frac{3}{8}$ (iii) $\frac{2}{7}$ (iv) 0.25
   (v) 0.95

9. (i) $\frac{11}{36}$ (ii) $\frac{5}{36}$ (iii) $\frac{1}{18}$
   (iv) $\frac{7}{18}$ (v) $\frac{2}{5}$
10. (ii) 0.512   (iii) 0.064   (iv) 0.479

Chapter 2: Statistics 1

Exercise 2.1

1. (i) Numerical   (ii) Categorical
   (iii) Numerical   (iv) Categorical
2. (i) Discrete   (ii) Discrete
   (iii) Continuous   (iv) Discrete
   (v) Continuous   (vi) Discrete
   (vii) Discrete   (viii) Discrete
3. (i) Categorical   (ii) Numerical
   (iii) Numerical; (ii) is discrete
4. Race time is continuous; Number on bib is discrete
5. (i) No   (ii) Yes
   (iii) Yes   (iv) No
6. (i) Contains two pieces of information
   (ii) No. of eggs
   (iii) Amount of flour
7. (i) Categorical   (ii) Numerical
   (iii) Numerical
   (iv) Categorical; Part (iii) is discrete; Bivariate continuous numerical
8. (i) True   (ii) True
   (iii) False   (iv) False
   (v) True   (vi) True
   (vii) True   (viii) True
9. Small, medium, large; 1-bed house, 2-bed, 3-bed; Poor, fair, good, very good.
10. (i) Primary   (ii) Secondary
    (iii) Primary   (iv) Secondary
11. (i) Secondary
    (ii) Roy's; they are more recent
12. (i) No. of bedrooms in family home and number of children in the family
    (ii) An athlete's height and his distance in a long-jump competition.

Exercise 2.2

1. (i) Too personal (it identifies respondent)
   (ii) Too vague/subjective
2. (i) Too personal   (ii) Too leading
   (iii) Overlapping
3. QA: Judgemental and subjective
   QB: Leading and biased
4. Not suitable; too vague, not specific enough
6. B and D are biased; B gives an opinion; D is a leading question
7. (i) Do you have a part-time job?
   (ii) Are you male or female?

8. Explanatory variable: Length of legs
Response variable: Time recorded in sprint
9. Explanatory variable:
Number of operating theatres
Response variable:
Number of operations per day
10. (i) Group B (ii) The new drug
(iii) Blood-pressure
(iv) Designed experiment

Exercise 2.3

1. Census – all members of the population surveyed.
Sample – only part of the population surveyed.
A sample is more convenient and cheaper.
2. Any sample of size n which has an equal chance of being selected.
3. (i) Likely biased (ii) Random
(iii) Random (iv) Random
(v) Random
4. Selecting a sample in the easiest way;
(i) Convenience sampling
(ii) High level of bias likely; unrepresentative of population
5. (i) Convenience sampling
(ii) Systematic (iii) Stratified
6. (i) Very small sample; not random and not representative
(ii) Each member of the local population should have an equal chance of being asked. The sample shouldn't be too small. Sample should be stratified to ensure all age and class groups are represented.
7. (i) Convenience
(ii) Her street may not be representative of the whole population.
(iii) Systematic random sampling from a directory **or** Cluster sampling of travel agents' clients, i.e., pick one travel agent at random and survey them about all their clients.
8. (i) Assign a number to each student and then use a random number generator to pick n numbers.
(ii) (a) 23 (b) 8
9. (i) Quota sampling
(ii) Convenient as no sampling frame required.
Left to the discretion of the interviewer so possible bias.
10. (i) Cost and time, without a great loss in accuracy.

(ii) A list of all items that could be included in the survey.
11. (i) 52 Junior; 48 Senior
(ii) Stratified sampling is better if there are different identifiable groups with different views in the population.
12. (i) Cluster sampling (ii) Convenience
(iii) Systematic

Exercise 2.4

1. (a) (i) 8 (ii) 7
(b) (i) 7 (ii) 7
2. (i) 41 km/hr (ii) 39.45 km/hr
3. (i) 14 (ii) 14 (iii) 17
4. 14 **5.** 4, 6
6. (i) 25.857 (ii) 15; Median
7. (i) 195 (ii) 19
8. 79.2%
9. Median, since 50% of the marks will be above the median mark.
10. (i) 16.2 (ii) $x = 35$
11. (i) 25 (ii) 6 (iii) 5.6
(iv) 14 (v) 6
12. (i) 4 (ii) 4 (iii) 4.25
13. (i) 32 years (ii) (30–40) years
14. (i) 42.7 (ii) Mean will increase
15. (i) (a) B (b) C
(ii) Categorical data is not numerical
16. (i) 4.3 mm
(ii) 26.5 hours
(iii) 3 mm; 15 hours
(iv) 2.5 mm; 16.5 hours
(v) median rainfall and mean sunshine (least rainfall and highest sunshine)
17. 3.36 or 3.48

Exercise 2.5

1. (i) 8 (ii) 57
2. (i) 33 (ii) 29
(iii) (a) $Q_1 = 27$ (b) $Q_3 = 34$ (c) 7
3. (i) 13 (ii) 8
(iii) 15 (iv) 7
4. (i) 5 marks (ii) 14.5 marks
(iii) On average, the girls didn't do as well as the boys. The girls' marks were more dispersed.
5. (i) 25 (ii) 50
(iii) 65 (iv) 15
6. (i) $Q_1 = 3.2$; $Q_3 = 4.0$;
Interquartile range = 0.8
(ii) 5.5
7. (i) 3.5 (ii) 2.7 (iii) 3.9

8. 1.414; 1.414
    (i) New set is $x + 10$
    (ii) Both the same
    (iii) If all the numbers are increased by the same amount, the standard deviation does not change.
10. (i) 14; 14   (ii) Route 1: 2; Route 2: 2.3
    (iii) Route 1, as times are less dispersed
11. 1.6   12. 0.84
13. 1.9   14. 11; 4.36
15. (i) 25   (ii) 5.3
    (iii) 30.3 and 19.7   (iv) 3
16. (i) $\bar{x} = a + 2$ (ii) $a = 5$
17. (i) 80%   (ii) 20%
18. (i) No, as it does not tell you what percentage did worse than Elaine.
    (ii) 480
19. (i) 53.5   (ii) 74.5
    (iii) 10.5   (iv) 4 students
    (v) 40th percentile
20. (i) €55   (ii) €32
    (iii) 13   (iv) €59; 7
    (v) 53rd to 56th percentile
21. $a = 10 - b; a = 6, b = 4$

Exercise 2.6

1. (i) 4   (ii) 27   (iii) 8   (iv) 36
2. (ii) 8   (iii) 16
3. (i) 6   (ii) 4.3 sec
    (iii) 3.25 sec   (iv) 3.5 sec
4. (i) 62   (ii) 47   (iii) 67   (iv) 20
5. (i) 41   (ii) 32   (iii) 47   (iv) 15
    (v) 47
6. (i) 19   (ii) (a) 66   (b) 49
    (iii) 55   (iv) 26
7. (i) 76; 27   (ii) 68; 38
    (iii) Those who didn't smoke; lower median
8. (ii) 55   (iii) 66.5
    (iv) English; Higher median
9. (i) 31 mins   (ii) 17.5 mins
    (iii) 15 mins   (iv) 0.75
    (v) Both have median 17.5, similar ranges; hence no significant difference
10. (i) 52 mins
    (ii) (a) 52 mins   (b) 69 mins
    (iii) (a) 31 mins   (b) 55 mins
    (iv) Women in the survey have a higher median and a wider range.

Exercise 2.7

1. (ii) 12   (iii) (20–40) km
    (iv) 40%

2. (i) 10   (ii) (40–50) years
    (iii) 12   (iv) 60
    (v) (50–60) years   (vi) (40–50) years
3. (ii) 38   (iii) (12–16) mins
    (iv) (12–16) mins   (v) 30
    (vi) 8
4. (i) 19   (ii) 54
    (iii) (10–15) sec   (iv) (10–15) sec
    (v) 20   (vi) 20
5. (ii) (25–35) mins   (iii) (25–35) mins
    (iv) (15–25) mins   (v) 48 people
    (vi) 29 mins

Exercise 2.8

1. Symmetrical;
    (i) Normal   (ii) Peoples' heights
2. Positively skewed; Age at which people start third-level education
3. (i) c   (ii) a   (iii) b
    (iv) b   (v) c
4. Negatively skewed;
    (i) Mean   (ii) Mode
5. More of the data is closer to the mean in (A).
6. (i) B   (ii) B
7. (i) A   (ii) Equal
8. (i) B   (ii) A
9. (i) A   (ii) B
10. (i)

A	B	C	D
✗	✗	✓	✗
✓	✗	✗	✗
✗	✓	✗	✓
✓	✗	✗	✗
✓	✓	✓	✗

    (ii) D, as more of the data is located further from the mean.

Test yourself 2

A – questions

1. (i) Primary   (ii) Secondary
    (iii) Primary   (iv) Secondary
    (v) Secondary
2. (i) 13   (ii) 8   (iii) 15   (iv) 7
3. 10; 3.7
4. (i) Census surveys entire population; sample surveys only part of the population
    (ii) 25 students
5. (i) 32   (ii) €48   (iii) €25
    (iv) €29   (v) Males, higher median
6. (i) (b) because it has the greater spread
    (ii) 2; 1.14

7. (i) Stratified, then simple random sampling
(ii) 20 students
(iii) Give each student a number and then select 10, using random button on calculator.
8. (i) Yes. May not be representative as there is no random element to the survey.
(ii) Use stratified sampling based on gender, age, marital status, income levels, etc. and then use simple random sampling.
9. See definitions in textbook.
10. (ii) 4.7 mins   (iii) 4.05 mins; 1.2 mins

B – questions
1. David as standard deviation of his marks is smaller.
2. (i) $P_{40} = 57\%$ (ii) 75th percentile
3. (i) A, D   (ii) C, A   (iii) B
(iv) A   (v) A
4. 2.3
5. (i) Negatively skewed as most of the data occurs at the higher values.
(ii) A = mode; B = median; C = mean
(iii) Age when people retire
6. Large, 15; Medium, 25; Small, 20
7. (i) Mean = 3.74   (ii) $\sigma = 2.37$
(iii) In the later study, the average number of accidents has increased. The spread has also increased as the standard deviation is higher.
8. (i) Explanatory: Fertilizer; Response: Wheat yield.
(ii) Explanatory: Habitat; Response: Species.
(iii) Explanatory: Amount of water; Response: Time to cool.
(iv) Explanatory: Size of engine; Response: Petrol consumption.
9. A: Systematic; B: Convenience; C: Simple random; D: Stratified; E: Quota
10. (i) Median = 40; Interquartile range = 50
(ii) (a) Because zero would not be a typical average
(b) It would be distorted by the zeros or very high values.

C – questions
1. (i) (a) Median = 2 goals;
Interquartile range = 3 goals
(b) Mean = 2.56 goals; $\sigma = 1.66$
(ii) The mean is higher in the 2008/09 season and the standard deviation is also higher. The wider spread in the 2008/09 season suggests more open games. However, the median number of goals per game is the same for both seasons. Overall, there is little significant difference between the two seasons.
2. (i) 22   (ii) $X = 11$, $Y = 27$, $Z = 22.5$
(iii) Strand Road as the median is higher.
3. (i) Driver: Positively skewed as a lot of the data is clustered to the left in the (20–30) year age-group.
Passenger: From ages (0–40) years, it is a symmetrical distribution with a mean of approximately 20 years. The values fall away as you move away from the centre.
(ii) (a) Driver: 20 years
(b) Passenger: 18 years
(iii) A uniform distribution, suggesting casualties equally likely at all ages with moderate peak from (15–25) years.
(iv) The (17–25) years age-group. Most of the casualties among both drivers and passengers occur in this group.
4. (ii) **Similarity:** Both have the same mode (3).
Difference: Girls distribution resembles a normal distribution. For the boys, most of the data is concentrated at the lower values (1–3).
(iii) Though the medians are the same, the girls' distribution has a greater spread. The samples are sufficiently different to suggest that this could not happen by chance.
(iv) They could include more boys and girls who are not in GAA clubs. Include both urban and rural children so the sample would be less biased. Also, be more precise about what 'playing sport' means.
5. (i) A – run; B – cycle; C – swim
(ii) 25 mins   (iii) Approx. 3 mins
(iv) It would be very unusual for two or more athletes to have the same time as it is continuous numerical data (times were to the nearest 1000th of a second).
6. (i) Histogram – ensure that the class intervals are equal.
(ii) The distribution has a positive skew (tail to the right). Median = **225** days.
(iii) It is not a normal distribution and so z-scores are not appropriate. The distribution has a positive skew and hence it is not a normal distribution.
(iv) $\frac{24}{115}$ (or 0.21). This is the relative frequency of the next earthquake occurring between 100 and 200 days later.

(v) The idea of 1000 deaths is very subjective as earthquakes occur in areas of low population also. An earthquake relatively low on the Richter Scale could result in a lot of deaths in a densely-populated area. So the size of the earthquake, as measured on the Richter Scale, may be more relevant to a future analysis than the number of deaths. Finally, the data may be divided by region and the frequency plotted against the size of the earthquake.

Chapter 3: Probability 2

Exercise 3.1

1. (ii) $\frac{7}{12}$ (or $\frac{28}{48}$)
2. (ii) $\frac{13}{18}$ (iii) $\frac{5}{36}$
3. (i) $\frac{12}{35}$ (ii) $\frac{6}{35}$ (iii) $\frac{18}{35}$
4. (ii) $\frac{9}{25}$ (iii) $\frac{12}{25}$
5. (ii) $\frac{1}{3}$ (iii) $\frac{5}{18}$
6. (ii) $\frac{2}{27}$
7. (i) $\frac{7}{15}$ (ii) $\frac{8}{15}$
8. (ii) $\frac{2}{5}$ (iii) $\frac{3}{5}$
9. (ii) $\frac{13}{60}$
10. (ii) $\frac{4}{15}$
11. (i) 0.3 (or 30%)   (ii) $\frac{18}{25}$
12. $\frac{35}{216}$

Exercise 3.2

1. 10   2. 6.5   3. €12.75   4. 4
5. −0.2   6. 1.43   7. 1.5
8. Expect to win €$3\frac{1}{3}$; not fair as mathematical expectation $\neq 0$
9. €0; yes, since expected amount is zero.
10. €22.50; loss as bet is €25
11. €190
12. (i) 0.3   (ii) 2.9
13. Lose €16.67
14. (i) $p + q = 0.4$; $2p + 4q = 1$
    (ii) $p = 0.3, q = 0.1$
15. (i) 0.0456   (ii) €77.84
    (iii) €361.89   (iv) €427.50
16. $13\frac{1}{3}$
17. Play dice; cards (lose €6.25); dice (lose €3.33) Difference = €2.92

Exercise 3.3

1. (i) Fixed number of independent trials with two outcomes that have constant probabilities
   (ii) $\frac{1}{2}, \frac{1}{2}$; 8
2. (i) $\frac{5}{32}$ (ii) $\frac{5}{16}$
3. (i) $\frac{3125}{7776}$ (ii) $\frac{3125}{7776}$ (iii) $\frac{625}{3888}$
4. $\frac{560}{2187}$
5. $\frac{5}{16}$
6. (i) 0.028   (ii) 0.31
7. 0.124 $\left(\text{or } \frac{48384}{360625}\right)$
8. $\frac{1}{9}$
9. (i) $\frac{96}{625}$ (ii) $\frac{608}{625}$
10. (i) $\frac{81}{625}$ (ii) $\frac{96}{625}$ (iii) $\frac{544}{625}$
11. (i) $\frac{441}{1000}$ (ii) $\frac{189}{2500}$
12. (i) $\frac{144}{625}$ (ii) $\frac{72}{3125}$
13. (i) 750   (ii) 125   (iii) 1875
14. (ii) $\frac{1}{81}$ (iii) $\frac{1}{3}; \frac{32}{81}$
16. (i) 0.29071   (ii) 0.04845
17. (i) $\frac{3}{13}$ (ii) 0.0588
18. 0.08
19. (i) 0.27869   (ii) 0.11148
20. (i) 0.0563   (ii) 0.00309; 0.07508

Exercise 3.4

1. (i) $\frac{2}{5}$ (ii) $\frac{1}{3}$ (iii) $\frac{2}{15}$
2. (i) $\frac{1}{3}$ (ii) $\frac{1}{4}$
3. Yes; $P(A) \times P(B) = P(A \cap B)$
4. 0.1
5. 0.5
6. (i) 0.1   (ii) $P(A \cap B) \neq P(A).P(B)$
   (iii) $\frac{2}{7}$
7. (i) 0.56
   (ii) $P(A \cap B) = P(A) \times P(B) = 0.56$
8. (i) $\frac{2}{15}$
   (ii) $P(A).P(B) = \frac{1}{15}$ and $P(A \cap B) = \frac{2}{15}$
   $\Rightarrow$ not equal
9. (i) $\frac{2}{3}$ (ii) $\frac{1}{2}$
10. 0.49; No, as $0.49 \neq 0.42$
11. (i) 0.03   (ii) 0.2   (iii) 0.32
12. (ii) 0.2   (iii) 0.2
    (iv) Yes, as $P(A \cap B) = P(A).P(B) = 0.15$
13. (i) $\frac{1}{15}$ (ii) $\frac{11}{15}$ (iii) $\frac{1}{5}$
14. (i) Independent events; obtaining a head when a coin is tossed
    (ii) They are mutually exclusive; zero

15. (i) $P(A) = 0.48$; $P(B) = 0.3$
   (ii) $P(A).P(B) \neq P(A \cap B)$
   (iii) 0.36
16. $P(E \cap F) \neq 0$ and $P(A \cap B) \neq P(A).P(B)$

Exercise 3.5

1. (i) 0.025   (ii) $\frac{11}{4165}$ (or 0.00264)
   (iii) $\frac{46}{833}$ (iv) $\frac{44}{4165}$
2. 330; (i) $\frac{5}{11}$ (ii) $\frac{2}{11}$ (iii) $\frac{1}{66}$
3. (i) $\frac{1}{364}$ (ii) $\frac{1}{91}$ (iii) $\frac{9}{91}$ (iv) $\frac{55}{182}$
4. (i) $\frac{16}{81}$ (ii) $\frac{1}{6}$
5. (i) $\frac{2}{3}$ (ii) $\frac{5}{42}$
6. (i) $\frac{11}{46}$ (ii) $\frac{30}{49}$
7. (i) 120   (ii) 56   (iii) $\frac{7}{15}$ (iv) $\frac{14}{15}$
8. (i) $\frac{1}{2}$ (ii) $\frac{1}{40}$ (iii) $\frac{1}{20}$ (iv) $\frac{9}{20}$
9. $\frac{20}{147}$
10. (i) $\frac{1}{56}$ (ii) $\frac{3}{28}$ (iii) $\frac{1}{14}$ (iv) $\frac{11}{56}$

Exercise 3.6

1. (i) 0.8849   (ii) 0.1587
   (iii) 0.0274   (iv) 0.9282
2. 0.9222   **3.** 0.8133   **4.** 0.9793
5. 0.0228   **6.** 0.1056   **7.** 0.2266
8. 0.0107   **9.** 0.0968   **10.** 0.0166
11. 0.7123   **12.** 0.6826   **13.** 0.8664
14. 0.1980   **15.** 0.9534   **16.** 0.7159
17. 1.12   **18.** 0.34   **19.** 0.91
20. 1.42
21. (i) 0.8413   (ii) 0.6915   (iii) 0.6915
22. (i) 0.5948   (ii) 0.6844
23. (i) 0.1056   (ii) 0.0301
24. (i) 0.1370   (ii) 0.2902
25. (i) 0.1349   (ii) 0.0514
26. (i) 0.3830   (ii) 0.3721
27. (i) 0.0668   (ii) 0.3085
28. (i) 0.6554   (ii) 0.7257   (iii) 0.3056
29. (i) 0.0062   (ii) 0.1587   (iii) 0.6247
30. 0.5746
31. (i) 0.0764   (ii) 0.1895
32. (i) 6   (ii) 294
33. (i) 203   (ii) 111
34. (i) (a) 0.0668   (b) 0.7745
   (ii) 73%

Exercise 3.7

1. Allocate numbers 1 to 20 and use random number table.
2. Allocate numbers 1 to 8, giving 1 and 2 to fish; 3 to vegetarian; 4, 5, 6, 7, 8 to meat.

3. (i) 0.3125   (ii) 0.0625
4. Generate random numbers; 0 and 1 the cars turn right; 2 to 9 the cars turn left; generate using the random number key on your calculator.
5. (i) 14
6. 23   **7.** 0.52   **8.** 3

Test yourself 3

A – questions
1. 0.1762
2. (ii)
3. 0.4116
4. (i) 142506   (ii) 51300
   (iii) $\frac{950}{2639}$ (or 0.36)
5. 0.7338
6. $\frac{256}{625}$
7. (i) $\frac{2}{5}$ (ii) $\frac{3}{10}$
8. (i) 0.5   (ii) 0.8
   (iii) 0.9; $P(E \cap F) = P(E).P(F)$; 0.5
9. 23 cent
10. $\frac{1}{2}$

B – questions
1. $\frac{20}{27}$
2. 0.75
3. (i) $\frac{1}{35}$ (ii) $\frac{11}{35}$
4. (i) $\frac{3}{8}$ (ii) $\frac{2}{13}$ (iii) $\frac{27}{110}$ (iv) $\frac{13}{25}$
5. (i) 0.1359   (ii) $k = 1.12$
6. (i) 0.15   (ii) $\frac{7}{15}$ (iii) $\frac{1}{10}$
7. (i) $\frac{19}{27}$ (ii) $\frac{1}{2}$
8. Lose €5; not fair since expected payout not zero.
9. (i) 0.2 $\left(\text{or } \frac{3125}{15552}\right)$ (ii) 0.067 $\left(\text{or } \frac{3125}{46656}\right)$
10. (i) $\frac{1}{6}$
   (ii) $\frac{1}{4}$; Yes as $P(E \cap F) = P(E).P(F)$

C – questions
1. (i) ABEH, ACEH
   (ii) $\frac{3}{4}$ (iii) $\frac{3}{8}$ (iv) $\frac{1}{16}$
2. (i) 0.063   (ii) 0.309   (iii) 0.042
3. (a) (i) $\frac{1}{5}$ (ii) $\frac{5}{13}$ (iii) $\frac{17}{25}$
   (b) $\frac{1}{6}$ (independent of p)
4. (i) 0.0668   (ii) 0.052
5. (i) $\frac{1}{14}$ (ii) $\frac{97}{105}$ (iii) $\frac{37}{42}$
   (iv) $\frac{17}{21}$; no, since answers to (iii) and (iv) are different
6. (i) $k = 1.42$ (ii) (a) $\frac{1}{6}$ (b) $\frac{1}{4}$

7. (a) (i) 0.6   (ii) $a = 0.3$, $b = 0.3$
    (b) 3 boys (9 girls)
8. (i) Spinner: $E(x) = 4$; Dice: $E(x) = 3.5$;
    Spinners have better chance
9. (i) $\frac{5}{16}$ (ii) 0.149
10. (i) All the same
    (ii) Smooth bell-shaped, symmetrical,
    empirical rule applies
    (iii) (a) 0.0228   (b) 0.9544; 114
11. (i) $\frac{1}{3}$ (ii) $\frac{37}{45}$
    (iii) Yes, as $P(E \cap F) = P(E).P(F)$
    (iv) No, as $P(E \cup F) \neq P(E) + P(F)$

Chapter 4 : Statistics 2

Exercise 4.1

1. (i) C and E   (ii) A and F   (iii) B and D
    (iv) A; negative correlation
2. (i) B   (ii) C   (iii) D
3. (i) Strong positive
    (ii) The better a student does in the mock
    exams, the better he/she tends to do in
    the final exam.
4. (ii) Strong positive
    (iii) On balance, there is a tendency for
    those who do better at statistics to also
    do better at maths.
5. (i) Negative   (ii) Positive   (iii) None
    (iv) Negative   (v) Positive
6. (i) B   (ii) C   (iii) A   (iv) D
7. (i) Reasonably strong negative
    (ii) Yes; as the age of the bike increases, it
    causes the price to decrease.
8. (ii) Strong negative
    (iii) No; an increase in the sales of one does not
    cause a decrease in the sales of the other.

Exercise 4.2

1. A(0.6); B(−1); C(−0.4); D(0.8)
2. (i) 0.9   (ii) −0.8   (iii) 0
    (iv) −1   (v) −0.1   (vi) 0.2
3. (i) Line of best fit.
    (ii) Approximately equal number of points
    on either side of line.
    (iii) 55 kg
    (iv) Strong positive
5. 0.86
6. (iii) −0.9
    (iv) $y = 41 - 1.1x$ (by calculator)
    (v) Approx. 12
7. (ii) Strong negative correlation
    (iv) $y = -1.7x + 98$ (exact)
    (v) Approx. 68

8. 0.85
9. (iii) $y = 1.9x - 16$ (by calculator)
    (iv) Approx. 15 hours
10. (ii) Strong negative correlation
    (iii) −0.9250
    (iv) $y = -3x + 18$
    (v) 0.9
11. (ii) Fairly strong positive correlation
    (iii) 0.8591
    (iv) $y = 0.63x - 2.2$ (by calculator)
    (v) Approx. €18

Exercise 4.3

1. (i) 68%   (ii) 95%   (iii) 81.5%   (iv) 68%
2. (i) 34%   (ii) 16%   (iii) 81.5%
3. (i) 46 km/hr   (ii) 73 km/hr
    (iii) 82 km/hr
4. (i) $55 < x < 65$ (ii) [50, 70]
5. (i) [162 cm, 178 cm]   (ii) [146 cm, 194 cm]
6. (i) 95%   (ii) 2.5%   (iii) 570
7. (i) 8160 bulbs   (ii) 5700 bulbs
    (iii) 300 bulbs
8. 25
9. (i) (a) 95%   (b) 99.7%   (ii) 97 portions
10. (i) 1   (ii) −2   (iii) 1.5   (iv) −2.5
11. (i) A value which lies 2 standard deviations
    above the mean.
    (ii) A value which lies $1\frac{1}{2}$ standard deviations
    below the mean.
12. (i) Karl's mark is 1.8 standard deviations
    above the mean.
    Tanya's mark is 0.6 standard deviations
    below the mean.
    (ii) Karl, 97 and Tanya, 61
13. Height: $z = -1.5$; Weight: $z = 0.5$
14. (i) Maths: $z = 0.417$; History: $z = -0.8$
    (ii) Maths; higher z-score
    (iii) 83
15. (i) Her mark was 1.8 standard deviations
    above the mean
    (ii) 58.4   (iii) −0.7
16. (i) 1.75   (ii) 77
17. (ii) History: $z = 2$; Physics: $z = 1.5$.
    Yes, she did better in History.
18. First beach: $z = 1.43$; Second beach: $z = 1.25$.
    Her claim is correct.

Exercise 4.4

1. (i) 0.3   (ii) 0.04   (iii) $0.26 < p < 0.34$
2. (i) 34%
    (ii) $0.29 < p < 0.39$; 95% of samples would
    give this result.
3. $0.35 < p < 0.37$
4. $0.218 < p < 0.382$

5. $0.176 < p < 0.398$

6. (i) 400   (ii) 1111   (iii) 4444

7. $0.35 < p < 0.49$

8. $0.325 < p < 0.389$; No, as 0.4 is outside this range.

9. $0.489 < p < 0.579$; No, as 0.5 is within this range.

10. (i) 0.2166   (ii) 0.065
    (iii) 0.1667   (iv) Dice is fair.

11. No

12. $2.4\% < p < 24.5\%$; claim correct

13. $0.61 < p < 0.723$; Yes, it's justified.

14. (i) $0.09 < p < 0.21$
    (ii) If 100 samples were taken, we would expect 95 of them to have defective items ranging between 9% and 21% (or between 27 items and 63 items).
    (iii) 190

Test yourself 4

A – questions

1. 81.5%

2. (i) B   (ii) A   (iii) C
    (iv) A   (v) B

3. (i) $a = 160\,\text{cm}$, $b = 170\,\text{cm}$, $c = 180\,\text{cm}$, $d = 190\,\text{cm}$, $e = 200\,\text{cm}$
    (ii) $z = 1$
    (iii) 16%

4. (ii) Strong positive
    (iv) $y = 0.713x + 9.74$ (exact)
    (v) 33

5. 7.5 cm

6. (i) 0.06   (ii) $0.62 < p < 0.74$

7. (i) A measure of the strength of the linear relationship between 2 sets of variables.
    (ii) (a) $r = 0.916$
       (b) It is very likely that a student who has done well in Test 1 will also have done well in Test 2.

8. (i) 95%   (ii) 47.5%

9. (i) 0.8   (ii) 0.66
    (iii) Simon did better in French.

10. There may be a strong positive correlation between house prices and car sales but that does not imply that one increase **causes** the other.

B – questions

1. (i) 0.022   (ii) $0.241 < p < 0.286$

2. (i) 2.5%   (ii) 0.95   (iii) 5000 hours

3. (i) $r = 0.959$
    (ii) Very strong positive correlation.

4. (i) 3%
    (ii) $18\% < p < 24\%$; not sufficient to reject party's claim.

5. First tree: $z = 2$; Second tree: $z = -0.67$. He is correct since $z = -0.67$ has a greater chance of happening on the normal curve than $z = 2$.

6. (ii) Strong negative correlation.
    (iii) $y = -1.12x + 41.6$
    (iv) 38 mins
    (v) $r = -1$

7. (i) 0.05
    (ii) $11\% < p < 21\%$; no evidence to reject claim.

8. (i) 1.5   (ii) 153 cm

9. $66.9\% < p < 81.9\%$; NCCB's beliefs are borne out.

10. (i) 2%   (ii) $\hat{p} = 0.1096$
    (iii) $0.0896 < p < 0.1296$; yes, owner's claim is justified.

C – questions

1. (i) (a) 68%   (b) 81.5%
    (ii) 8150 nails   (iii) 0.16

2. (ii) $y = 0.7x + 25$
    (iii) $r = 0.737$
    (iv) There is a strong positive correlation between maths and physics results.

3. (i) 5%
    (ii) $83\% < p < 93\%$; **no**, their claim is not justified as 81% is not within the confidence limit.

4. (i) (a) 1.25   (b) -1 (c) 0   (d) 4
    (ii) 2.5%
    (iii) 80 years
    (iv) Since $z = -2.5$, its very unlikely. The probability will be less than 1%.

5. (i) $r = -0.85$
    (ii) 37 years; 139 bpm
    (iii) 180 bpm
    (iv) -0.8
    (v) $MHR = 216 - (0.8 \times \text{age})$
    (vi)

Age	Old rule	New rule
20	200	200
50	170	176
70	150	160

For a younger person (20 years) the *MHR*'s are roughly the same; for an older person (50 years or 70 years) the new rule gives a higher *MHR* reading.

    (vii) At 65 years of age, the old rule gives $MHR = 155$ and the new rule gives $MHR = 164$. To get more benefit from exercise, he should increase his activity to 75% of 164 instead of 75% of 155.

Chapter 5 : Inferential statistics

Exercise 5.1

1. (i) Sampling distribution
    (ii) decrease
    (iii) μ
    (iv) $\dfrac{\sigma}{\sqrt{n}}$

2. Ⓐ Represents the distribution of the sample means

3. (i) Normal distribution; The Central Limit Theorem
    (ii) Sample size is sufficiently large (i.e. >30)
    (iii) Mean = 12;
    Standard deviation $= \dfrac{2}{\sqrt{36}} = \dfrac{1}{3}$

4. (i) (4, 6), (4, 8), (4, 10), (6, 8), (6, 10), (8, 10)
    (ii) Means are: 5, 6, 7, 7, 8, 9
    (iii) Statistic
    (iv) Both = 7

5. A parameter is a numerical property of a population.
    A statistic is a numerical property of a sample.

6. (i) Positively
    (ii) Normal distribution
    (iii) Sample size is sufficiently large ($n > 30$) to apply the theorem.

7. 0.0228
8. 0.0262
9. (i) 0.209   (ii) 0.1635
10. (i) 0.3   (ii) (a) 0.0228   (b) 0.4706
11. 0.894
12. $P(\bar{x} > 8 \text{ years 1 month}) = 0.0228$;
    Number of samples = 1
13. 0.3214
14. C = 80, D = 96, E = $78\frac{2}{3}$
15. $n = 26$
16. (i) 0.0793   (ii) $n > 170$
17. (i) 0.0228   (ii) 0.822   (iii) 0.086;
    Answer (iii)

Exercise 5.2

1. $62.17 < \mu < 63.83$
2. $279.1 < \mu < 288.9$
3. (i) $225.2 < \mu < 228.8$
    (ii) 5%
4. $60.9 < \mu < 64.5$
5. (i) $5.097 < \mu < 5.143$
    (ii) 5.10 and 5.14
    (iii) The "95% confidence" means that the mean lies in the range 5.10 to 5.14 95 times out of 100.
6. €269.71 $< \mu <$ €290.29

7. (i) $28.99 \text{ cm} < \mu < 29.41 \text{ cm}$
    (ii) No, as the sample size (180) is sufficiently large to apply The Central Limit Theorem.
8. (i) 0.0125
    (ii) 0.932 g
    (iii) $0.9075 < \mu < 0.9565$
    (iv) The confidence interval would be
    $[0.9124 < \mu < 0.9516]$
    (v) A larger sample results in a smaller confidence interval.
9. (i) $4.28 < \mu < 4.92$
    (ii) 601 cars
10. (i) $747.42 < \mu < 748.58$
    (ii) $n = 23$
11. (i) $68.12 < \mu < 69.88$
    (ii) $n = 28$
12. (i) 0.629
    (ii) $46.2 \text{ g} < \mu < 51.0 \text{ g}$
    (iii) At least 70
13. (i) $\bar{x} = 57.4$
    (ii) $\sigma = 15.1$

Exercise 5.3

1. $0.1096 < p < 0.1904$
2. $0.293 < p < 0.427$
3. $0.260 < p < 0.379$
4. $0.122 < p < 0.358$
5. $0.294 < p < 0.386$
6. (i) $0.654 < p < 0.812$
    (ii) $0.765 < p < 0.917$
7. (i) 34%
    (ii) $29.4\% < p < 38.6\%$; On 95% of samples the true proportion will lie in this interval.
    (iii) 2156
8. $0.245 < p < 0.295$
9. (i) $0.08 < p < 0.22$
    (ii) 2180

Exercise 5.4

1. No; $z = 1.68$; so not greater than 1.96
2. Yes; $z = -2.66$
3. (i) H_0: The mean age of the patients is 45 years.
    H_1: The mean age of the patients is not 45 years.
    (iii) $z = 1.89$
    (iv) No; $z = 1.89$; so not greater than 1.96
4. (i) H_0: The mean length is 210 cm
    H_1: The mean length is not 210 cm
    (iii) Yes: $z = 2.5$
    As $z = 2.5$ is in the critical region, we reject the null hypothesis.
5. No: $z = 1.955$; so z not greater than 1.96

6. Yes: $z = -2.11$, which is < -1.96
7. Yes: $z = -2.54$, which is less than -1.96
8. (i) 0.0836
   (ii) 0.0562
   (iii) 0.099
   (iv) 0.0394
9. (i) $z = 1.77$
   (ii) p-value $= 0.0768$
   (iii) No, as p-value > 0.05
10. (i) $z = -1.5$
    (ii) p-value $= 0.1336$
    (iii) No, as p-value > 0.05
11. (i) $z = 1.5$
    (ii) No, as $z \not> 1.96$
    (iii) p-value $= 0.1336$
    (iv) Yes, as p-value is not less than 0.05; so we accept H_0 that the mean time required is 12 mins.
12. (i) $z = 2.5$
    (ii) 0.0124
    (iii) Yes, as p-value < 0.05
13. Standard error $= 0.0036$; $4.993\text{mm} < \mu < 5.007\text{mm}$; Yes as $z = 2.22$ and so $z > 1.96$.

Test yourself 5

A – questions
1. 0.89
2. Mean $\mu = 2.85$;
   Standard error $= \dfrac{0.07}{\sqrt{20}} = 0.016$
3. $24.42 < \mu < 27.98$
4. $260.0\,\text{ml} < \mu < 272.2\,\text{ml}$
5. $0.522 < p < 0.678$
6. $0.45 < p < 0.65$
7. Yes; $z = 2.113$ and $z > 1.96$
8. (i) The mean $460.3\,$g has not changed.
   (ii) $z = 2.18$
   (iii) Since $z = 2.18$ and $2.18 > 1.96 \Rightarrow$ the new mean is different from the known mean.
9. (i) Normal distribution; Central Limit Theorem
   (ii) Sample size is large (i.e. >30)
   (iii) None.
10. (i)

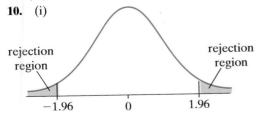

rejection region   rejection region

-1.96 0 1.96

   (ii) $z < -1.96$ and $z > 1.96$
   (iv) p-value $= 0.1096$

B – questions
1. $n = 10$
2. (i) 0.401
   (ii) 0.691
   (iii) 0.494; unaffected as $n > 30$
3. $30.6\,\text{kg} < \mu < 32.2\,\text{kg}$
4. (i) Since $n \geqslant 30$, the Central Limit Theorem can be applied.
   (ii) $0.057 < p < 0.343$
5. (i) If 100 samples of the same size are taken, then the true population mean or proportion will lie in the given interval on 95 occasions out of 100.
   (ii) $3.16\,\text{km} < \mu < 13.88$
6. (i) H_0: $\mu = 1.2$ sec; H_1: $\mu \neq 1.2$ sec
   (ii) Critical regions are: $z < -1.96$ and $z > 1.96$
   (iii) $z = -3$. Yes as $z < -1.96$ and so is in the critical region.
   (iv) p-value $= 0.0026$
   Since $p < 0.05$, we reject the null hypothesis that $\mu = 1.2$ sec.
7. (i) 0.118
   (ii) 0.69
   (iii) $0.576 < p < 0.812$
   (iv) The sample proportion, 0.8 is within the confidence limit and so we accept the school's claim.
8. (i) H_0: The mean weight is 25 kg.
   H_1: The mean weight is not 25 kg.
   (ii) $z = -2.36$
   (iii) p-value $= 0.0182$
   (iv) Yes, as the p-value < 0.05
   (v) "The p-value is the smallest level of significance at which the null hypothesis could have been rejected".
9. (i) 68 kg; 0.6 kg
   (ii) 17 samples

C – questions
1. (i) H_0: The mean weight is 500 g.
   H_1: The mean weight is not 500 g.
   (ii) $z = 1.666$
   (iii) p-value $= 0.095$
   (iv) Since p-value $\not< 0.05$, we accept the null hypothesis. The result is not significant.
2. (i) 0.0533
   (ii) $0.245 < p < 0.454$
3. (i) $\bar{x} = 81.4\,$g
   (ii) $\sigma = 15\,$g
4. (i) 10.6%; 6.7%
   (ii) $z = -1.58$
   (iii) p-value $= 0.114$

(iv) $p = 0.114$ is not less than $0.05 \Rightarrow$ the mean weight of the sample is not different from the population mean.

5. (a) Mean $= \mu$; Standard deviation $= \dfrac{\sigma}{\sqrt{n}}$

    (i) Normal distribution.

    (ii) Normal distribution.

    The Central Limit Theorem can be applied to any distribution if n is large ($n > 30$). The distribution of the sample means will always be normal when the underlying population is normal.

    (b) (i) 0.278   (ii) 695

6. (i) $\frac{3}{4}$

    (ii) 0.2966

    (iii) Normal distribution; $\mu = 22.05$; $\sigma = 0.7524$

    (iv) 103

7. (i) 0.773

    (ii) 0.631

    (iii) 2.89 kg

    (iv) 0.936

8. (a) (i) 0.0228

    (ii) 0.440

    (iii) 0.785

    (b) (i) Mean only 1.08 standard deviations above zero.

    For a normal distribution this gives a probability of about 0.14 of negative times, which are impossible.

    (ii) Large sample $\Rightarrow$ mean approximately normally distributed.

9. (i) 0.1587

    (ii) 0.1736

    (iii) 63 g